DATE DUE

SEP 2 7 1989	OCT. 29 1993
OCT 3 1 1989	MAY 1 7 1994
JAN 0 2 1990	
JAN 2 9 1990	
FEB 1 0 1990	
MAR 0 3 1990	
APR 0 1 1990	
JAN 0 3 1991	
MAR 0 5 1991	
OCT 7 1992	
OCT 2 7 1992	
APR. 2 2 1993	
MAY 2 0 1993	

Frank Lloyd Wright's Usonian Houses

THE CASE FOR ORGANIC ARCHITECTURE

Frank Lloyd Wright's Usonian Houses

THE CASE FOR ORGANIC ARCHITECTURE

BY JOHN SERGEANT

WHITNEY LIBRARY OF DESIGN, an imprint of
WATSON-GUPTILL PUBLICATIONS/New York

For my father, Nigel, and Bob Berger

Paperback Edition
First Printing 1984

Copyright © 1976 by John Sergeant
All drawings of work by Frank Lloyd Wright
Copyright © 1976 by The Frank Lloyd Wright Foundation
except for drawings on the following pages:
Pages 34, 35 © 1976 by Madeline Thatcher
Pages 20, 183 Copyright © 1976 by Richard MacCormac
Pages 24 lower, 58, 72, 73, 80-81 lower, 110, 163,
164, 169, 184 Copyright © 1976 by John Sergeant

First published 1976 in New York by Whitney Library of Design,
an imprint of Watson-Guptill Publications,
a division of Billboard Publications, Inc.,
1515 Broadway, New York, N.Y. 10036

Library of Congress Catalog Card Number: 76-7281
ISBN 0-8230-7177-4
ISBN 0-8230-7178-2 pbk.

Distributed in the United Kingdom by Phaidon Press Ltd., Littlegate
House, St. Ebbe's St., Oxford

Manufactured in U.S.A.

3 4 5 6 7 8/88 87 86 85

Edited by Susan Braybrooke, Susan Davis, and Naomi Goldstein
Designed by Michel Goldberg
Set in 10 point Helvetica by Gerard Associates/Graphic Arts, Inc.

Contents

Chronological List of Frank Lloyd Wright's Chief Designs, 1929–1943   **6**

Foreword by Lionel March   **7**

Preface   **9**

Introduction   **11**

1   The Usonian Concept   **15**

2   Housing Usonia   **31**

3   Education, Design, and Construction   **95**

4   Broadacre City   **121**

5   Popularizing Organic Architecture   **137**

6   Implications of Organic Design   **159**

Notes   **171**

Appendix A   A Spatial Analysis of Usonian Houses   **183**

Appendix B   The Personal Architectural Services of Frank Lloyd Wright   **189**

Appendix C Agreement between Contractor and Owner for Construction of Usonian Buildings   **191**

Appendix D   Organic Architecture Meets the International Style   **197**

Appendix E   Taliesin Memorabilia   **199**

Appendix F   Broadacre City Petition, 1943   **201**

Bibliography   **203**

Index   **205**

Chronological List of Frank Lloyd Wright's Chief Designs, 1929–1943

(Authorities whose dates differ from Pfeiffer's are given in parenthesis)

1929 Jones house, Tulsa Oklahoma
Project: St. Mark's-in-the-Bowerie apartment tower, New York, New York

1930 Kahn Lectures delivered at Princeton University

1932 Foundation of Taliesin Fellowship
Publication of *An Autobiography*
First study of Broadacre City

1934 Willey house, Minneapolis, Minnesota

1935 Kaufmann house, "Falling Water," Bear Run, Pennsylvania
House projects: Hoult, Lusk (1936, Hitchcock), Marcus

1936 Hanna house, Palo Alto, California
Jacobs house, Madison, Wisconsin (1937, Drexler and Hitchcock)
Roberts house, Marquette, Michigan
Administration building for Johnson Wax Company, Racine, Wisconsin

1937 Johnson house, "Wingspread," Racine, Wisconsin

1938 Rebhuhn house, Great Neck, New York
Taliesin West, Scottsdale, Arizona
Florida Southern College, Lakeland, Florida
House projects: Jester, Jurgensen, for *Life* magazine

1939 Armstrong house, Ogden Dunes, Indiana
Rosenbaum house, Florence, Alabama
Schwartz house, Two Rivers, Wisconsin
Sturges house, Brentwood Heights, California
"Suntop Homes," Quadruple Housing, Ardmore, Pennsylvania
Winkler-Goetsch house, Okemos, Michigan
Project: Usonia 1 housing

1940 Baird house, Amherst, Massachusetts
Bazett house, Hillsborough, California
Christie house, Bernardsville, New Jersey
Euchtman house, Baltimore, Maryland
Lewis house, Libertyville, Illinois
Manson house, Wausau, Wisconsin
Pauson house, Phoenix, Arizona
Pew house, Madison, Wisconsin
Sondern house, Kansas City, Kansas
Stevens plantation, Yemasee, South Carolina
House project: Oboler

1941 Affleck house, Bloomfield Hills, Michigan
Griggs house, Tacoma, Washington
Oboler gatehouse, Los Angeles, California
Richardson house, Glen Ridge, New Jersey
Wall house, Plymouth, Michigan
House projects: Petersen, Sundt

1942 Jacobs second house, Middleton, Wisconsin
House projects: Burlingham (1940, Drexler; 1941, Kaufmann, Jr.), Cooperative Homesteads, Cloverleaf Quadruple Housing

1943 Guggenheim Museum, New York, New York
House project: Hein

Foreword

This book is the first serious study of the Usonian home, a concept which stands in Frank Lloyd Wright's works where *l'unite d'habitation* stands in the works of Le Corbusier. Both concepts are the culmination of their architect's patient research into appropriate forms for housing in the 20th century. Both are conceived within a comprehensive urban framework—*la ville radieuse* in Le Corbusier's case and Broadacre City in Frank Lloyd Wright's, which is excellently described in Chapter 4 of this book. Both are transformations, indeed idealizations, of existing, common housing types—*l'apartement* and the villa, respectively. And both exemplars have enjoyed the contagion of success throughout the world's metropolitan areas.

But whereas many planners have argued that high-rise apartment buildings hold the solution to the problem of housing rapidly increasing urban populations in a situation of diminishing land supplies, few have advocated the widespread adoption of the single-family home, predominantly one-story and occupying on the average an acre of land per plot. Indeed the proposition seems absurd, if not downright irresponsible. If conventional wisdom is held to, then a study of the Usonian home will be of mere academic interest and of no relevance to public policy. At most a small, moderately wealthy class able to buy expensive land might find such a book of practical interest.

I believe that this is not the case and that John Sergeant's study is both timely and relevant. I hold the view that Frank Lloyd Wright's vision of the home and city is by far the most realistic in human, ecological terms of all the proposals for urban development put forward by planners and architects in this century and as such demands much more serious attention than has hitherto been given it by those politicians and professionals whose actions shape the futures of countless urban regions.

John Sergeant shows how Wright answered the challenges of rapid urbanization and population growth. While most designers came to accept the practical problem as that of accommodating "average households" in "residential units," Wright steadfastly stood by the idea of each individual family having its own distinctive home. Even those designers who have come to question the solution of mass production of housing types, and who advocate the construction of megastructures within which individual users might have degrees of freedom to adapt the environment to their particular needs, fail to touch the profound significance — appreciated by Wright —of family homes as autonomous estates in a presently shiftless, rootless mass society and as a plurality of centers for the restructuring and humanization of that society.

It was the Renaissance theorist, Alberti, who pointed out the appropriateness of the villa for family living: "A private house is manifestly designed for use of a family. . . . There is a great number of persons and things in a family, which you cannot distribute as you would in a city as well as you can in the suburbs. In building in town, your neighbor's wall, a common gutter, a public square or street, and the like shall all hinder you contriving it just to your own mind; which is not so in the country, where you have as much freedom as you have obstruction in the town."

The best "megastructure" for the home in Alberti's and Wright's opinion is the earth itself. But if this is accepted as an ideal, it raises two questions of a practical kind: first, is there enough land to accommodate people without crowding, and second, if populations are spread about so loosely, will not transportation and public utility costs be excessive? Neither question can be answered precisely, but some idea of the magnitude of the problem in these terms can be given.

Visualize an example: take a population and accommodate it as Wright suggests in his proposals for Broadacre City. It is a fact that the whole of the population of the United States requires no more land than that covered by maps of the Interstate Highway system where the roads are drawn to a scale representing a 4-mile band in reality, or 4 percent of the land surface. No other urban land would be required! Indeed half of the land so laid out would be for intensive agricultural and forestry uses anyway. Wright's proposal is to see the future nation as a single city. Today each separate city has to be linked to every other in an elaborate network of transport and communication channels. At the intersections and nodes there is congestion; between these there are channels that are underutilized. In Broadacre City the loads are spread along the network so that the system is in balance at every point. From a number of recent research investigations of a quantitative kind it seems that Wright's idealism is also highly practical as far as land use, transport, and communication are concerned.

Yet there remains one further question: who designs the individual homes? A simple calculation shows that the architectural profession could not possibly design homes for each individual family's needs. Wright knew this. Perhaps the most radical aspect of his work is to be found in his attitude to home building and self-help that John Sergeant brings to light in this book. Wright could see that people endowed with fine talents may set examples and that that is a social responsibility they must bear, but they have no right to enforce their opinions on anyone.

Wright saw the dissemination of innovative ideas through radio and television. He proposed setting up decentralized design stations that would promote research, advice, and education through the media. In particular such stations would concern themselves with local problems and with

fostering a distinctive *genius loci* in keeping with the area's natural resources, climatic conditions, and cultural development.

John Sergeant clearly sets out the sources of Wright's urban concepts that are deeply embedded in the American tradition, while at the same time he shows how Wright practiced what he preached. Sergeant has carefully demonstrated the organic nature of this great designer's life and works as made manifest in a brilliant galaxy of small and beautiful homes.

Lionel March
Cambridge, England

Preface

The dwelling of this century would be a very different matter without the work of Wright. The Prairie Houses countered the maelstrom of social and technical change in America before the First World War by emphasizing *rootedness* and the security of hearth and family. They did this with a planform and imagery which both shocked taste of the day and became an important component of the *ethos* of modern architecture. They possess an alluring blend of monumentality, engineering skill and reflections on Japanese architecture and the Arts and Crafts. The Usonian Houses endeavored to realize similar goals for the smaller budgets and much-changed conditions of the time of the Second World War.

The first edition of this book was intended to fill what I saw as a gap in studies of Frank Lloyd Wright. These were mainly descriptive, and it was not possible to consult any analysis of the late work. It was however written in the mid-1970's, at the very particular moment of the Energy Crisis, and reflects this concern. Were I to undertake the task now I should enlarge the formal study which was started in the first Appendix: the spatial analysis. It is one of the perennial strengths of Wright's design that it is able to sustain study from widely different viewpoints and is amenable to varying interpretation. The American organic tradition, although it used the slogan 'Form follows Function', never suffered from the crude rationalism of the mainstream Modern Movement, and throughout made use of symbol and metaphor. This resulted in a richness of imagery which is likely to appeal to changing architectural interests. There is however a fundamental proposition behind all aspects of Wright's work, not least in its energy implications, and this is in its holistic attitude toward life and Nature. We are, with our culture and our technology, a part of a fragile creation and not separate from or above it. In Wright's view this should inform not just the siting and concept of our buildings, but the way in which we approach all tasks.

This study did not have the advantage of access to Frank Lloyd Wright archives. It was therefore necessary to travel far to unearth collections of Wright's letters, interview surviving clients and apprentices, and measure as many Usonian houses as possible. The plans have all been redrawn to the same scale to aid comparison, and summaries of building and client information have been added. I trust that the calculations of net area, measured inside the outside walls, are accurate to within 5 percent.

The dating that I have adopted for Wright's houses refers to the date of design. Completion occurred later, and in some cases, notably those of the self-build homes, up to 15 years later. I am following the method of Pfeiffer, who is archivist for the Frank Lloyd Wright Memorial Foundation, as used in his chronological listing of Wright's *opus*, published at the end of Olgivanna Wright's book, *Frank Lloyd Wright: His Life, His Works, His Words.* Pfeiffer adopts the date of the drawing signed by Wright. My work has uncovered discrepancies with the dating of some clients' drawings. However, since Pfeiffer is, to all intents and purposes, the only person allowed access to Wright's archives and 9,000 drawings, the matter must rest there, until scholars are permitted to work on the material.

Only study of Wright's correspondence with his clients will clarify dating inaccuracies. Wright was not adverse to changing the dates on drawings to make them earlier. Russell Hitchcock's research at Taliesin in the summer of 1941 disputed Wright's chronology so that certain drawings have two dates, Wright's and Hitchcock's. Pfeiffer's datings occasionally conflict with evidence of former apprentices who worked on them.

Wright's thought was both broad and far-ranging. The same mind that related the detail of the buildings to their concept placed his house designs in a total social context. This book has therefore been difficult to write. Any thread of argument loses the depth of Wright's "lateral thinking." I have tried to make the footnotes a commentary on the text, as well as informative, and I hope the reader will use them.

My approach to many aspects of Wright's work in the 1930s and 1940s has benefited directly from the advice of Curtis Besinger, professor in the School of Architecture and Urban Design, University of Kansas, and my grasp of Wright's historical background has been enlarged and guided by Lionel March, professor in the Department of Systems Design, University of Waterloo, Ontario, and lecturer in the Cambridge University School of Architecture. Both have allowed me to make use of their own material and have been of incalculable help.

I am also very grateful to a large number of people for making it possible to write this book:

The initial research was partly funded by grants from Liverpool University and the Liverpool Architectural Society.

The final field work was the result of the help of Professors Gardner-Medwin and Tarn and a leave of absence from Liverpool University.

David Lea, London, for his continuous encouragement.

Professor Colin Rowe, Cornell University; Francis Jones, Frank Horton, and Malcolm Quantrill, the Liverpool School of Architecture; Professor Newton Watson and Dean La Tourelle of the School of Environmental Studies, University College, London; Professors Dougan and Leonard Eaton of the University of Michigan; and Professor George Beal, University of Kansas, for their suggestions and advice.

Bob Twombly, professor in the Department of History, City College, New York, for his help and references.

John Pritchard of the Liverpool School, David Kent of the Cambridge School of Architecture, and Madeleine Thatcher for their draftsmanship.

Susan Braybrooke and Susan Davis, my editors at the Whitney Library of Design, for their patience and enthusiasm.

John Howe, Minneapolis; Herbert Jacobs, Berkeley, California; and Blaine Cliver of the National Trust for Historic Preservation, Washington, D.C., for their correspondence.

The staffs of many libraries, especially the Avery Library, Columbia University, and the Kenneth Spencer Research Library, University of Kansas.

The many owners of Wright and Goff homes that I visited, for their kindness and help, especially Stanley and Mildred Rosenbaum of Florence, Alabama.

None of the fieldwork would have been possible without the generosity and home-from-home of Betty and Martin Fisch; and the whole six years' work would not have come to fruition without Ronni, my wife, who accompanied me along the miles of desert and mosquitoes, and whose criticism and insight saw the book through many drafts.

10

Introduction

Since I started this study, the architectural world has changed. The qualities of Frank Lloyd Wright's post-Depression houses that attracted me — their use of natural materials and cool, shaded interiors, and their close relationship with their sites — have become points of departure for new buildings. But the concept of organic architecture for which Wright fought — the idea of building with nature rather than against it — has largely been ignored during the last two decades. Building sites have been regarded as surfaces to be manipulated, and cheap energy has encouraged deficiencies in building design to be made up by reliance on the heating and cooling plant. An esthetic of building, that of steel, aluminum and glass, has been established, requiring materials that will become increasingly scarce and that utilize enormous energy inputs in their manufacture. This architectural esthetic expresses waste and a belief, it is to be hoped now dead, in a human-dominated nature.

When I first visited the United States I, like many Europeans, was surprised equally by the extremes of the climate and the overcompensation for this in American buildings. In Houston, Texas, people carried heavy woolens with them to survive the numbing cold of air conditioned public buildings. In San Francisco in 1964, I asked the head of the design section of Skidmore, Owings & Merrill, for whom I briefly worked, why all four sides of their office buildings were always constructed in the same way — so that the north facade was heated and the south facade simultaneously cooled. It was not merely naiveté that made me ask this, but the belief that the elements of buildings should vary with their locale. I remembered the example given by Buckminster Fuller some years before in London,[1] when he declared the Bell Telephone kiosk to be his archetype for successful building. This prefabricated capsule gave equal comfort in the sub-zero dark of Alaska and in the heat of the Arizona desert.

It struck me at the time that Fuller's proposition implied an increasingly sterile and unvaried world. Architects now practicing were influenced by this and other similar pronouncements. In 1965, one analysis suggested that there was then so much mechanical equipment in houses that it could be used to support a lightweight skin, dispensing with the building shell entirely.[2] I was therefore startled to discover that the inhabitants of Wright's post-Depression houses, those of a type of construction used from 1936–1943 to which he gave the name Usonian, had only background heat. They lit fires and even put on sweaters in very cold spells. In summer the Usonian house gave shade and breeze, but the occupants' tempo had to alter with hot weather. Conditions were comfortable but not artificially so. The thermal mass of masonry and heavy floors and roof themselves prevented the structure from suffering extremes of temperature. The energy implications of this are no less important than the way of living it suggests.

By contrast, the mobile home was, by 1970, almost as ubiquitous as the telephone booth. It was deployed in every state without variation or regard for location, and accounted for nearly one-quarter of the entire housing stock. The lower-income groups of homebuyers, for whom this was the only choice, are today confronted with enormously increased utility and maintenance costs for lightweight, poorly insulated construction.

The federal Department of Housing and Urban Development attempted in 1970 to meet the housing shortage by encouraging prefabrication. Under its Operation Breakthrough program, modular homes were shipped 3,000 miles from Pennsylvania to the state of Washington. There they still undercut local west coast building costs despite the added cost of shipping complete house units. This was possible because of cheap energy and therefore transportation. In order to distribute industrialized homes, components had to be lightweight and therefore without thermal mass. One of the most cherished beliefs of modern architecture—the ability to utilize mass production in housing — now seems in question.

In 1964 I visited Wright's Bazett and Hanna houses. I found them to be homes that air conditioned themselves, for the fabric of the building shaded, lit, and insulated itself. These houses expressed a warmth and naturalness for which I was totally unprepared. I had come into contact with an architectural ability that I sensed had generated the relationships with trees and contours and twists and turns, all of which gave me such enjoyment. I also found built-in seats where the building made me pause. I found soft lighting from within the fabric, and above all an extraordinary flowing, contained, and varied sense of space. When I tried to relate these houses to what I knew of Wright's work I found it very difficult to do so. There was Wright's book, *The Natural House,* but no study that placed this late domestic design in a wider context.

Five years later I began traveling to study Wright's late houses and discovered that the qualities that had attracted me originally were all more fully developed the further I progressed along my 29,000-mile pilgrimage. Like English vernacular buildings, Wright's houses varied in materials and siting to suit their localities. Few of them were air conditioned. Their name, Usonian, was nowhere fully explained. As I learned something of Wright's plan for urban decentralization, known as Broadacre City (which originated at the same time as the Usonian homes), I found that this plan was dismissed as impractical utopianism in everything I read. Yet in all those weeks on the highway I was constantly traversing roadside commercial strips and far-flung residential areas that seemed very close to Wright's predictions.

There seemed to be a determination on the part of all the critics I consulted not to recognize the obvious. Whether this might have been caused by the character of the man, I did not know. I read that he was conservative, yet his private life was not exactly conventional. He was a friend of Clarence Darrow, the liberal lawyer and advocate for the socially deprived, and was associated with a group of men at the University of Wisconsin who were leading American radicals. Then I read of Wright in John Dos Passos' *USA: The Big Money:*

... an erect spare white-haired man, his sons are architects, apprentices from all over the world come to work with him, drafting the new city (he calls it Broadacre City). Near and Far are beaten (to imagine the new city you must blot out every ingrained habit of the past, build a nation from the ground up with the new tools). For the architect there are only uses . . . and needs.

(Tell us, doctors of philosophy, what are the needs of a man. At least a man needs to be notjailed notafraid nothungry notcold not without love, not a worker for a power he has never seen —that cares nothing for the uses and needs of a man or a woman or a child.) Building a building is building the lives of the workers and dwellers in the building. . . .[3]

There seemed to be a need for a book on what can be called Wright's second career, a book that tried to relate the man's architectural work to his philosophy. His concept of organic architecture has certainly been given a new relevance by the realization of "ecological principles," and it might be that the underlying political convictions merited a hearing. Wright himself said:

We are very slow to take things on that occur at home. It has always been the idea of our people that culture came from abroad and it did, so you can't blame them for thinking so. They didn't want to hear of its developing here in the tall grasses of the western prairies.[4]

The period of Wright's work that is under discussion here is generally marked by the Depression at the beginning and the Korean War at the end.

The year 1929, when Wright was 62, is easily identified as the year his architectural practice, like almost everything, collapsed and he started work on his planning proposals. By his eightieth year, in 1947, he had formulated principles for the design of the small house and made the overall plans for a number of residential communities. There were some remarkable exceptions, but his chief contribution to domestic design had already been made.

As he grew older, Wright frequently returned to the concept, which he had expressed in 1908, of houses being as different as their owners. In expressing their individuality and way of life, enhancing the beauty of their sites, and increasingly using local materials, he was building "organically." Some late houses, usually those for clients whose characters especially attracted Wright, or for spectacular sites, achieved an extraordinarily unique quality. However this was by no means restricted to Wright's work. Although the homes designed by other architects were visually very different, and of another order of design skill, I found that ownerbuilders all over the country were expressing the same concept, often achieved on very low budgets and with salvaged materials. For example, in the Southwest I found that there was a body of work in which Bruce Goff, together with his clients, was building original designs and creating works of art that demanded recognition.

The chief advance of the Usonian houses was to evolve a *way* of building, which was subsequently varied to suit differing sites and clients. It included open planning in the living areas; small bedrooms, well supplied with built-in closets; as well as a zoning of the plan to maximize whatever spaciousness a small home might have. All these features were used again and again. The relationships of the house mass to the carport and terrace, of the living areas to the central kitchen and bedroom wing remained remarkably constant. The houses could be expanded easily and were made according to a method of construction that eliminated finishing trades and "decoration," revealing the materials of which they were made. Each house was different, yet each one used what Wright called the same "grammar."

The standard American house of this century, the traditional North American home, was framed of wood, plastered inside and clapboarded out, and set upon an excavated basement that was located well below the frost line and contained the heating plant. Wright's late houses were radically different from this standard; they were organized horizontally, allowing a closer relationship with the outdoors, lacking completely the "boxing in" of compartmentalized rooms, and they dispensed with the basement. They even dispensed with massive, conventional foundations, which was a daring, cost-saving innovation. They were uncluttered by radiators, since they were heated from the floors by "gravity heat."

Wright was opposed to air conditioning. He argued, "external changes in temperature that tear down a building also tear down the human body."[5] The seasonal changes that occur almost everywhere in the United States are extreme, and buildings that do not rely on machinery to achieve comfort need to react very closely to this climatic change. For Wright this factor was viewed as an opportunity for design to work with natural conditions, indeed to express them. It is a complex task, for not only do continental conditions vary considerably, but body reactions to temperature depend upon these variations. The body can lose heat to its surroundings by direct radiation to nearby surfaces, by convection to the air, or by evaporation of moisture from the skin. So, like anyone who has lived in Chicago, Wright knew that a bald statement of temperature was meaningless without knowledge of prevailing wind speed and the degree of

humidity. A temperature of 70°F can feel like 50°F in a strong wind, but like 85–90°F in still, humid air.

The climate of southern Wisconsin, where the Usonian house originated, is that of the temperate zone, roughly encompassing the Midwest and Northeast. The temperature range is from subzero to the upper nineties; the summer is humid and the winter, especially in the northern Midwest, is like that of the tundra, the source of the northern winds. In spring and fall the changes of temperature can be sudden, causing building materials to expand and contract equally suddenly. In the southern prairies these changes can be violent, involving temperature changes of 45°F in one day, torrential rain, or damaging hailstones. Frost extends 2 ft or more into the ground, and where moisture is present, can move and crack buildings. In this zone, Usonian houses were generally successful.

The Southwest and Southeast can be broadly classified a humid zone, with generally higher temperatures than the Midwest and Northeast. These may be above 100°F with up to 100 percent humidity, so it is important to open a building to cooling breezes or to induce or entrain them. In the Western arid zone, the air is dry, but temperatures, especially those between day and night, can fluctuate greatly. In both zones, reflected solar heat and glare can be insufferable, and the transition from building to site can substantially affect the interior conditions. The Usonian houses were generally successful, although in some instances Wright made too great a use of glazed areas. In some northern locations this increased heat losses; and in the south because of solar gains, some homes have had air conditioning subsequently installed by their owners.

Wright's concept of organic architecture, however, meant very much more than building homes that work with the climate to produce conditions of comfort by natural means. Wright endowed

the word "organic" with such cultural meaning that the remainder of this book would be required to attempt a whole definition. He gave some idea of his interpretation in a conversation with Mies van der Rohe, reproduced in the first *Taliesin* publication of 1940.

Like every other architectural scheme which is real, Broadacre City is here presented as a transitional scheme. All genuinely great building is transitional building. Only as we can plan to take advantage of the law of change in the process of growth can we do justice to human nature. Through the law of cause and effect, we must proceed to interpret the present in terms of the future. So this is not intended to be an ultimate pattern, but one so free of major and minor axes as never to become the usual academic fixation, and always to have sufficient reflex to accommodate inevitable organic change. In other words it is not "classic." It is organic.[6]

One dictionary definition of "organic" is "having systematic coordination, organized, forming an organic whole." Wright's idea is nearer to the concept defined in the dictionary as "pertaining to a certain organization not accidental" and in the biological sense "derived from living organisms." The Wrightian dictum "out of the ground and into the light!" nicely contains the layers of meaning involved. "Out of the ground" refers to the roots or origins of organic action, the inner nature of the context or problem generating design. "Into the light" is the ever-changing present that action meets, while between the two is a structured process of growth. It is the last that has been imperfectly understood.

It is the first principle of any growth that the thing grown be no mere aggregation. Integration as entity is first essential. And integration means that no part of anything is of any great validity in itself except as it be an integrate part of the harmonious whole.[7]

For Wright, an organic whole is not a state, but a dynamic process, and it is for this reason that he believed that "no organic building may ever be 'finished.' The complete goal of the ideal of organic architecture is never reached."[8]

13

This viewpoint has its counterpart in philosophy. The universe is, according to Whitehead, dynamic and self-integrating: "The proper test is not that of finality, but of progress."[9] According to Paul Henshaw, "Life is defined as a kind of sustained interaction among the elements of nature—one in which the forces for organization are greater than the forces for disorganization, leaving a margin for life and thereby the attributes of behavior."[10] And as Edward Frank states, in an excellent paper on Wright, "Organic philosophy accepts the position that man is an experiencing being, or better yet, an experiencing becoming, whose nature is dynamic and therefore rejects the view of man divorced from the world and aloof from the flow of life."[11]

It was this attitude of mind that produced an architecture that is never understood at once, in the manner of a classical building. Organic architecture engages the senses, since it can only be appreciated if the viewer walks around it and perceives the action of the time upon it and the mind, because the physical is left purposely incomplete to be mentally resolved by the observer. At this point Wright's approach to design met the insight of Lao-Tse:

The use of clay in molding pitchers comes from the hollow of its absence

Doors and windows in a house are used for their emptiness

Thus we are helped by what is not to use what is.[12]

This expresses Wright's idea of free space in architecture and untroubled attitude to the present, "the ever moving infinite that divides Yesterday from Tomorrow."[13] It is the difference between the growth of Taliesin, which is a rambling genetic process with every stage a fresh occasion in time, and the growth of the Bell Telephone Laboratories at Holmdell, New Jersey, which were built by stages, each of which was an aggregation toward a predetermined, finite form. This contrast has been lucidly expressed by Edward Frank.

When Mies [van der Rohe] remarked that he would never design a dome since he could not know what sort of space he was creating, he defined precisely the difference in world conceptions between Wright and himself. To Mies a dome, or any other curved surface, is a succession of isolated, infinitely small points, each creating its unique space. This infinitely variable space cannot possibly be intellectually comprehended by a man crossing it. To Wright however, it is the whole man, including his intellect, who experiences the act of traversing the space. To one, space is an objective fact: to the other, it is a subjective experience. Henri Bergson distinguishes these different approaches to reality by writing "We attribute to the motion the divisibility of the space which it traverses, forgetting that it is quite possible to divide an object, but not an act." . . . To Mies architecture is the distillation of the known; to Wright architecture is an adventure, within the greater adventure of life and evolution, into ever more profound depths of nature.[14]

Wright's clients were people who felt that the Usonian houses expressed the way that they wished to live. For them he was meeting a need for a more informal family life. His homes allowed easy and maximal use of a small site. They had no "sense of the grand," but were designed for the celebration of the family coming together. They were not formulated for servant-help, but were planned for ease of maintenance with a central kitchen from which conversation could be maintained with guests. In the 1930s organic houses anticipated a lifestyle for which only a few were ready — those who had adapted first to social change. "When a man wants to build a building he seeks an interpreter, does he not? He seeks some man who has the technique to express that thing which he himself desires but cannot do."[15] The interpretation of the need for a small, informal house was the greatest achievement of Wright's late architectural career. However, it was formulated in post-Depression America at a time when an organic architecture in which each person was free to express his or her needs was clearly impossible. It was to Wright's great credit that he was impelled to find a means by which society could be changed to allow this to happen, which meant society must itself become organic.

. . . but we cannot have an organic architecture unless we have an organic society. We may build *some buildings for a few people* knowing the significance or value of that sense of the whole which we are learning to call organic, but we cannot have an architecture for a society such as ours now is.[16]

Therefore a study of Wright's late houses must also be a study of Broadacre City. His concern did not stop with those who could afford his services, but included a formulation of the emergent decentralized city in which every citizen could reach his or her full potential.

CHAPTER 1 The Usonian Concept

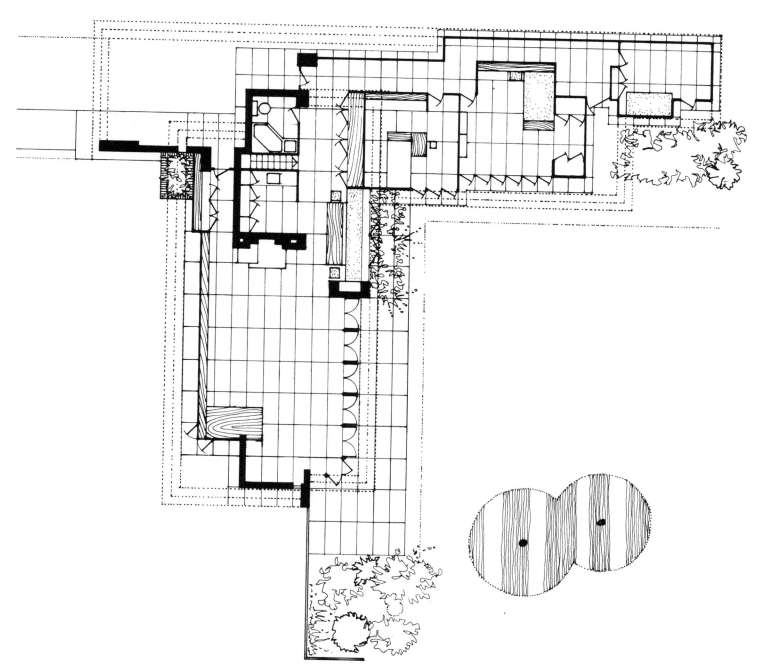

The house of moderate cost is not only America's major architectural problem but the problem most difficult for her major architects.[1]

Notwithstanding all efforts to improve the product, the American "small house" problem is still a pressing, needy, hungry, confused issue.[2]

Wright was an undeniably brilliant designer of large and expensive houses, which, because they have attracted much critical interest, have tended to divert attention from his most important body of work — his small houses. For 20 years after the Depression, Wright struggled with the problem of low-cost housing against a background first of shortages of resources, then of rising costs. During this period he continually created places of great beauty and sought to bring about an architecture of warmth and humanity. He demonstrated a staggering number of innovations, from sheet steel to earth walling, and from self-build homes to cooperative communities. These have received little attention and have never before been brought together in one volume. The very name that he gave to all the buildings of this second creative period of his life, Usonian, calls for insight into its use and their meaning. To study Wright's Usonian houses is to observe fragments of their designer's vision of society and the city. They summarize all his skills as a designer and are directly related to Broadacre City, his mature life's work.

Usonia

The name "Usonia" presents a slight mystery. As Wright himself put it, "We had no real name for ourselves." He ascribed this better word for the "States United" to Samuel Butler's novel *Erewhon,* where it does not, in fact, appear. It has been suggested that Wright picked up the name on his first European trip in 1910 when there was talk of calling the U.S.A. "U-S-O-N-A," to avoid confusion with the new Union of South Africa.[3] However, Wright made "Usonian" as much his personal word as he did "organic,"

and indeed, the two came to mean much the same for him. "Usonia" was his name for the reformed American society that he tried for the last 25 years of his life to bring about. (See Chapter 4 for a thorough discussion.) "Organic" referred to the way in which this change was going to occur. Ultimately, both spring from Wright's deep conviction that a culture or an individual should proceed integrally from its core or roots, "out of the ground and into the light."

The Jacobs House

In 1936, both Falling Water, the Kaufmann weekend house at Bear Run, Pennsylvania, and the Administration Building for Johnson Wax Co. in Racine, Wisconsin, heralded the resurgence of Wright's practice. They also overshadowed the publication the next year of the first Usonian home, the Herbert Jacobs house in Madison, Wisconsin.[4] However, this humble 1,500-sq-ft home built for $5,500 was to be of more lasting significance than either of the larger projects.

Usonian Manifesto

In the January 1938 edition of *Architectural Forum,* which was completely designed by Wright, the solution to the "small house problem" was demonstrated not only by the plans and photographs of the dwelling but also by the characteristically pragmatic manifesto that accompanied it.

What would be really sensible in this matter of the modest dwelling for our time and place? This house for a young journalist, his wife, and small daughter is now under roof. Cost: Fifty-five hundred dollars including architect's fee of four hundred and fifty. Contract let to Bert Grove. To give the small Jacobs family the benefit of the advantages of the era in which we live, many simplifications must take place. Mr. and Mrs. Jacobs must themselves see life in somewhat simplified terms. What are the essentials in their case, *a typical case?* It is not necessary only to get rid of unnecessary complications in construction, necessary to use work in the mill to good advantage (off-site prefabrication), necessary to eliminate, so far as possible, field labor, which is al-

ways expensive: it is necessary to consolidate and simplify the three appurtenance systems — heating, lighting, and sanitation. . . . At least this must be our economy if we are to achieve the sense of spaciousness and vista we desire in order to liberate the people living in the house.[5]

Wright goes on, ". . . and it would be ideal to complete the building in one operation as it goes along, inside and out." With only a hint at the reality of the sheer beauty and utility of the home, Wright sought to show its relevance in the down-to-earth terms of building construction. In fact, he demonstrated, as one would expect, very clear understanding of the building process.[6]

The significance of the Jacobs house lies not only in the fact that in it Wright realized all his technical innovations, but also that these were quietly integrated into a plan and lifestyle that delighted his clients and met the need for an informal house to suit the changed social habits of the late 1930s. The simplifications and improvements that Usonian houses offered were later incorporated into the broad mass of subsequent American homebuilding.

Planning Innovations

At a minimal cost, the Jacobses obtained a home that ensured their privacy from the street, maximized the garden area on a small suburban lot, and gave them a spacious interior. The way in which this was achieved was novel and intriguing. In its site planning, the house fronted closely on the street and one boundary. This reduced the expense of a driveway and increased the depth of the garden behind the house. Its L shape created an inner world to which the family and all usable rooms related.

The design rejected the overblown practice (still current in America) of setting a miniaturized plantation house on an infinitesimal and unusable lawn.[7] The resulting problems of potential overlooking from the street that this caused were solved brilliantly by turning the house's back to the street, with

16

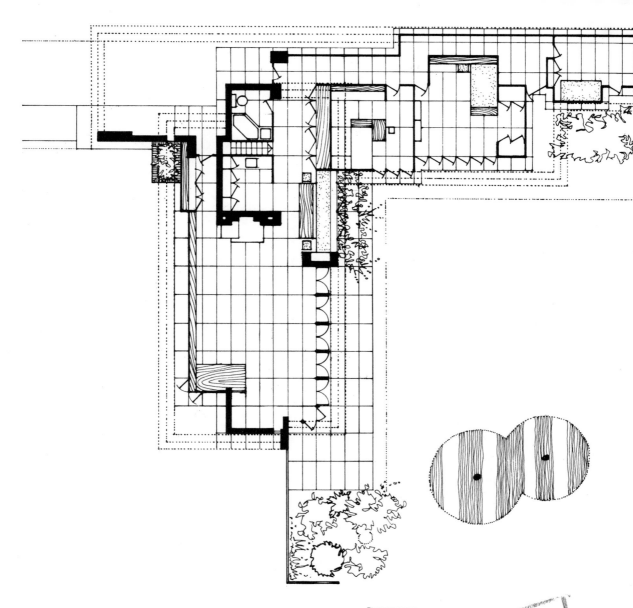

Clients: Mr. and Mrs. Herbert Jacobs
Profession: Journalist, author
Location: Madison, Wisconsin
Year of design: 1936
Best source: *Architectural Forum,* January 1938; Henry Russell Hitchcock, *In the Nature of Materials*
Builder/supervisor: Taliesin Fellowship
Cost: $5,500
Floor area: 1,340 sq ft; 124.5 sq m

4 0 4 8 12 16 feet
1 0 1 2 3 4 5 metres

The Jacobs house, exterior, Madison, Wisconsin, 1936. Photograph by Pedro E. Guerrero.

only high-level windows on that facade. The bedroom wing, with a narrow corridor leading outside past the third bedroom, made up one side of the garden, and the great sweep of living area, with its fireplace, bookshelves, table, dining alcove, and terrace, made up the other. Centralizing the services immediately placed the kitchen and bathroom at the "hinge" of the plan, with convenient access to both doors. Anyone working in the kitchen was then in a central but open position—an advance of some sociological significance.

Kelly Smith and Twombly have both commented on the way in which the social organization of the Usonians changed from Wright's earlier Prairie houses.[8] The homes of the period between 1900 and 1910 expressed the unity of the family, with their open plans pinwheeling about a central chimney core, but they contained contrasting elements of an informal livingroom and almost ritualistic diningroom.[9] Dining was the prime social event of the period, so that by her organization, choice, and direction of servants, the hostess could display those qualities identified by Veblen as "conspicuous consumption."[10] After dinner, company moved to the livingroom and interacted more freely.

By 1937, Wright had abolished the diningroom. It became merely a specialized area of the livingroom in the same sense that places for music or reading were subtly suggested spatially and delineated by furniture. It is a noteworthy point that Usonian houses could contain little conventional furniture; reclining chairs, coffee tables, and pianos were most commonly used, as immovable pieces were all built-in. This followed Wright's sixth proposition, from the 1938 *Forum* mentioned previously, that "furniture, pictures, and bric a brac are unnecessary except as the walls can be made to include them or be them."[11]

Mrs. Jacobs, by contrast with earlier hostesses, was comparatively eman-

cipated. From her kitchen (which Wright soon began to call the workplace), she could watch the children on the terrace, bring food to the table almost without moving, and join in conversation with guests. This centralized position contrasts with the Prairie house kitchen, located in a corner of the house for the use of a servant or "hired girl."

The whole Usonian living area was designed to encourage informal use. Mrs. Leighey, in a later Usonian, described how the dining table was too small for formal dining but could be used for buffet entertaining.[12] And Mr. Jacobs remembers how his home could occasionally accommodate parties for the whole Taliesin Fellowship.[13]

The key to all this lay in the tightly designed "service core" of brickwork. The kitchen was efficiently laid out inside the service core like a ship's galley, with all walls used for storage or appliances and the ceiling carried up to clerestory windows above the surrounding roofs. Odors were thus removed, while cooking activities went on out of sight but within conversing distance. The bathroom lay alongside, and a short flight of steps led down to a small cellar for heating, fuel, and laundry. Attached to the exterior was Wright's invention, the carport.

Novel Construction Techniques

The Jacobs house incorporated three major construction features that were used in all subsequent Usonians: the board and batten walls; a planning grid, which simplified both architect's and builder's work; and a novel form of underfloor heating.

Board and Batten Walls

With the exception of minimal masonry load-bearing or wind-bracing points, the exterior walls were either glazed or of the famous Usonian sandwich panel. These board and batten walls, of pine in the Jacobs house, but subsequently of beautifully grained cypress wood, formed both the interior and

exterior finish. The need for plastering and decoration was thus removed at a stroke. The core of plywood was covered on each side by a dampproof membrane, and the battens screwed to it on both sides were so shaped as to hold the boards, while allowing them to expand. This composite wall was strong, gave insulation, and, Wright claimed, was "vermin proof and practically fireproof." In origin, the strong horizontal appearance referred to a traditional American form of barn wall or single-skin fencing as well as to Wright's own early work.[14]

Wright's preferred practice with Usonians was to construct the roof first, supported by the brick masses and window-wall posts, then to insert the wall panels, which could be assembled off-site or under the shelter of the roof, a traditional practice of Japanese architecture. This board and batten system was also integrated with the detailing in a direct and very clear way. The dimensions of board and batten gave a regular "stripe" or vertical module of 1 ft 1 in, and this controlled the heights of window transoms, sills, the "decks" for concealed lighting, bookshelves, eaves, clerestory windows, and chimneys. Elements of millwork were interwoven like basketry so that upper battens were aligned through the head of door frames, while the boards overlapped their jambs.

The Planning Grid

A horizontal 2 by 4 ft module or grid controlled the plan. This grid appeared on the architect's drawing as well as on the concrete floor itself, enabling the builder to locate walls and glazing units easily. For Wright the grid had pragmatic advantages — its dimensions were chosen to coincide with those of its materials, such as plywood, and thus reduced cutting and waste. He had always used grids. In the Prairie houses these were of complex tartan configurations and delineated the open interiors and exterior portecocheres and porches that echoed their cruciforms. Masonry piers punctuate and articulate

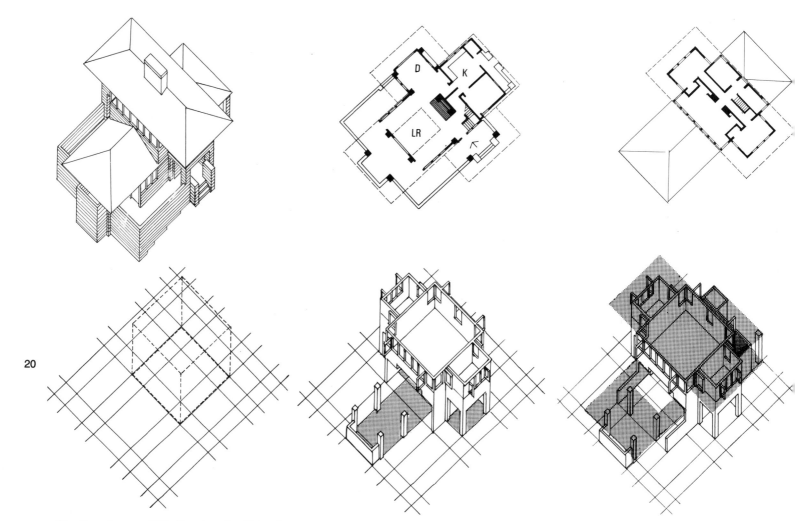

20

The Ross house, 1906. Drawings by Richard MacCormac.

these planning grids both on a drawing and in the experience of the spaces themselves. The entire working of the plan and its visual form are derived from these grids. They are the key to terse, simple plans like the Evans house, built in 1908, as much as to such complex overlays as the Martin house, built in 1904.

A valuable paper by Richard MacCormac demonstrated the educational toys of Wright's childhood as the origin of these grids.[15] These block-arranging games, invented by Froebel, and named "Gifts" by him, encouraged a search for unity and correlation of abstract pattern with three-dimensional form that became Wright's principal design tool. (This is discussed in detail in Appendix A: A Spatial Analysis of Usonian Houses.) By 1937, the simplified grid, or "unit system" as Wright called it, had also become the dimensioning system. At a time when a building's perimeters were elaborately dimensioned in the traditional way and working drawings were time-consuming pictures, Usonian walls and openings were simply centered on, or aligned with, or related to, subdivisions of the grid.[16] Not only did the grid allow drawings to be rationalized, but without it no concept of utilizing off-site prefabrication was possible.

Underfloor Heating

The lightweight floorslab of the Jacobs house was no less radical. The traditional basement, with masonry carried well below the frost line, was dispensed with. Wright substituted the thin concrete "floormat" that, with only slight edge-stiffening, sat upon a drained gravel bed. By incorporating steam or hot water piping, it became possible to heat the floor and abolish radiators. The elaborate millwork needed to conceal radiators in the Prairie houses could therefore be eliminated, while the Usonians contained the sweep and flow of their interior space even though on a smaller scale. Moreover, the result was an overall heat without draft or temperature variation of the most delightful type —cool head and warm feet.[17]

21

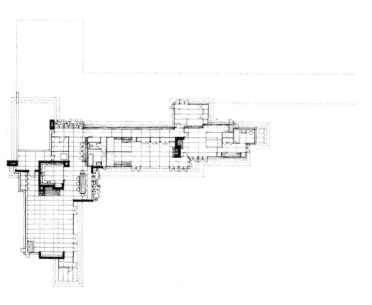

The Garrison house project, long-tail plan, Lansing, Michigan, 1939.

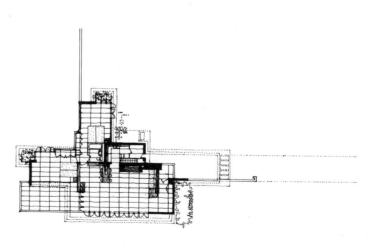

The Hause house project, short-tail plan, Lansing, Michigan, 1939.

A Kit for Growth and Change

After World War II, when Wright moved on from board and batten and brickwork construction, all his houses were called Usonian. However, within its original meaning the Usonian house was a rationale for going about "the small house problem." It was a kit of parts. Designs were sensitively varied according to clients' needs as well as siting and local building materials, but were recognizably "of a family," both in planning concept and construction. Wright himself described how they might also ". . . without deformity, be expanded later for the needs of a growing family. As you see from the plans, Usonian houses are shaped like polliwogs [or tadpoles] . . . with a shorter or longer tail. The body is the living-room and adjoining kitchen — and the whole Usonian concentration of conveniences. From there it starts out, with a tail: in the proper direction, say one-two bedrooms, three, four, five, six, bedrooms long; provision between each two rooms for a convenient bathroom."[18]

To reduce the tail and the home's external surface area, and to keep up with a growing family, double-decker bunks were fitted in children's rooms. Bedrooms were always very small and relied for their utility on large amounts of beautifully detailed built-in storage. The gallery or corridor (which was also used for continuous storage of books or clothes and was a space in its own right) was also very narrow.[19]

The bedroom wing might contain a playroom for children, as in the unbuilt Garrison project, and a study was commonly attached to the main "body" of the building, as in the Baird and Rosenbaum houses.

Satisfied Customers

For the most part, the original "kit" Usonians (which numbered 26 by 1948 when some were published in *Architectural Forum)* have survived the cycle of growing family, children leaving home, retirement, and visits by grandchildren. Most have not only survived well, but still house their original owners, who are now in their middle or old age. The Jacobses finally had three children and had to build again. The Hanna house in Palo Alto, California, was designed to allow the interior to be radically replanned. Other Usonians were enlarged. The Sondern house in Kansas City, for example, changed hands and was extended by Wright. The Rosenbaum house in Florence, Alabama, was given a unique court-yard addition to accommodate guests and a growing family.

Jacobs was the first in a select band of people whom Wright called "lower middle" clients who knew they were pioneers when they built their homes. They were immensely happy with their homes, and many wrote articles and even books saying so.[20] On first approaching Wright, the Jacobs thought of him as a "rich man's architect." This expectation was shared by nearly all the subsequent Usonian clients, who typically thought that he would not be interested in their humble problems and restricted budgets. All found the opposite to be the case.

The Evolution of the Usonian Concept

Herbert Jacobs gave Wright the opportunity to test the ideas that he had formulated during a decade. The notion of a variable, but constructionally standardized, low-cost dwelling with centralized services can be most directly traced to the "minimum houses" that accompanied the presentation of Broadacre City in 1935[21] and the "zoned houses" of 1934. The first magazine put out by the early Taliesin Fellowship contains a letter to Wright from housewife Dorothy Johnson Field. The letter makes an important planning point on the need to zone the house for children. This made a clear impression on Wright and in turn inspired the "two-zoned house" with its centralized services. He described these in *Taliesin* magazine.

"The utility stack has economically standardized and concentrated within it all the appurtenance systems entering into modern house construction: oil burning boiler and fuel tanks, air compressors, oil and gasoline supply for car, heating and air conditioning units, electric wiring and plumbing, vent and smoke flues. . . . Each bathroom, entire, is a one-piece standardized fixture directly connected to the stack; kitchen sink, ranges, and refrigeration likewise. Here as the nexus of the arrangement is a complete standardization in factory production of the wasteful tangled web of wires and piping at present involved in the construction of the ordinary dwelling."[22]

Although the "minimum houses" were designed to be built of sheet steel, both they and the "zoned houses" shared the concept of modularly related component assembly. Ultimately they relate to the blockwork houses of the 1920s, which also greatly developed such planning advances as the open living area without a separate diningroom that had appeared in some Prairie houses. The sensitive site planning of the Jacobs and other Usonian homes was obviously endemic to Wright throughout his career. However the maximization of site for a garden was a post-Depression concern, related to important ideas of self-sufficiency, as well as to Wright's own lifestyle at Taliesin, and the "centerline" of his model for reform of American society, Broadacre City.

The Dean Willey house of 1934 in Minneapolis, Minnesota, was the first essay in what became an exercise in land use, developed through many Usonians to the "quadruple" homes of 1939–1940. The house was called "The Garden Wall" and quite literally "wraps around the northwest corner of a lot sloping to the south—a fine vista in that direction."[23] This house with its angled wide eaves, hipped roof, internally battened ceiling, and symmetrical planting boxes, marks a fascinating link between the Prairie houses on the one hand, and the Usonians on the other, which it evokes in its untouched materials (cypress and brick), simple fireplace, brick-covered floormat, and prototype livingroom–bedroom "tail" plan. At this point the floors were solid, although not incorporating buried heating, and heating was by means of radiators.

This important house led to the projected Hoult house of 1935, in Wichita, Kansas. The Hoult design is designated by Pfeiffer to be the first Usonian house. John Howe substantiates this claim.[24] Although it has never been published, it was taken to working drawings and appears to have been very similar to the Jacobs design. Howe describes the house as having "the materials and method of construction determined by Mr. Hoult's being in the lumber and millwork business."[25] These techniques were first published in the design for the Lusk house in Huron, South Dakota, of 1935–1936.[26]

The Lusk House

The Lusk house was projected for the proprietor of the *Evening Huronite,* who asked Wright to replace the burned-out Sylvan Lake Hotel. Lusk's intention was to import the very best talent to bring national publicity to the Black Hills. This area attracted growing tourism following President Coolidge's vacation there in 1926 and after Gutson Borghum started his gigantic carvings on Mt. Rushmore. The hotel was designed but never built.[27] Wright loved the area and wrote poetically about it.[28] The house is remarkable for its mature, "long-tail" Usonian plan, admirable site-planning on a small corner lot, and feeling for locale and the northern climate.[29] The beautiful perspectives of the house show clearly the board and batten construction of all later Usonians, as well as two features that were not repeated: the "sawtooth" monopitch rooflights that were to break the flat roofline and the highly articulated chimneys and brick masses, which projected in a more expres-

23

sionist manner than subsequent Usonians, where increasing horizontality
and subservient chimney masses became the norm.

The Lusks visited the Willey house in
Minneapolis, weekended at Taliesin,
and entertained the entire Taliesin Fellowship on annual migration from
Taliesin West. Their enthusiasm was
to no avail, however. Their builder said
that "despite the module specifications" he could not build for the
$10,000 budgeted, and worst of all, the
Federal Housing Authority (FHA) declared that the "very uniqueness of the
design put it beyond the scope of their
approval."[30] This established an unfortunate precedent that dogged all
Wright's efforts until after World War II.
Many Usonians were to be abandoned
for lack of acceptance of features that
have since become standard elements
of the American housing scene.

The Jacobs house, therefore, brought
together all Wright's hopes and skills
represented in a number of unbuilt projects. That he had correctly deduced a
long-felt need was beyond doubt.
Nearly all the clients for the subsequent Usonians until 1943 had conceived an interest in Wright from reading his *Autobiography.* This interest
was turned into action by the publicity
given the Jacobs house[31] and appears
to have been shared by those clients
whose designs only went as far as
working drawings.[32] The most common reasons for cancellation were the
economic difficulties and conservative
attitudes of fund-giving institutions at
the time. Gene Masselink, secretary at
Taliesin throughout the Usonian
period, reported in the Madison *Capital
Times* of January 15, 1937, that Wright
was inundated with letters following national coverage of his work.[33] In addition, the geographical spread of Usonians — they were built in fourteen
states — together with the local publicity they produced, undoubtedly had
a snowballing effect that contributed
greatly to the continued flow of work at
Taliesin after 1946.

24

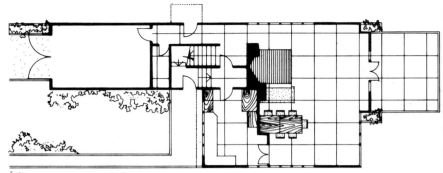

The one-zone plan, 1934.

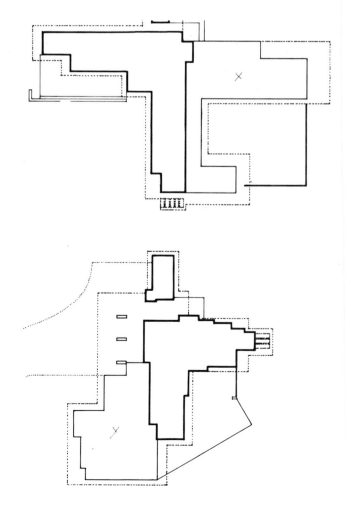

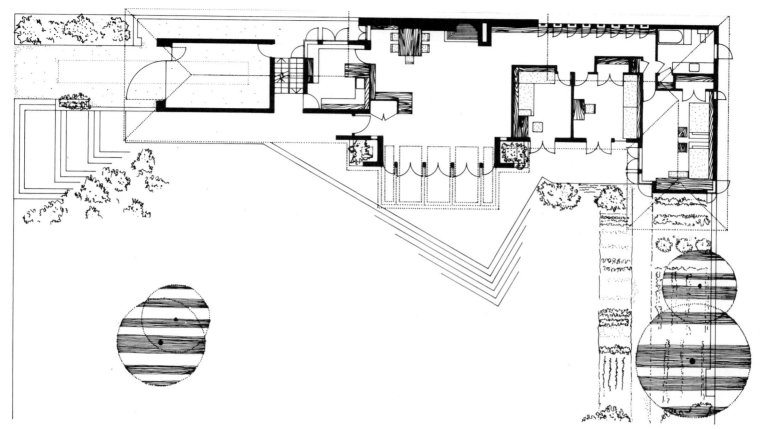

Clients: Mr. and Mrs. Malcolm Willey
Profession: Economist, college dean
Location: Minneapolis, Minnesota
Year of design: 1934
Best source: *Architectural Forum*, January 1938; Henry Russell Hitchcock, *In the Nature of Materials*
Builder/supervisor: Yen Liang, Edgar Tafel, and Taliesin Fellowship
Cost: Not known
Floor area: 1,800 sq ft; 167.2 sq m

The Sondern house, extended plan, Kansas City, Kansas, 1940.

The Rosenbaum house, extended plan, Florence, Alabama, 1939.

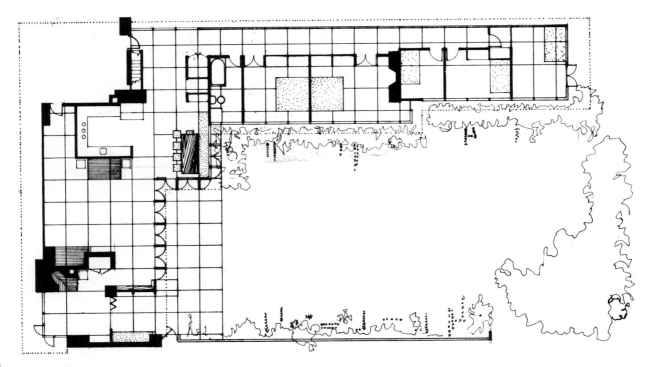

26 The Lusk house project, Huron, South Dakota, 1935–1936. The plan is a developed L form, with an extended bedroom wing.

The Jacobs house, interior, Madison, Wisconsin, 1936. The boards are of pine, with redwood battens. In most subsequent Usonians cypress was used throughout. Photograph by Pedro E. Guerrero.

Why the Usonians Were Successful

The success of the Usonians was a combination of low building costs and the very nature of the home.

Low Building Costs

The Jacobses, along with other Usonian clients, gained initial satisfaction from the low building cost of the Usonian house. For the most part, early Usonians were completed within the budget. Considering the degree of craftsmanship involved, this was chiefly a result of the clarity of the construction process.[34] The Jacobs house was unusual in that it was not only supervised by Taliesin but by Wright himself.[35] It lay on the direct route from Spring Green to Racine, Wisconsin, where the Johnson Wax Administration Building was simultaneously under construction. Wright was so determined to achieve a low budget that the $5,500 figure was adhered to by making certain concealed savings. Surplus or marginally substandard bricks were brought in from the Racine work.[36] Mr. Jacobs himself fitted all the interior ceiling panels and external soffits.[37] And, in Herbert Jacobs' words, after "we paid the contract fee, including Wright's fee of $500 . . . in the spring of 1938 we discovered that the house had no screens (flies and mosquitoes are bad in Wisconsin). When we called this to Wright's attention he told us to use the final installment of his fee ($125) for the screens, and we did."[38]

Nature of the Home

The second cause for satisfaction among Usonian clients or, to put it more accurately, their growing delight, was the nature of the home. The materials and spatial characteristics of the Usonians gave a sense of serenity, variety, and security that were well recognized by their owners.[39] This was so true that for many clients, their home became one of the most important elements of their lives. Certainly the fact that 50 percent of the original clients still live in their homes after 35 years seems unusual if death and war are taken into account.

The Jacobs house, like its antecedents, gives a clear sense of identity from the street and private domain once within. The exterior's strong horizontality gives a sense of repose and ease with its site. Inside, the warm, red, solid floor is quiet and suggests permanence. All around are natural materials and the beauty and scent of wood. There is at once an unusual sense of scale. Areas of the house vary spatially. Intimate areas, such as bedrooms, feel confidential in their small dimensions, delicate ironmongery, low ceilings, and tiny doors. The living area, where large numbers can gather, is celebrated with heightened ceilings, the sweep of bookshelves, and a flood of light. Built-in furniture, manipulations of wall, or ceiling height differentiate the space for separate activities (such as dining).

The space in the Jacobs house is not static. Its boundaries are complex and ambiguous. There is always an area of overlap—a part of the space for sitting is also a part of the dining area or even kitchen, lobby, or terrace. Corner glazing, with glass mitered directly to glass, reinforces this and "sets the corner free or open for whatever distance you choose."[40] This continuity was essentially what Wright meant by "breaking the box."

The resulting impression of spaciousness, within small dimensions, goes very much further, however. The fourth dimension of time is involved. Because a space cannot be said to terminate (its boundaries always slip beyond view), it is necessary to move about to comprehend it. So the house has a reticent, endearing way of revealing itself. This leads ultimately to the idea of the interior space being the reality of the building: "Unity Temple was when I thought I first had it," Wright declared. "It came to me quite naturally from my Unitarian ancestry and the Froebelian kindergarten training in the deeper primal sense of the form of the interior or heart of the appearance of 'things.'"[41]

For Wright, the philosophical basis for his work was Eastern; it lay in Lao-Tse and Okakura. "The reality of a room was to be found in the space enclosed by the roof and walls, not in the roof and walls themselves."[42] It is this Taoist, Zen world that studies of Wright have not explored. "True beauty could be discovered only by one who mentally completed the incomplete."[43]

The Jacobses and other clients might use other words to describe their homes, but they are absolutely aware of these qualities. The spatial experience is augmented by the quality of light. At various times of day the same place can feel quite different, with shafts of sunlight seeming to appear in unexpected places. After it has rained, sunlight can bounce off the roofwater and reflect a glowing, rippling light through the high-level windows upon the ceiling. These and other qualities, such as scent and texture, are all a part of Wright's aim, of "liberating the occupants." This richness of experience is not a superficial veneer, some divorce of building "package" from its "message." It is the result of the integral expression of the house's concept. It gives some understanding of all that Wright meant by organic architecture.

Performance of Usonian Construction

The innovations in the construction of the Jacobs house performed well. The board and batten walls have proven to be durable and strong.[44] Although their acoustic performance has not been ideal — for example, between bedrooms — it has been comparable with plasterboarded studwork. The solid floors are responsible for the Usonian houses' superior acoustic privacy. Because the houses are protected by overhanging eaves, they have not needed excessive maintenance.[45] Because they are not "decorated" and because of their construction, they have also been easy to change. For example, to add shelving the batten could be unscrewed to obtain fixing.

Although the walls lacked thermal mass, insulation has been quite adequate.[46] The interior finish of wood is of high specific heat and pleasant in winter, while the roof overhangs shade the boarding and prevent summer solar radiation. The joinery, both large- and small-scale, has been as successful as its good design and construction

can make it. The big mainspans of three 2 x 4s stitchnailed together have been stable, and the cantilevers have remained firm. The progressive step-back and termination of each 2 x 4 element of the composite mainspan beam here not only makes good sense structurally, but is also one of the most characteristic elements of all Usonians.

The Heating System

The efficacy of gravity heat is attested to by its widespread use since it was introduced by the first Usonians. Indeed, the floor slab design, with its cost savings over foundations, its integral heat, and integral finish, is one of these buildings' least recognized successes.[47] The looped piping buried under the slab has proven to be the chief limitation.[48] Usonians for the most part had wrought-iron pipes. Only later was copper commonly used, which is important to the life of the system. By warming massive materials, such as concrete floors and brick masses, gravity heat prevented the occupant of a space from losing body heat by radiation. As a result, conditions were still comfortable even if internal air temperature was only in the mid-60s. It was easy to supplement this heat with fires, and moreover, on a crisp winter's day, it was possible to open windows and completely freshen the house without losing the stored heat of the heavy elements of the structure.

This principle was carefully investigated at the time in a house built along Usonian lines by William Bernoudi, an ex-Taliesin apprentice, in St. Louis, Missouri in 1939.

The gravel bed acts as an insulation and little heat is lost into the ground. Actual tests made last winter showed that temperature, taken at varying levels, indicated little more than a degree of difference through the house. Temperatures were also taken of walls and ceiling to complete the tests. Practically all inside wall surfaces showed a higher temperature than the air in the room, due to the absorption of radiant energy upon their surfaces. In radiant heating the object is to raise the mean radiant temperature of the surfaces of the enclosure which is to be heated to a point where it will produce a feeling of comfort. . . . In the house under discussion the floor is the radiant surface which delivers heat directly (by absorption) to the walls and ceilings. Since the energy rays of heat travel in a straight line, they are not affected by air currents. Air velocity or movement is low and there is consequently little stratification of hot air near the ceiling. Tests showed that where the floor temperature was 69°F air temperature was 61°F. As the boiler temperature increased and the floor surface approached 80°F, air temperature rose to 64°F and created a feeling of comfort since it balanced the 14 BTUs per square foot per hour heat loss given off in radiation from the body. In cold weather the heating system is started slowly to allow the expansion of pipes with the concrete. Where most householders reduce air temperature late at night it was found to be more advantageous to shut off the system at 4 P.M. and start at midnight. The house is heated by an oil-fired hot water boiler.[49]

This principle is in direct contrast to the practice that has occurred since, where the inadequacies of lightweight materials, which heat up and cool down rapidly, have been remedied by greater and greater reliance on an energy-consuming plant. Wright's homes certainly allow for an awareness of the local climate and require dress to be varied accordingly, rather than the ecologically disastrous alternatives of shirt sleeves and thermostat.

This concept, while likely to be perfectly acceptable by the late 1970s, for energy cost and shortage reasons, met with some predictable opposition at the time. An old friend and client of Wright's, Lloyd Lewis, typified this opposition and complained at the inadequacy of his heating. Wright answered him by pointing out that Lewis's expectations were conditioned by working in the offices of the *Chicago Daily News,* which were maintained at an unassailable 85°F.[50]

Certainly, in terms of energy usage, the load for air conditioning homes is great-

er than that for heating them, and in this important area the Usonian homes were successful.[51] The 12-in insulated roof-space cushions overhead radiation, and roof overhangs shade walls and glass. Cross-drafts can be obtained at high level from the clerestory windows, and summer circulation of air is ensured by the open fireplace flues, which serve as vents. During the summer the thermal flywheel effect of the masonry and concrete floors works in reverse of their winter role, providing expanses of cool, hard surfaces. In servicing terms, the building itself, rather than its plant, does most of the work. This is now of fundamental importance under conditions of energy shortage. Homes are one of the few types of building in constant twenty-four hour use that can take advantage of thermal mass.

Least Successful Aspects of Usonians

It was in the area of electrical services that the Usonian kit was least successful. The Jacobses exposed lighting was serviceable, but was only repeated once. The small, bare bulbs spiraling round a straight, overhead conduit resembled a sparkling horizontal shaft of light. However, they were not as subtle, nor were they as easy to vary, as the fretted, concealed light strips that superseded them. The concrete floor and unadorned brickwork caused difficulties with the power circuit. Because there were no finishes such as plaster to conceal conduiting, it was necessary to install the conduiting very early in construction. Not only did concrete have to be poured around the conduiting, but this had to be very accurately located to allow correct positioning for floor supply of subsequent outlets in the board and batten walls. For the most part, vertical wiring could be run within the brickwork core and all distribution then carried in the ceiling.

Concealment of conduit and junction boxes within the sandwich walls caused the most problems. Since it was specified that the face of switches and outlets should be flush with the boarding, the plywood core and back of the inner boards had to be cut away, and the very flat junction boxes could themselves be difficult to wire. The builder of the Pope house commented on this difficulty.[52] In use, however, the electrical services, especially in the variety of lighting, were successful. They merely necessitated extra time and labor that did not fully meet with Wright's intention of highly simplified construction and operation of building trades.

Privacy and the Family

In a social sense, the Usonian concept set standards that American housing only incorporated after World War II. It proposed a single-story form that allowed privacy at suburban densities (22 persons per acre of Jacobs houses), and was an heroic integration of social ideas, optimal site use, and construction innovations. The notion of a model that could be varied for different sites and clients was older than the Usonian idea, however, and this raises the most important shortcoming, as well as the most intriguing anomaly, in Wright's thinking.

In 1934, his zoned house appeared, itself a development of two early designs: the "fireproof house for $5,000" project of 1906 and the Hunt house, LaGrange, Illinois, of 1907. The following year *Taliesin* magazine published the designs for the two-zone house with city, suburban, and country versions. The latter designs were based on the ideas in a letter from housewife Dorothy J. Field. Her letter accompanied the designs in the Taliesin publication. The letter is important in that it lights on precisely the issue that gave later Usonian clients most dissatisfaction: the kitchen's small size, lack of view outside, and the attendant problem of children taking over the living space.

Mrs. Field criticized the one-zone design whose "floor plan consists of one large room, an ell of which is for dining, with one corner partitioned off for kitchen and back pantry." She found this "pleasant to live in *when kept tidy,* but the children own the whole house" [italics supplied]. She went on to say, "A house has no one center. It has two. A center of Activity and a center of Quiet. The kitchen is not the laboratory of the house. It is the center of feverish activity from sun-up to sun-down, year in, year out. Enlarge upon this feature and make it a real room—for the family to work in, and play in. The livingroom is the center of quiet in the house. Here is a fireplace for winter cheer, the desk, the garden almost creeping in the windows, the books, the peace."[53]

After a sideswipe at other architects, Mrs. Field (who had just enthusiastically read *Broadacre City* and *An Autobiography*) put her viewpoint to Wright: "A housewife spends 90 percent of her time in the kitchen no matter how many gadgets she has . . . . When anyone is dead tired there is always the relief of knowing that on the other side of the door is peace and quiet and a tidy room."[54]

Because he was so open to suggestions for domestic design, Wright then developed Mrs. Field's ideas into his two-zone house.[55] It is therefore curious that the Usonian norm was based, not on two zones, but on one. Wright rationalized his alternative later by writing in 1954, "Back in farm days there was one big living room with a stove in it, and Ma was there cooking—looking after the children and talking to Pa—dogs and cats and tobacco smoke too—all gemutlich if all was orderly, but it seldom was; and the children were playing around. It created a certain atmosphere of a domestic nature which had charm and which is not, I think, a good thing to lose altogether."[56]

The reason for this change was probably the need to economize (the two-zone houses were large), while simultaneously trying to create a living area of spatial variety. Wright was always ready to change his houses if his clients felt that they could be improved upon, and alterations did in fact center on changes to the kitchen. In any event, the direction the Usonian houses took was firmly toward the "polliwog," or head-and-tail plan form.

After the Jacobs house, the ways in which the Usonian idea were developed for different clients and sites, climate and materials, together constitute a definition of what Wright meant by organic design. It is therefore necessary to follow these changes in architectural form and to explore their context, in terms of both the clients' involvement with the design and construction processes and the methods by which Wright, through Taliesin, had them built. Ultimately Wright's contribution to domestic design must be seen in terms of how it influenced the mass of contemporary American housing at the time.

CHAPTER 2 Housing Usonia

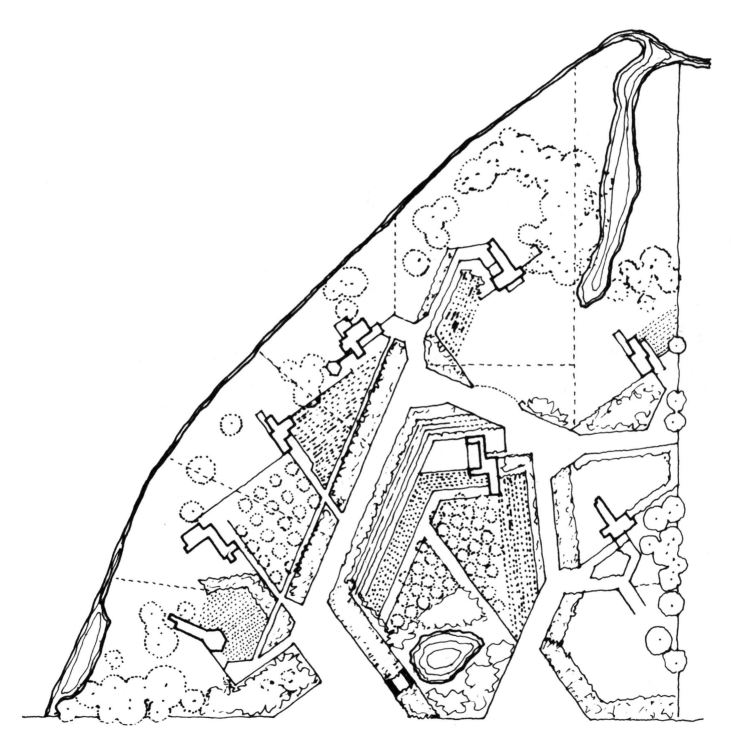

Having built the Jacobs house in 1937, Wright spent the remainder of his life (with the most creative period being that between 1937 and World War II) exploring the nuclear family's needs in climates as different as those of the Pacific Northwest, the Great Lakes, and the Mississippi basin. He also built for people in other kinds of relationships, for groups of families and for organized cooperatives; and while they were also royal courts, he built two communes in his two Taliesin homes. Beautiful, unusual materials were employed and unorthodox forms of contracting and supervision were utilized. The results made up a body of work of staggering inventiveness that gave immense satisfaction to what Wright, and Thoreau before him, called their "in-dwellers," and which still have freshness and relevance 35 years later.

Development of Usonians

It took Wright from 5 to 10 years to develop the Usonian design. The length of this gestation period is borne out by Wright's sureness and confidence with the idiom. Even while the Jacobs house was being built, the same concept was being framed to form a radically different building 2,000 miles away—the Hanna house. Completed in 1937, the latter was the first of Wright's hexagonal designs and initiated a search for greater spatial freedom that was to run through his work until his death. Setting out from the geometric fluidity of the hexagon, Wright developed toward the curve and circle, touched on free-form planning, and finally engaged in an obsessional struggle with the spiral—seen in the endlessness of the Guggenheim Museum.

Hexagonal Planning

Wright frequently described the hexagon as being more natural to human movement than the square. When employed in planning a building, it gives a honeycomb grid constructed of 60°–60° triangles. These may be visualized as hexagon clusters, diamond modules, or as a triagrid. Walls following the resulting 60°–120° angles feel entirely different from those arranged on a rectilinear grid, and spaces achieve more nearly the "breaking of the box" and continuity that Wright had in mind. The degree of difference is quite marked. It might be analogous to the experience of Africans from a round-hut culture when exposed to the Western right angle.[1] Understanding this concept is especially difficult for many European architects whose training emphasized that plans could be appreciated quite independently of the building as an experience. To an architect with such a background, the plan of the Hanna house suggests perversity and absolutely unsatisfactory spaces, when in fact it possesses a three-dimensional discipline related to its planning grid. As an experience the building has an inevitability and ease, and entering the forecourt is like encountering a warm embrace.[2]

The Hanna House

The Hanna house was built at Palo Alto, California, for the family of a teacher of child education, now a professor at Stanford University. It is one of the greatest of Wright's houses and has been continuously inhabited by its owners. The Hanna house is, for me, more important than the Kaufmann weekend pavilion, "Falling Water," because it is attuned to a growing family and is less exhibitionist. It has been fully documented in the January 1963 edition of *House Beautiful,* which is devoted to it.

In his first California home since the 1920s Wright serenely applied all the Usonian elements to a combination of falling site and hexagonal plan form. The building wraps around the contours to form a curved hollow of garden on its private side, the welcoming entrance court to the north, and downslope view out to the west. As the ground falls, the brick base becomes more massive and is revealed in the form of planters and retaining walls.

"The house is essentially a roof poised lightly above a two-level, paved terrace on the side of the hill."[3] Curtis Besinger's article in the January 1963 *House Beautiful* is necessary reading for an understanding of this, the largest Usonian, and indeed the whole building type. His perceptive description could almost substitute for an actual visit.

The vertical module of the boarding, 1 ft 1 in., is twice the length of the hexagon side, 2 ft 2 in. This, as well as the strongly ridged roof plane, together with the ubiquitous hexagonal grid, unify and interrelate the parts of a plan that amble around trees and about corners and levels in a seemingly artless way. Where the rectangular grid and small dimensions of the Jacobs house allowed Wright a degree of ambiguity, here the 60°–120° angle and vistas of up to 80 ft gave him a greater opportunity. The living areas fan around a bow-like fireplace, constantly overlapping with spaces that are partly glimpsed, over the sofa-bookcase, through an eaves trellis, or beyond a fold in the board walls. Once these spaces are reached, something that was previously revealed becomes concealed; the participant is at the center of experience. This sequential space is further layered and interpenetrated by changes of floor level, the undulating window plane, and the ceiling overhead; lower flat decks contrast with higher sloping ceilings.

That every element is under control and was anticipated, is a daunting thought for an architect. To a house guest it is merely natural.

The dominant feeling was of wonderful, secluded shelter, with the kind of aura I knew in the big old houses of my childhood. . . . In view of the fact that no house of my childhood was ever so casually joined to the outdoors, so profusely fenestrated and skylighted, or so varied in levels and ceiling heights, I was surprised that I was so emotionally familiar with the place. To feel so secure without the dark and gloom of restricting walls, yet I felt free. Not the kind of airiness associated with open,

The Hanna house, Palo Alto, California, 1936. This is the first Usonian with a pitched roof. Ceilings are not boarded, but covered with Filipino matting.

glass walls, which makes me feel as though I might fall out the windows, but a feeling of having space to move around in and somewhere to go.[4]

The Hannas were more than delighted by the house and particularly by the way in which it accepted all the changes their lives required. They described it simply as "Our love affair with our house." The statement carried weight because it was made by practical people who chose to go into long-term debt in building it.

For Wright, "the flow and movement in this design (was) a characteristic lending itself admirably to life." But he was not satisfied. "The hexagon has been conservatively treated, however. It is allowed to appear in plan only and in the furniture which literally rises from . . . the floor slab upon which the whole rests. To me, here is a lead into a new, fascinating realm of form—although it is somewhat repressed on the side of dignity and repose in this first expression of the idea."[5]

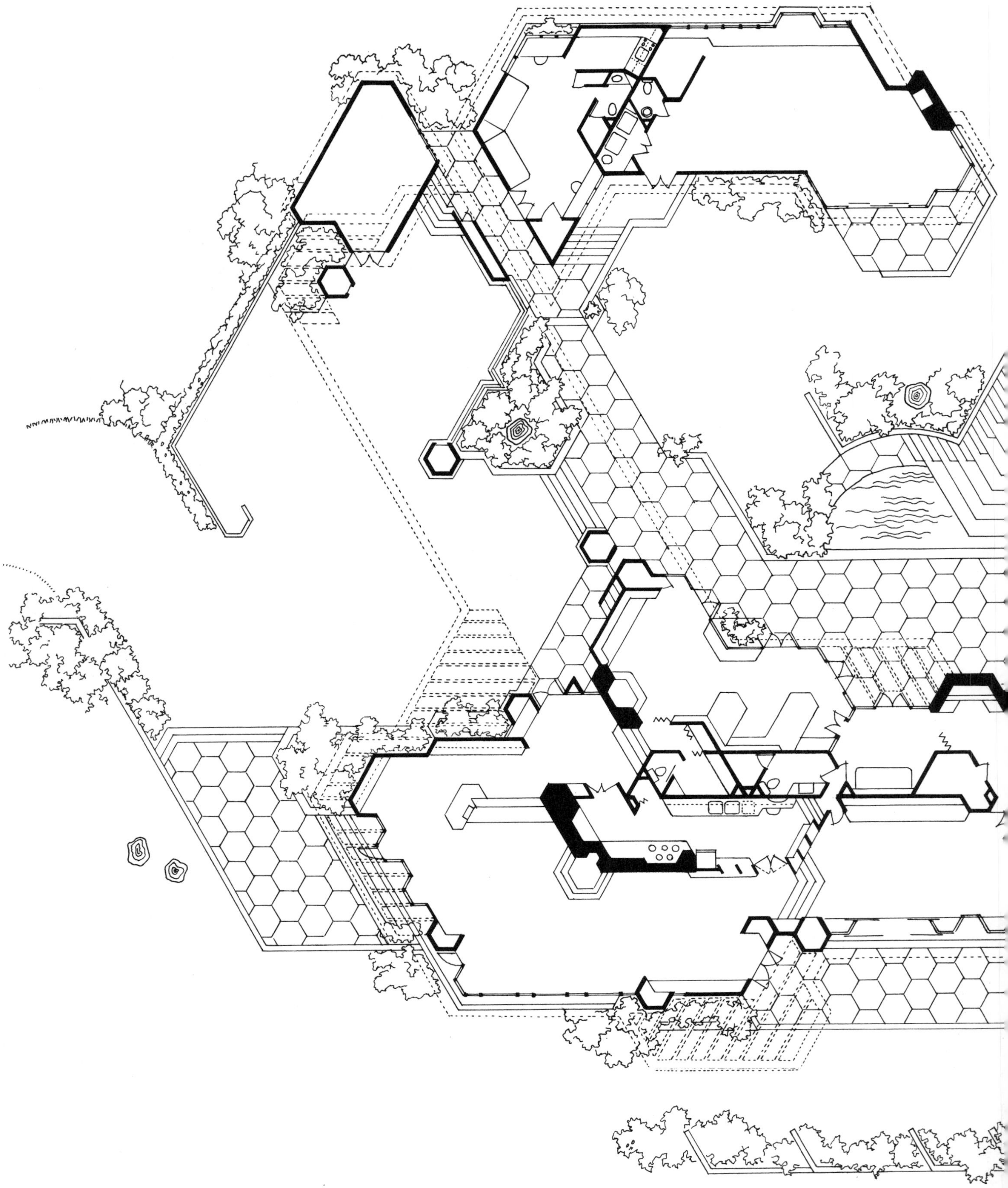

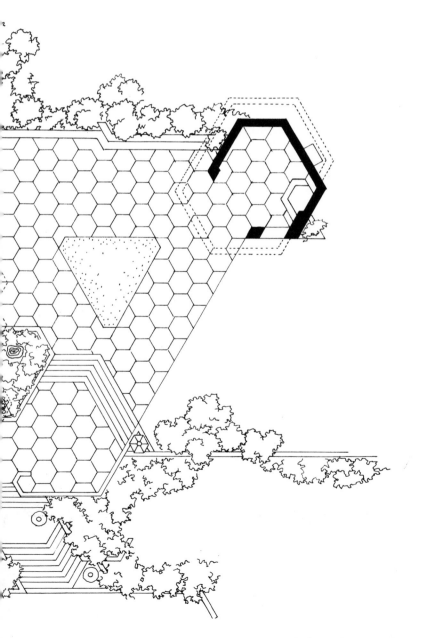

Clients: Mr. and Mrs. Paul Hanna
Profession: Pedagogist, college professor
Location: Palo Alto, California
Year of design: 1936
Best source: *Architectural Forum,* January 1938; Henry Russell Hitchcock, *In the Nature of Materials*
Builder/supervisor: Harold Turner
Cost: Not known
Floor area: 4,825 sq ft (includes guest house, etc.); 448.3 sq m

The Jester House

While the Hanna house was under construction, Wright had already started exploring yet more fluid forms in his project for Ralph Jester at Palos Verdes, California, in 1938. The house was never actually built, however. It was designed for a coastal, desert climate and bachelor client who was an assistant director in the movie business. (Jester later assisted Cecil B. de Mille in the production of "The Ten Commandments.") For this very particular set of needs, Wright designed an unprecedented solution. In a small, gulch-like depression was to be placed a terrace and above it a shade-giving flat roof. Under and around this anchoring idea then bubbled and swirled a joyous succession of circular forms, or rather experiences.

Since plywood was even stronger when bent than in the folded walls of the Hanna house, this material was to frame the walls of rooms, here separated according to activity, but all linked by continuous glazed doors to the covered patio.[6] It would therefore be necessary to go "outside" between rooms, this experience being conceived of as the theme of the house. By day the patio would have been cool and shaded, with breezes induced by the Venturi effect of air movement between the "room-drums." When the temperature dropped at night, each room could be closed off.

Access from the car court to this cool patio or outer "room" was to be through a gate. Once within the shade, the eye was led through trellis-like pergolas to the delights of the bedroom-garden complex (with circular bed, bath, and breakfast table) and the swimming pool. Like the engaging variety of a cluster of blown bubbles, the pool, with attendant diving platform, curved around the patio and filled the ravine. When it rained the pool would gently overflow into the landscape. Ralph Jester could swim to this extreme edge and from the water, 15 feet up, survey the view. Sadly, high bids were re-ceived for construction of this house, and Jester's needs changed when he married. He commissioned Wright's son, John Lloyd, for the home he finally built.

The Jester house project, Palos Verdes, California, 1938. Wright attempted to build versions of this design for other clients. In a project for the second home for Gregor Affleck, this model was altered from the original brick and plywood to include stone.

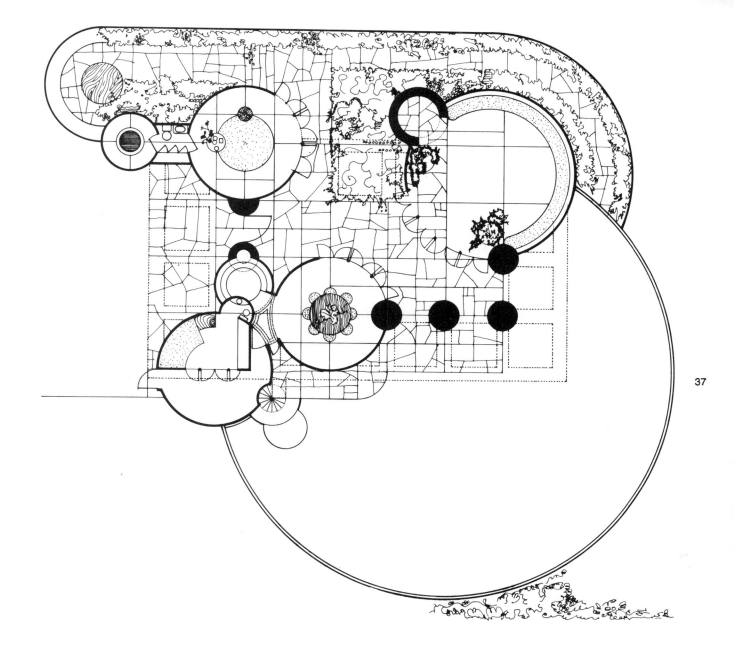

The Jester house project, Palos Verdes, California, 1938.

The Lloyd Burlingham House

Wright briefly abandoned the discipline of grid and machine-sized building materials in favor of free form. The Lloyd Burlingham house, projected for El Paso, Texas, in 1941, was to be built of adobe, the indigenous clay-mud construction of the Southwest. It complemented the site, which, Wright wrote, was "piled with sweeping sands, continually drifting in swirling lines that suggest waves of the sea."[7] The curving forms that resulted, with the house a reflex ellipse within the continuous curve of outer wall and forecourt, would have achieved a remarkable sympathy with the landscape, and its massive construction, shaded overhangs, and green courts, with the climate.

Context for the Usonians

The three designs of the Hanna, Jester, and Burlingham houses serve as points of reference for later geometric variations on the Usonian norm. The bulk of Usonians commissioned were simpler and more similar to the Jacobs house both in concept and type of client than to the Jester or Burlingham houses. Typically, the Usonian clients were independent-minded, journalists, academics, and small businessmen. Their homes were usually built in the face of great financial difficulty. Increasingly Wright encouraged or attracted clients who shared an interest in the solutions to post-Depression America that he himself was applying in his own home at Taliesin in Spring Green, Wisconsin, and at his winter camp at Taliesin West, near Phoenix, Arizona. Wright's solution was self-sufficiency. For this reason, and also to ensure that there was ample natural landscape to interact with his designs, he insisted that clients have acreage and that their sites be nonurban.[8] Construction might also involve the clients themselves acting as general contractors or doing physical labor. In actuality, few clients grew their own produce or built their own homes, as did the apprentices at Taliesin, but the prewar period did see these ideas formulated and designs made for the first Usonian cooperative, which consisted of six homes built around a shared farm unit.

It was after World War II, under conditions that were initially discouraging for private home construction, that some clients began to build their own homes, and even, in some cases, to quarry their materials. Throughout the period, construction costs were relatively low, while raising finances was prohibitively difficult. Mass unemployment after the stock market crash of 1929 ensured a comparatively cheap supply of highly skilled craftsmen, upon whom certainly the hexagonal Usonian, and to an extent all Usonians, depended.

Following postwar demobilization, similar conditions briefly prevailed, until rising prosperity began to drive building costs higher. At this point, around 1950, three tendencies arose: (1) the conventional Wright house (still called Usonian by him, although often not of board and batten construction) required increasingly rich clients; (2) more clients were willing to bypass building costs by partial or wholly self-build techniques; and (3) Wright himself searched urgently for cheaper methods of construction, both by labor-intensive and prefabricated approaches.

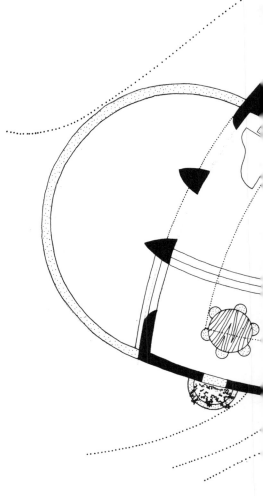

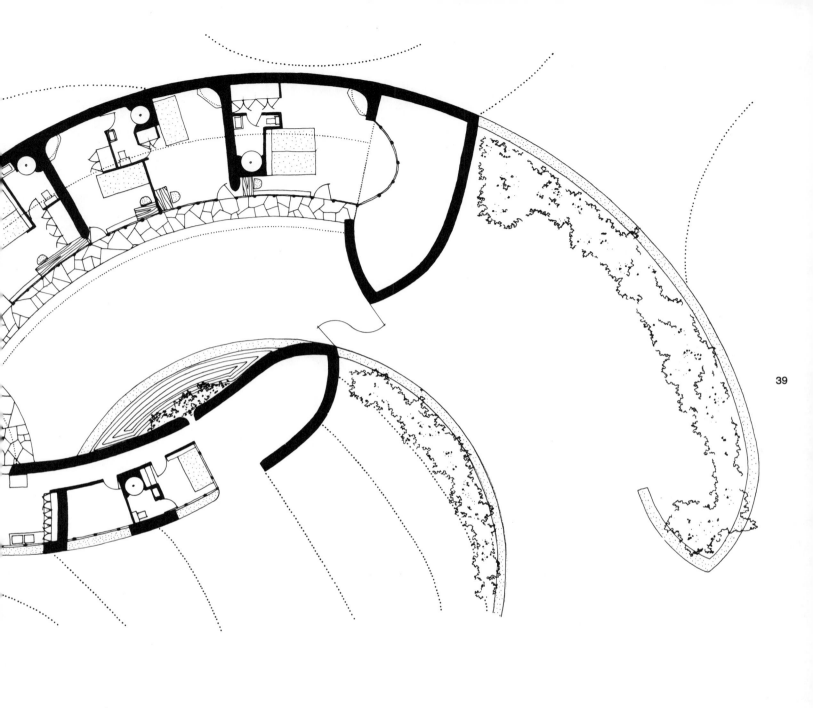

39

The Burlingham house project, El Paso, Texas, 1942. Construction was to be in adobe, and the free-form plan was intended to complement the sweeping sands of the site.

Five Types of Usonian House

The twenty-six completed Usonians, and some thirty-one unbuilt Usonian house projects of the prewar period,[9] have a singularity that is only apparent by making an 11,000-mile journey around the United States. The designs for these houses should also be studied in the Taliesin archives; something that is unlikely to be possible until Wright's request for a vault and museum to house them is carried out by Taliesin Associated Architects.[10] However, certain categories are helpfully apparent. There is the flat site "polliwog" plan of the Jacobs house type—of L or T plan—with one or more wings. There is a similar type in which the rectangular grid is "invaded" by the diagonal geometry of a wing. There is also a contracted, single-block or "inline" plan incorporating bedrooms, a hexagonal version of all these, and a rectangular grid type that is raised upon masonry piers.

The Polliwog Usonian

The Jacobs polliwog – type house (or tadpole design) was most frequently employed. Applied on a luxurious scale in the Rebhuhn house in Great Neck, New York, in 1938, in a T-shaped plan, it was most elegantly developed in the Rosenbaum house in Florence, Alabama, in 1939, and in the Schwartz house in Two Rivers, Wisconsin, in the same year. It was still realized for low cost in 1940 in the Pope house in Falls Church, Virginia,[11] and in the Sondern house in Kansas City, Missouri. The Christie house in Bernardsville, New Jersey, built in 1940, was of larger scale and was set on a sweeping rural site. All the last were L-shaped plans.

The Rebhuhn House

The Rebhuhn house was built for a collector and publisher of erotic literature. It is a two-story, truncated cruciform and contains subtle changes of level about a massive fireplace core. The bedroom wing is projected above the garages and entrance by timber haunches, reminiscent of those in con-

The Rebhuhn house, exterior, Great Neck, New York, 1938.

Clients: Mr. and Mrs. Ben Rebhuhn
Profession: Publisher
Location: Great Neck, Long Island, New York
Year of design: 1938
Best source: Never published
Builder/supervisor: Harold Turner
Cost: Not known
Floor area: 3,000 sq ft (estimated); 278.7 sq m

crete at "Falling Water." The flat-roofed kitchen-breakfast area forms another wing, beautifully screened by built-in fitments for displaying books and artwork. The house contains a spiraling entrance route that is subtley defined by changes of level in both floors and ceilings. Turning the final 90° around the chimney core lies a noble, double-height living area running from the fireplace, to immense windows, to the garden—a room that was probably a prototype for the similar but less formal space in the Rose Pauson house built in Phoenix, Arizona, in 1940, now lost by fire.[12] This links the last quadrant, consisting of the study-library, with a gallery above that slides back across the head of the great room, around the core, and back to the bedrooms. The plans have never been published. The house was immaculately built by Harold Turner, Wright's itinerant builder who supervised all the more luxurious Usonians.[13]

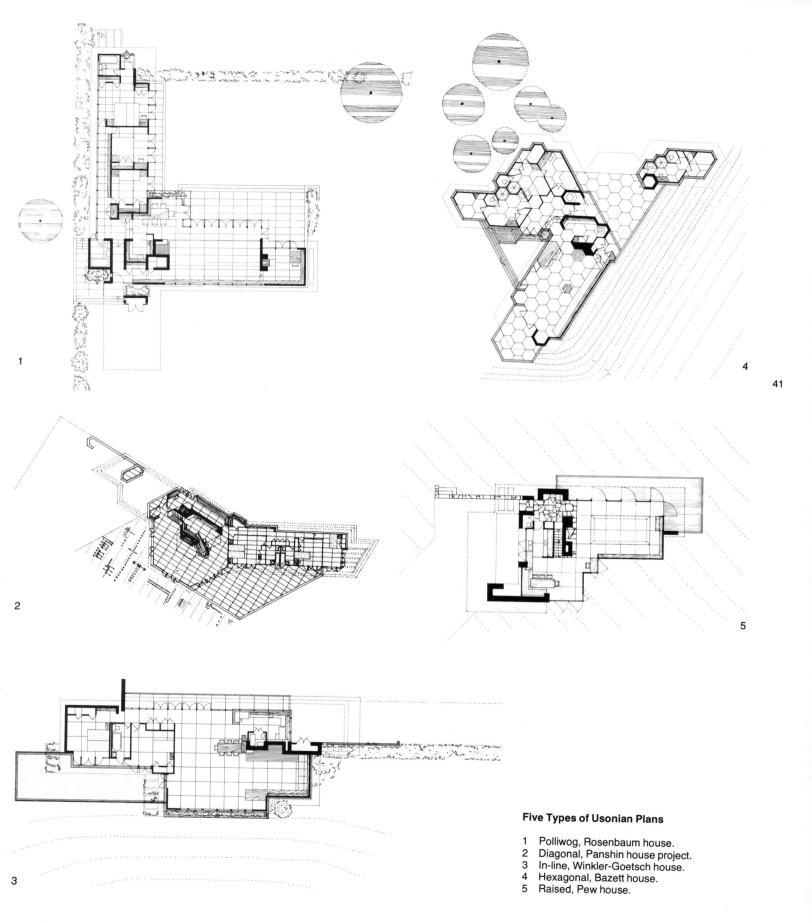

1

4

41

2

5

3

Five Types of Usonian Plans

1 Polliwog, Rosenbaum house.
2 Diagonal, Panshin house project.
3 In-line, Winkler-Goetsch house.
4 Hexagonal, Bazett house.
5 Raised, Pew house.

The Rosenbaum House

The Rosenbaum house was built for a scholar who, at the time the house was commissioned, was running a family business. Rosenbaum is now on the faculty of the State College at Florence, Alabama. The house plan was similar to the Jacobs house with improvements and variations. The living areas were more spacious, with an enlarged dining alcove, a 100-sq-ft study, and redesigned service core. By incorporating the heater at floorslab level, Wright was able to omit the small basement, together with its stair. This allowed extra circulation space and made the core an island with alternative routes about it, enhancing the house's apparent spaciousness. The bedroom wing of three rooms was terminated by a second bathroom.

The house is the purest example of the Usonian. It incorporates detailing improvements and combines all the standard elements in a mature and spatially varied interior.[14] Its exterior has an almost overpowering horizontality. The street facade forms a cypress wall from which springs the carport, a 20-ft cantilever utilizing concealed steelwork. Ten years after construction, the Rosenbaums had Wright extend the house. It thus became the first Usonian to be radically altered, something which owners of Wright houses were loath to do, but which he himself always saw as potentially inherent in an organic building. This addition backed a second L onto the first, containing a Japanese garden. With four sons in the family, extra sleeping accommodations were required. A quiet guest room terminated one arm, and the other contained a family kitchen, bunk-playroom, and utility room with second carport.

The Rosenbaum house, exterior, Florence, Alabama, 1939.

42

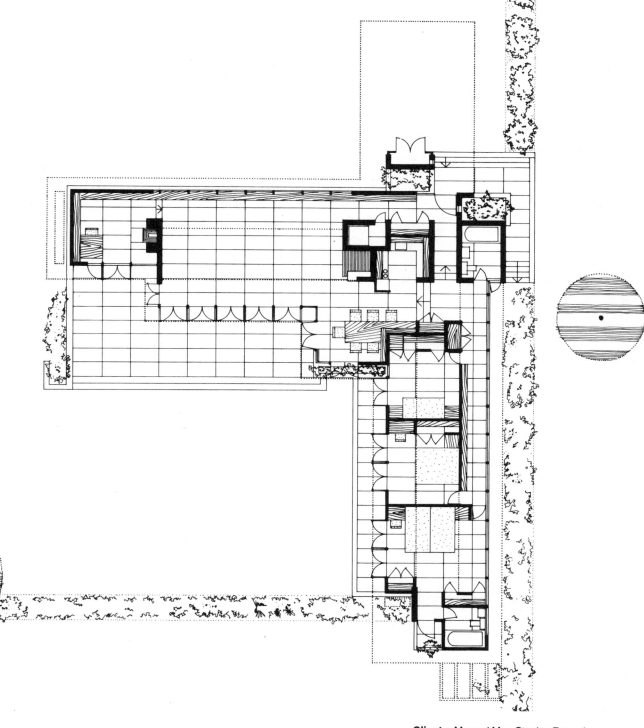

43

Clients: Mr. and Mrs. Stanley Rosenbaum
Profession: College professor
Location: Florence, Alabama
Year of design: 1939
Best source: *Architectural Forum,* January 1948; Henry Russell Hitchcock, *In the Nature of Materials*
Builder/supervisor: Burton Goodrich
Cost: $12,000
Floor area: 1,540 sq ft; 143.1 sq m

44

1

2

3

4

5

6

The Rosenbaum house
1   Study and livingroom from the terrace.
2   Dining area from the fireplace.
3   Entrance looking past the core.
4   Bedroom, with clerestory and bookcase details.
5   Livingroom bookcase and clerestory.
6   Bedroom wing from the dining area.

The Schwartz house, exterior, Two Rivers, Wisconsin, 1939.

The Schwartz House

Bernard Schwartz runs a small textile business in Two Rivers, Wisconsin. At the time of commissioning Wright to build his family's house, his business was not yet started. He saw the 1938 copy of *Time* magazine with Wright on its cover, studied the edition of *Life* magazine of the same year with its article, "Houses for Different Incomes," and went to Taliesin to request a version of Wright's contribution, "A House for a Family of $5,000 – $6,000 Income."[15] Schwartz's association with his architect was colorful, and a building that differs little from the house in *Life* was the happy result. The house is angled to the street, whereas all the neighboring homes line it; the bend on which it is located is thus also complemented. Lake Michigan lies behind.

This oblique relationship to the street was something Wright was to use often. It creates diagonal movement on the lot and an angled, rather than frontal, relationship with other dwellings and the lake. At Two Rivers, such a house is a landmark in that elemental region north of Manitowoc. The street facade of the Schwartz house is two stories high and forms the base of an L-shaped plan, with cantilevered carport. From the bedroom gallery, the high, single-story living areas can be seen through a double height. Because of the angled site planning, the terrace enclosed by the L of the living and dining areas faces south (where neighboring homes regard an eastern view of grey waves). The interior has

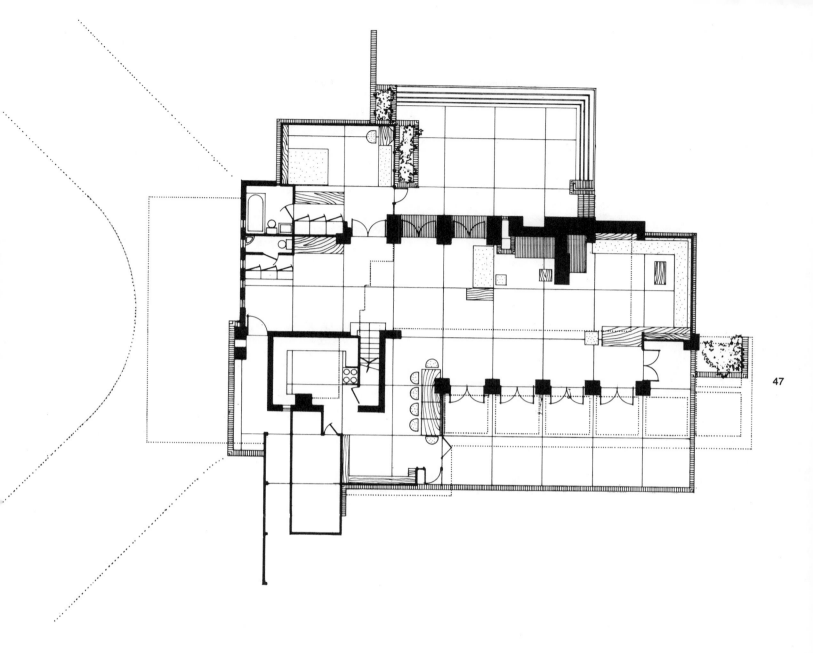

47

Clients: Mr. and Mrs. Bernard Schwartz
Profession: Businessman
Location: Two Rivers, Wisconsin
Year of design: 1939
Best source: Henry Russell Hitchcock, *In the Nature of Materials*
Builder/supervisor: Edgar Tafel
Cost: $18,000
Floor area: 3,000 sq ft; 278.7 sq m

48

The Christie house, exterior, Bernardsville, New
Jersey, 1940.

great spatial variety, intimacy, and grandeur — with brick piers punctuating the view to the lake, clerestories sailing overhead, and a dining area where the fretted plywood windows fill a wall and interweave with china shelving. A narrow stair is drawn out of the living space to turn onto a gallery to the bedrooms. At each door, the balcony steps out, widening until terminated by a desk.[16]

Small Polliwog Plans and Projects

Both the Pope and Sondern houses of 1940 were of small dimensions. The former was originally built around a shade-giving tulip tree, while the latter was perched on a bluff. The Pope house was built for the family of a journalist on the *Washington Evening Star*. It was located in Falls Church, Virginia. Because of its subsequent adoption by the National Trust for Historic Preservation, and reerection at Woodlawn Plantation, Virginia, the house is the best documented of all Usonians, and the only one for which the full correspondence between client and architect has been released by Taliesin.[17]

The Pope house is unusual in that it has a five-step drop down into a two-way living area, where its bookshelf seating looks north and the dining alcove looks south. Its workspace also has an external window.[18] Loren Pope himself wrote a fine description of his home, showing an insight into Wright's intentions typical of many Usonian clients.[19]

The Christie house in Bernardsville, New Jersey, and the Sondern house in Kansas City, Missouri, both of 1949, were similar standard L plans. The Sondern house was radically changed after World War II when new owners asked Wright to double its size. Considerable restoration of the original building was needed at this time. This would indicate that the fabric had been less than successful in the notorious

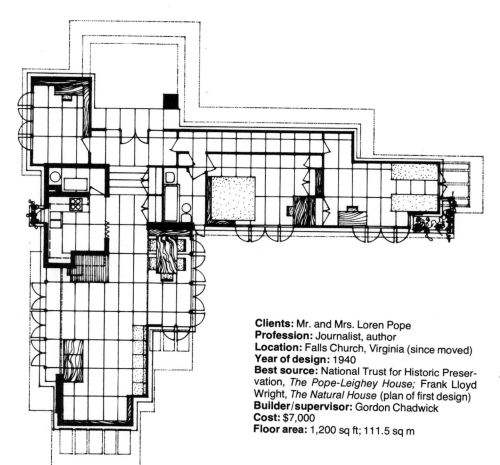

Clients: Mr. and Mrs. Loren Pope
Profession: Journalist, author
Location: Falls Church, Virginia (since moved)
Year of design: 1940
Best source: National Trust for Historic Preservation, *The Pope-Leighey House;* Frank Lloyd Wright, *The Natural House* (plan of first design)
Builder/supervisor: Gordon Chadwick
Cost: $7,000
Floor area: 1,200 sq ft; 111.5 sq m

49

Sondern plan unavailable.

Clients: Mr. and Mrs. Clarence Sondern
Profession: Chemist
Location: Kansas City, Missouri
Year of design: 1940
Best source: Henry Russell Hitchcock, *In the Nature of Materials*
Builder/supervisor: Jack Howe
Cost: Not known
Floor area: 1,270 sq ft; 118 sq m

The Brauner house project, Lansing, Michigan, 1939. The Brauners built a different design in 1950.

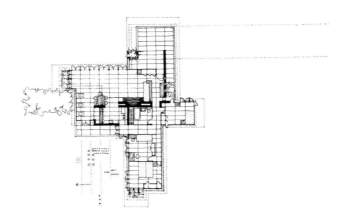

The Garrison house project, Lansing, Michigan, 1939. The bedroom wing includes a children's nursery.

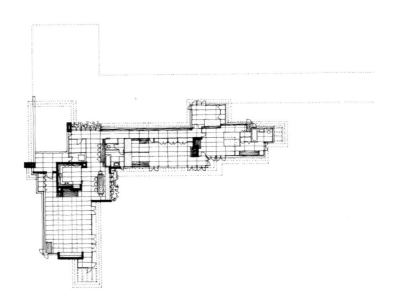

The Newman house project, Lansing, Michigan, 1939.

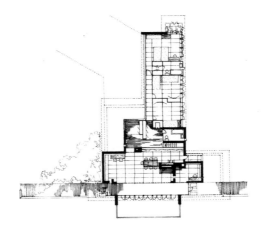

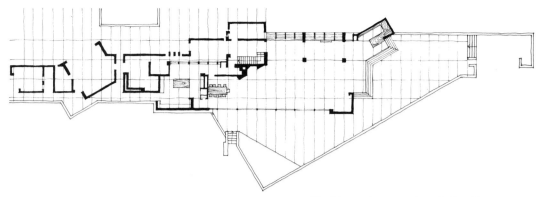

The Marcus house project, Dallas, Texas, 1935.

climate of the Kansas City region, with its heaving frosts, blistering heat, high winds, and hailstones, all changing with punishing rapidity. The Brauner, Garrison, and Newman projects in 1939 also fell within this most typical plan-type.

The Diagonal Usonian

The second Usonian plan, the polliwog with diagonal elements, was frequently used in postwar designs. Without the complication of the hexagonal module, a change of geometry could differentiate zones of the house, such as daytime from nighttime functions, as in the Armstrong house, built in 1939 near Ogden Dunes, Indiana, and the Manson house built in 1940 in Wausau, Wisconsin.[20] The Jurgensen[21] and Panshin[22] projects developed the idea of a simple diagonal wing. The former juxtaposed 90° – 180° enclosing walls with a 45°, 4-ft square grid running across them. Subtle intersections and triangular overlays resulted. The latter, for a prospective member of the first Wright cooperative, placed a hexagonal "head" of livingrooms onto a rectangular bedroom tail, both with their own 2 by 4 ft grids at 45°, a rare

incidence of Wright not capitalizing on the potential tensions of planning geometry — the zones of the house remained unresolved.

The earliest and largest design of this type was the 1937 project in Dallas, Texas, for Stanley Marcus.[23] An immensely long, horizontal house with a 28 by 64 ft living area was designed to attune with the "breadth of vista" of the Texas prairie. To combat local climate it was based on "natural air conditioning" by means of a central (chimney) exhaust stack and terraces with insect screens hung from sweeping cantilever beams above the roofs. The movement pattern of cars set up a 60° geometry, causing the garage to nudge gently into the 4-ft square planning grid. This was echoed in the study area. The exterior terrace took up this line in such a way as to suggest that the whole house had been set upon a diagonal base that transparently showed through in the retaining walls and line of the fireplace. It is this multilayering of plan geometry that Wright used to heighten and discipline the experience of his buildings. Certainly the Jurgensen and hexagonal Sundt designs utilize this multilayering characteristic in an unforgettable way.

The In-Line Usonian

This single-block plan was similar to the basic Usonian, but had shorter circulation routes and a smaller external perimeter. In the Sturges house of 1939, in Brentwood Heights, California, the plan was very compact, with the living area operating as circulation space for the bedrooms beyond. The kernel of the design was the broad terrace with its view southward across Los Angeles. To achieve this, the building is perched on the edge of the hill in a two-thirds cantilever. Its dramatic character is similar to that of "Falling Water" and is made possible by the same masonry masses at the rear. At Sturges, a workshop is concealed below in the cantilever bracing. Here also the Usonian board and batten wall was varied. The plywood core was omitted and sloping studs substituted so that each external board successively lapped those below it. Unseasoned 'green' redwood was used, stained rust-red. Above the roof level the boards battened inward with special bridging "drip" battens. The design has a certain inexorability, and is a terminal statement in Wright's search, stated in the 1920's, for a house that is indigenous to the Los Angeles basin.

Here the Sturges house is viewed from below 20 years after construction.

The Sturges house, exterior, Brentwood Heights, California, 1939. Rough-sawn, overlapping redwood boards were substituted for the usual Usonian plywood core with board and batten walls. Photograph by Pedro E. Guerrero.

Since the Sturges house has no clerestory lantern, Wright obtained his characteristic double-level space by separating the secondary roof spans from the primary beams by short posts. Photograph by Pedro E. Guerrero.

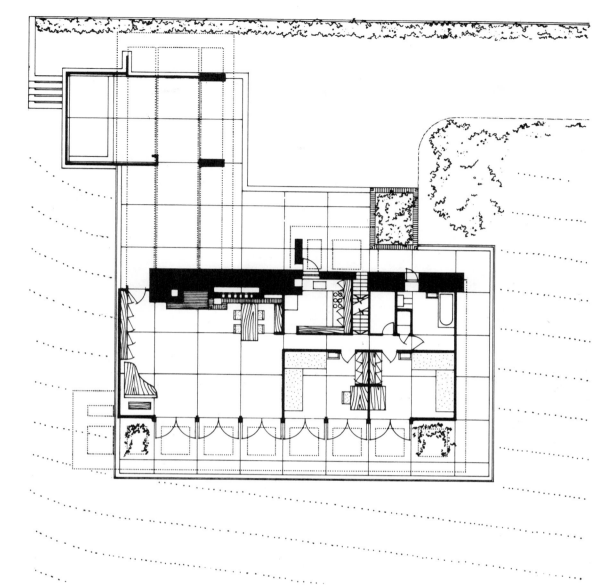

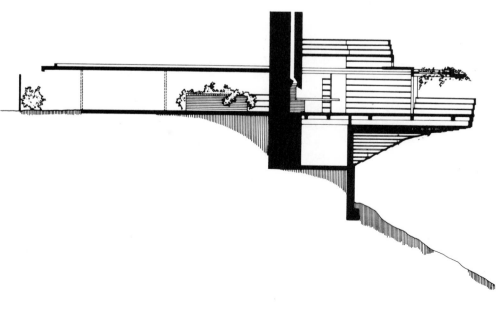

Clients: Mr. and Mrs. George Sturges
Profession: Not known
Location: Brentwood Heights, Los Angeles, California
Year of design: 1939
Best source: *Architectural Forum,* January 1948; Henry Russell Hitchcock, *In the Nature of Materials;* Frank Lloyd Wright, *The Natural House*
Builder/Supervisor: Paul Speer & Company: John Lautner
Cost: $9,000
Floor area: 870 sq ft; 80.8 sq m

The Winkler-Goetsch house, exterior, Okemos, Michigan, 1939.

The Winkler-Goetsch house, built in 1939, in Okemos, Michigan, was designed for two women on the faculty of Michigan State University. It is similar in plan to the Sturges house. However, its site is flat and the building is very horizontal. Entry is past the carport and along a broad sheltered walk down the northeast facade and into a gallery off the living area. A brick mass prevents further progress. The house is then found to float among trees (a characteristic of Wright's) as the windows to the south overlook a drop in the land. The living area is expansive, with boundaries that are difficult to define because they are beyond view. The house is organized in strips — workspace to gallery, chimney and dining area to side wall, sitting alcove to glazed doors and walled lawn beyond, and south range of window bay with planters. The crossview from one window wall to the other counters this "stripping" of the space, and the alcove is a snug and safe haven.

The whole building is a very assured statement of the Usonian type, with a 4-ft square grid, triple-tiered cantilevered eaves, and conventional detailing. This gives an exterior of simplicity, great horizontality, and contrasting brick and glass surfaces that have invited comparison with the work of Mies van der Rohe and the Internationalists.[24]

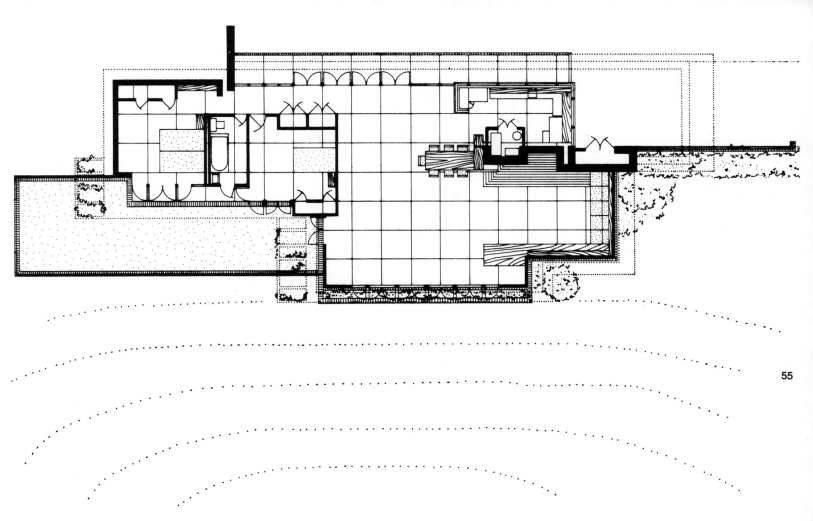

55

Clients: Ms. Katherine Winkler and Ms. Alma Goetsch
Profession: Faculty of the University of Michigan Art Department
Location: Lansing, Michigan
Year of design: 1939
Best source: *Architectural Forum,* January 1948; Henry Russell Hitchcock: *In the Nature of Materials;* Frank Lloyd Wright, *The Natural House*
Builder/supervisor: Harold Turner
Cost: Not known
Floor area: 1,350 sq ft; 125.4 sq m

The Baird house, exterior, Amherst, Massachusetts, 1940.

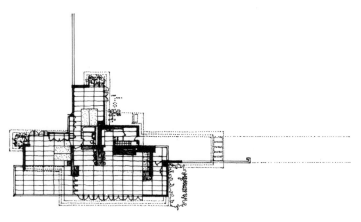

The Hause house project, Lansing, Michigan, 1939.

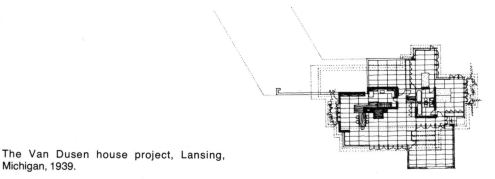

The Van Dusen house project, Lansing, Michigan, 1939.

The Baird house, built in 1940, in Amherst, Massachusetts, was constructed for a professor at Amherst College. It is a longer version of the Sturges plan. It lines the rear with services, kitchen, and bathrooms, and locates day and night activities on either side of a circulation space. The big two-way fireplace conceals a study beyond, and the pavilion workshop is separated from the carport and house by a walled dog yard. The Euchtman house of the same year, in Baltimore, Maryland, has a similar plan but is smaller, its diagonal carport built around an existing tree, complete with copper flashing. The Hause and Van Dusen projects for Usonia (a coop designed in 1939 in Lansing, Michigan) vary the plan-type, as do the Peterson (formerly Edith Carlson) and Hein projects of 1941 and 1943 respectively. The Rose Pauson house in Scottsdale, Arizona, and Arch Oboler "Eaglefeather" (Scheme 1) for Los Angeles, both of 1940, were different because of the relationship of their compact plans with steeply falling sites.

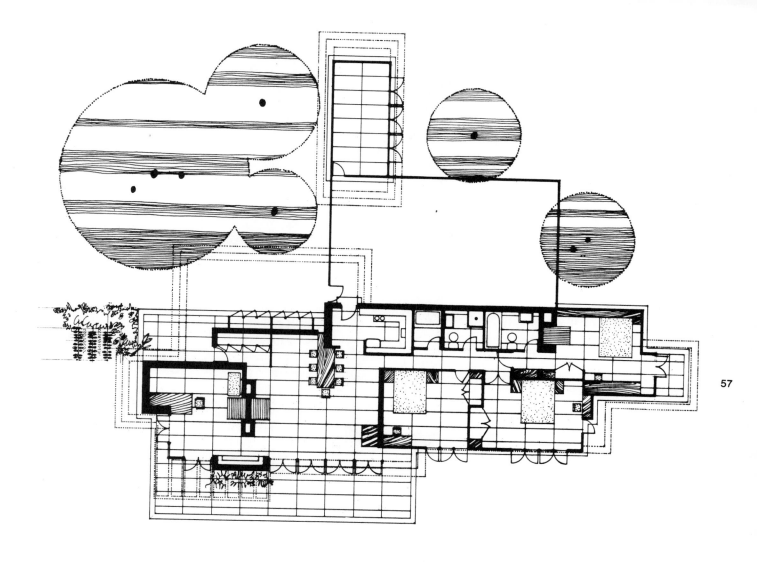

Clients: Mr. and Mrs. Theodore Baird
Profession: Shakespeare scholar, college professor
Location: Amherst, Massachusetts
Year of design: 1940
Best source: *Architectural Forum,* January 1948
Builder/supervisor: General contractor, Wesley Peters; supervised by J. C. "Carey" Caraway and Edgar Tafel
Cost: Not known
Floor area: 1,200 sq ft; 111.5 sq m

The Pauson house, now gutted by fire, disobeys Wright's dictum: never build *on* a hill, build around it.[25] This magnificent exception straddles a small hill in the desert above the road. It screens the view of the mountains behind and crowns the stepped walkway up to the house like some Toltec relic. The rose-colored stone masses (all that is now left) were banded by lapping boards into a massively based block. The head of the walkway plunged through the house and emerged as a balcony overlook at the far side. From here, the desert panorama was replaced by a turn along the side of the house. There followed a tiny entrance hall and, after a check by the chimney and two more turns, the double-height living room with a fully glazed directional view off the crest to the desert and mountain beyond.

"Eaglefeather," Wright's name for "Oboler's dream of an eagle's nest on a mountaintop" in California, is best known for his dramatic pencil rendering of the huge cantilever seen from below.[26] This project would have been of similar materials to the Pauson house — native stone built into the mountaintop, containing a reservoir and anchoring down the successive lapped board levels and balconies. Access would have been past a pool, and the bedrooms were to have been built up at the very edge of a steep drop, near a stair to a livingroom. This was placed upon an immense boarded deck whose cantilevered prow was to jut some 50 ft above the mountainside and 30 ft beyond the house itself. In essence, however, both the Pauson and Oboler houses were compact, two-story plans, the one with narrow double-height livingroom and line of upper bedrooms, the other with a horizontal living area, lavish decks, and bedrooms below. In both designs the architecture extends to the limits of the site and its generating idea reaches beyond into the landscape.[27] The organization of movement patterns enhances both houses' relationships with their sites to produce a unique feeling of place.

Because the Pauson house was destroyed by fire, this interior is lost. Photograph by Pedro E. Guerrero.

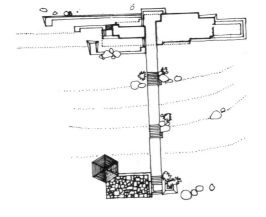

Client: Ms. Rose Pauson
Profession: Not known
Location: Scottsdale, Arizona
Year of design: 1940
Best source: *Architectural Forum*, January 1948; Henry Russell Hitchcock, *In the Nature of Materials*
Builder/supervisor: Robert Mosher
Cost: Not known
Floor area: 3,600 sq ft; 334.5 sq m

The stepped approach shown here was an integral part of the Pauson design. The house concealed a view of the mountain behind it. Then it led to an axial view off the crest to the right. Photograph by Pedro E. Guerrero.

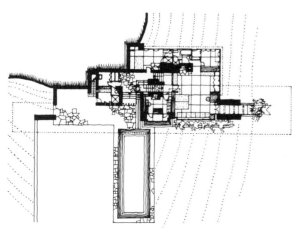

Oboler ground floor plan.

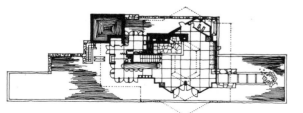

Oboler upper floor plan. A masonry reservoir is an integral part of the house.

The Oboler house project, "Eaglefeather," Los Angeles, California, 1940. Only the gatehouse was built.

The Hexagonal Usonian

The Hanna house, built in 1936, was the earliest and largest of the hexagonal plan-form Usonians. In it Wright extended the hexagon grid over a whole site to integrate a number of buildings, including the house, a guest house, workshop, garden house, and later, carparking terraces. The same discipline was used in the sprawling and mysterious Leigh Stevens plantation "Auldbrass" of 1940 near Yamassee, South Carolina. The intricate and unconventional construction,[28] the site buried in a moss-hung swamp, and the undisclosed nature of Steven's government work combined to give the project this air of mystery.[29] Diagonals were not restricted to the plan but were also utilized in the sloping walls. The 1- by 12-in. sloping stanchions, supporting 2- by 6-in. rafters in pairs, were clad in diagonal 1-in. cypress boarding incorporating ventilation slots at top and bottom. Over the normal heated concrete floors were slung lapped copper-clad roofs treated blue by chemical process.[30]

The Stevens house was not occupied fulltime, and the complex included caretakers' and guest houses, a farm, and cottages for black farm workers and their families. These last structures were highly ingenious pieces of miniaturized design, containing a livingroom with fireplace, a kitchen, seat beds and storage, and a screened sleeping porch with washing area and privy adjacent, beneath the exterior eaves.

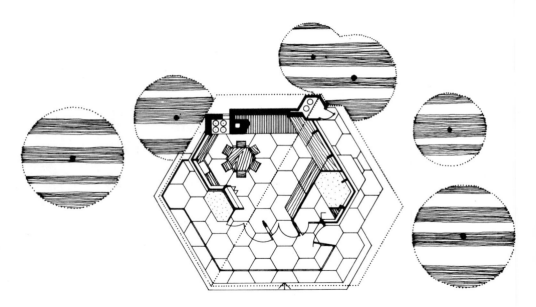

60

Clients: Mr. and Mrs. Leigh Stevens
Profession: Government official
Location: Yamasee, South Carolina
Year of design: 1940
Best source: *Architectural Forum,* January 1948; Moser and Verner, eds., *Sixty Years of Living Architecture;* some revised drawings in *Drawings for a Living Architecture*
Builder/supervisor: Peter Berndston
Cost: Not known
Floor area: 2,000 sq ft (main house); 185.8 sq m

The Bazett house, built in 1940 at Hillsborough, California, is basically an hexagonal version of the Jacobs plan. The 60° angle of the two wings wraps about the corner of the garden. The carport, which links with the guest house, terminates in a balcony walk overlooking the steep drop to the southeast, and this walk leads into the entry. The floor drops into a long living-room, delicately lit, with a modulated, glazed wall to the garden on one side and a 20-ft built-in seat and book-shelves on the other. At the fireplace, the lines of cypress-panelled ceilings from three roof areas meet. Wright makes one of his most characteristic contrasts between this public zone and the tiny scale of the bedrooms, where almost every wall conceals storage or washing facilities (such as custom-made, hexagonal, stainless steel shower tubs).

Clients: Mr. and Mrs. Sidney Bazett
Profession: Not known
Location: Hillsborough, California
Year of design: 1940
Best source: *Architectural Forum*, January 1948; Henry Russell Hitchcock, *In the Nature of Materials*
Builder/supervisor: Blaine Drake
Cost: Not known
Floor area: 1,480 sq ft (includes guest house); 137.5 sq m

"Snowflake" was the name Wright gave to the Wall house of 1941 in Plymouth, Michigan. This house possibly ranks as modern architecture's greatest wedding present.[31] The plan was of head and twin tail form (now extended), and its hexagonal planning grid was projected as a diamond module. Like Wright's other south Michigan houses, the building occupies one of the occasional hillocks in that flat region. Its hexagonal living space is raised upon a brick plinth and this in turn extends, as the land falls, to form massive stepped retaining walls enclosing a raised grass terrace. Walking its edge accentuates what topography there is. Symmetrical implications of the wigwam roof-form of the living area are immediately combated by the off-center core and built-in seat and table. This space is entered in a curving fashion alongside its perimeter, which takes on a meandering character, especially in wrapping around the core to reach the dining area, lit through three small winter gardens. Above this the cedar boarding swirls in waves, and throughout are the marks of the elaborate Usonian — again built by Turner — 60° brick specials and immaculate millwork piano hinges, corner opening doors, and built-in radiogram speakers.[32]

62

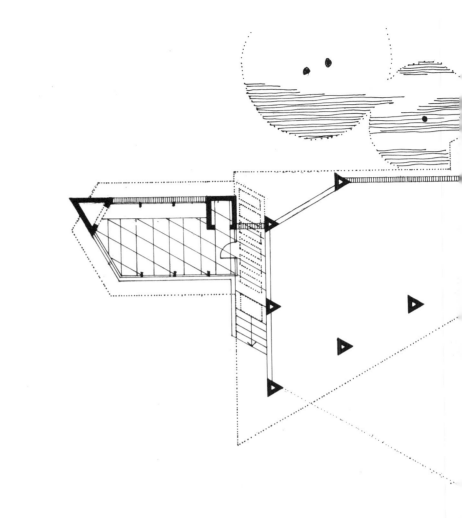

The Wall house, "Snowflake," exterior, Plymouth, Michigan, 1941. The massive masonry retaining walls supporting the terrace and lawn set a precedent for many later Wright designs.

Clients: Mr. and Mrs. Carl Wall
Profession: Corporate officer
Location: Plymouth, Michigan
Year of design: 1941
Best source: *Architectural Forum,* January 1948
Builder/supervisor: Harold Turner
Cost: Not known
Floor area: 2,000 sq ft; 185.8 sq m

The last hexagonal plan-type and the most resolved in its design, was the Vigo Sundt project of 1941 in Madison, Wisconsin, which was never built.[33] The exquisite perspective drawing of the house indicates a site with a boat basin at the edge of one of the two Madison lakes.[34] The plan is functionally of arrowhead form with the livingroom at the point, the workspace-utility-carport in one barb, and the bedrooms in the other. The acute corners were to be brick masses containing fireplaces, ducts, and storage.

It is in the interworking of the plan's functions with its geometry that the project attracts attention. It consists of a superimposition of many triangles, some shifted and others overlapping in the manner of an afterimage. These allow spaces to interlock in an unprecedented way. An outer triangle containing the carport and entrance loggia partially overlaps the triangular livingroom and the bedroom wing. The three corners of the livingroom were to be masonry recesses—each top-lit—that were satellites to the main glazed space with its raised coved ceiling. The fireplace marked the sitting zone. The workplace served the dining area, while bookshelves, a desktop, and seat delineated the third zone for study and writing. The central area flowed out, on two sides through glazed doors to terraces, and on the third side down steps to the loggia. The spatial ambiguity of the plan would have given the house that quality which the Hannas called "endless fascination."

Although the Sundt design was not built, it was however essentially realized in the Richardson house in Glen Ridge, New Jersey. Until access to Wright's archives is permitted it will not be certain whether the latter followed the former. Certainly the Sundt design and plans were those published by Wright, and they are much more strongly related to their site.

World War II prevented the Richardsons from building their home until 1951, when it was constructed on a different site from its intended location in Livingston. As built, the house is a mirror-image of the Sundt plan, with an additional study and longer bedroom wing. It substitutes brickwork for board and batten in the terrace walls, and boasts a remarkable three-way boarded cypress livingroom ceiling that laps downward in contrast to the upward-coving of the Wisconsin project. Its beautiful millwork evokes the spirit of the pre-war executed work.[35]

64

The Richardson house, exterior, Glen Ridge, New Jersey, 1941. Rainwater pipes have been substituted for the original drip outlets, which caused damp and efflorescence in the brickwork.

Richardson interior.

Clients: Mr. and Mrs. Stuart Richardson
Profession: Engineer
Location: Glen Ridge, New Jersey
Year of design: 1941; built 1951
Best source: Not published
Builder/supervisor: Local contractor
Cost: Not known
Floor area: 2,000 sq ft (estimated); 185.8 sq m

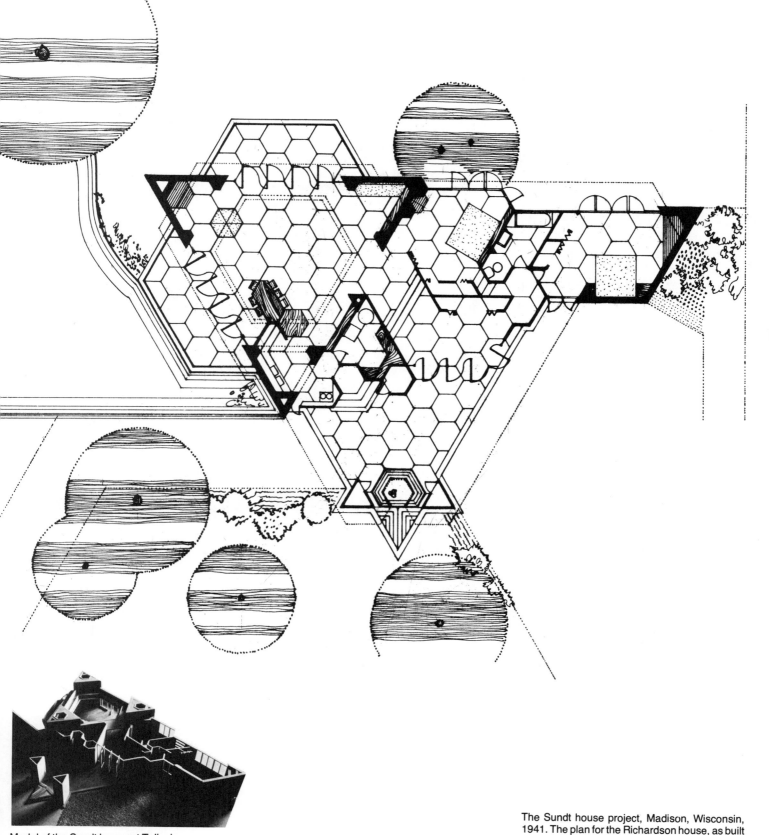

65

Model of the Sundt house at Taliesin.

The Sundt house project, Madison, Wisconsin, 1941. The plan for the Richardson house, as built in 1951, is similar to this project.

The Raised Usonians

The fifth broad category of Usonian plans was the masonry piered plan. It was used on the edge of ravines or water. In the Lloyd Lewis house, built in 1940 at Libertyville, Illinois, Wright raised the building well off the ground, since the site on the bank of the Des Plaines River was subject to dampness and possible flooding. "That type of house I believe ideal for a prairie site on low, damp, land of that type. But no such proceeding could be called cheap."[36] Lloyd and Kathryn Lewis were very old friends of Wright.[37] Lloyd was a member of a group that included the poet Carl Sandberg, the critic Alexander Woolcott, and playwright Charles MacArthur.[38] Both Lewises were journalists.

66

The Lewis house has a Florentine scale. From the carport there is an unusually grand entry sequence along a formal loggia, whose brick piers mark the cross-rhythm of three terraced flower beds. This leads to a broad stair with top-lit planter giving access to the generous upper livingroom and screened porch. The bedroom "tail" is reached at the midpoint of the stair. The restful proportion of these spaces, subtle changes of level, and assured cypress detailing make this one of Wright's simplest and most successful Usonian interiors. Its scale suited the Lewises' occasional large parties in what Wright wryly called "those fashionable woods." He wrote, "The tragedy that befell so many of my clients happened to the Lloyd Lewises. They just liked to stay in their house and didn't care to go out anywhere unless they had to."[39]

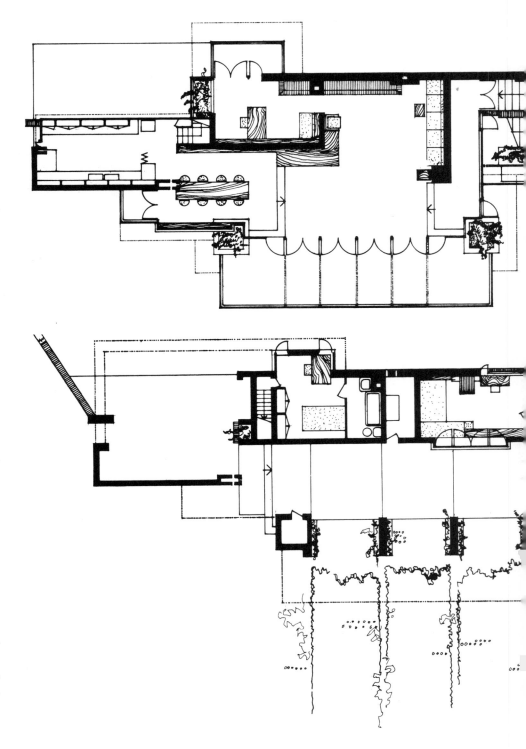

Clients: Mr. and Mrs. Lloyd Lewis
Profession: Journalists
Location: Libertyville, Illinois
Year of design: 1940
Best source: *Architectural Forum,* January 1948; Henry Russell Hitchcock, *In the Nature of Materials*
Builder/supervisor: Edgar Tafel
Cost: Not known
Floor area: 2,350 sq ft; 218.3 sq m

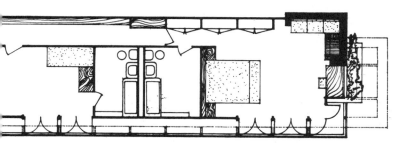

Lewis upper floor plan.

Lewis carport.

Lewis ground floor plan.

The Lewis house, exterior, Libertyville, Illinois, 1940. The house overlooks the Des Plaines River to the southwest. The upper deck of the Lewis house is permanently screened with steel supports, painted red.

The Pew House

The Pew and Affleck houses represent a strategy of site treatment quite different from "building round the hill" at Taliesin. In the latter, the buildings progress gently along the contours. In the former, the building starts level with the slope but stands out from the landform as it falls away.[40] The Pews moved to Madison, Wisconsin, from Cleveland, Ohio, in 1930. Clarence Pew was a research chemist with the University of Wisconsin Forest Products Laboratory, and the house was built in 1940.[41] Their 75-ft-wide lot, with frontage on the north shore of Lake Mendota and $8,500 budget were all that they could afford.[42] As with the Schwartz house, Wright placed the Pew house diagonally upon the lot in such a way as to differentiate it from its neighbors and improve the orientation and view.[43] So narrow was the site that Wright was obliged to place the bedrooms on the first floor. However, these difficulties were resolved in a masterful design.

Conceptually the building acts as a staircase to the view, while it is simultaneously a part of the lakeshore and poised above it. It is approached from above, but cars are suitably stopped, and the entrance indicated, by a low stone wall. The chimney, service core, and supporting pier of the house course out from the horizontal strata of the site in local honey-colored stone.[44] This core is also paved with the same stone, while the remainder of the house is of clear-spanning timber incorporating steelwork. Like the Lloyd Lewis house, heating is by steam pipes in the floor, one loop every two feet. The floor boards were laid with gaps to allow the passage of warm air.

Functionally the plan is small and efficient. The workspace is a through-unit with access to the front door and windows to the carport, an improvement over most Usonians. The livingroom leads directly to a broad terrace, as does the tightly planned bedroom floor above. This raised terrace is the heart

The Pew house, exterior, Madison, Wisconsin, 1940. The house is set diagonally on its narrow site. The long deck overlooks Lake Mendota to the northwest. Photograph by Robert Twombly.

of the concept. Its lapped cypress rail echoes the far lakeshore and contrasts with the verticality of the northern woods, while its straight line parallels the axis of the livingroom from fireplace to opposing pier. A raised section of coved ceiling midway across the room reinforces this centrality, holding down and counterpointing the meandering rear wall, which eventually returns through the workspace to the entry mass.[45]

The owners' personalities and fondness for their house give the space a quality of repose enhanced by the scent and fresh color of the beautiful millwork and stonework.[46] The house has a simplicity and intimate scale that is immediately appreciated, yet it also has recesses and boundaries that are difficult to recall without actually sitting there. The brutal strength of its concept, the utility of the plan, the control of all sensations in an utterly ingenuous way, and the delicate handling of its materials all make the Pew house, for me, the greatest of Wright's late career.[47]

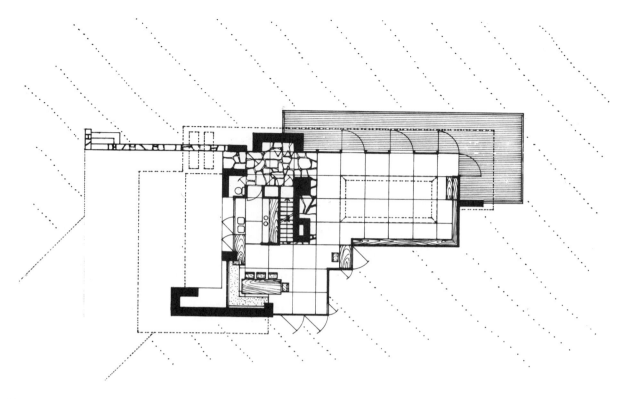

Pew ground floor plan.

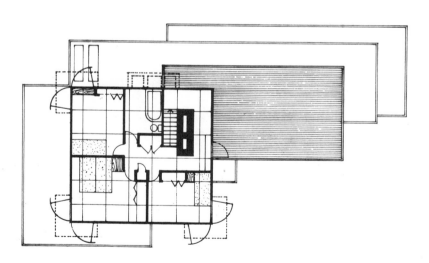

Pew upper floor plan.

Clients: Mr. and Mrs. Clarence Pew
Profession: Research chemist
Location: Madison, Wisconsin
Year of design: 1940
Best source: *Architectural Forum,* January 1948; Henry Russell Hitchcock, *In the Nature of Materials*; Frank Lloyd Wright, *The Natural House*
Builder/supervisor: General contractor, Wesley Peters; supervisor, J. C. "Carey" Caraway
Cost: $8,500
Floor area: 1,216 sq ft; 112.9 sq m

The Affleck House

Gregor Affleck grew up in Spring Green, Wisconsin, not long after Wright had gone to Chicago. He knew the Lloyd-Joneses, Wright's maternal family. Affleck was a chemical engineer, a self-confessed "total survival of the Protestant work ethic,"[48] but also a devout Catholic. He "discovered how to make money," in his own words, and commissioned Wright at the age of 50. The house was built in 1941 in Bloomfield Hills, Michigan. It follows the familiar L plan. The workspace, services, carport, and bedroom are built up on the edge of a small ravine, which the living area spans. The house is entered from a top-lit loggia, whose open well overlooks a pool and streamlet that eventually runs into a pond. The broad, boarded terrace, very similar to that of the Pew house, overlooks this pond. This interrelationship with the fold of the site through many levels generates the house's special quality.

The high, well-lit loggia is overlooked by guest room windows at a higher level, and is itself higher than the sweeping 40-ft livingroom that stretches beyond. Plants climb up the fretted plywood rooflights and tumble down the well to meet still other plants growing up from the pool below. The shady undercroft is equipped with two seats connected by a bridge and provides a framed view of woods and pond. The whole house is a constructional tour-de-force and monument to Harold Turner's art.[49] The cypress work is not so much akin to mill work as to cabinet making, since all the board walls are lapped, the plywood cores are inclined, and the 12 by 1 in cypress boards are specially milled to chamfer and overlap. The skill required to construct corners and door frames (complete with lapped doors), all with mitered joints and two-way slopes, can be imagined. The testimony of a visit to the house, which exudes a sense of ease and naturalness, belies this virtuosity. The Afflecks brought up their family in the house and lived there until they died.

Here is the Affleck exterior as seen from the southwest.

The Affleck house, interior, Bloomfield Hills, Michigan, 1941. Here is the top-lit entry loggia. The inclined, lapped cypress walls can be seen by the windows of the guest room. In the foreground is a glazed lightwell overlooking a pool by the stream below.

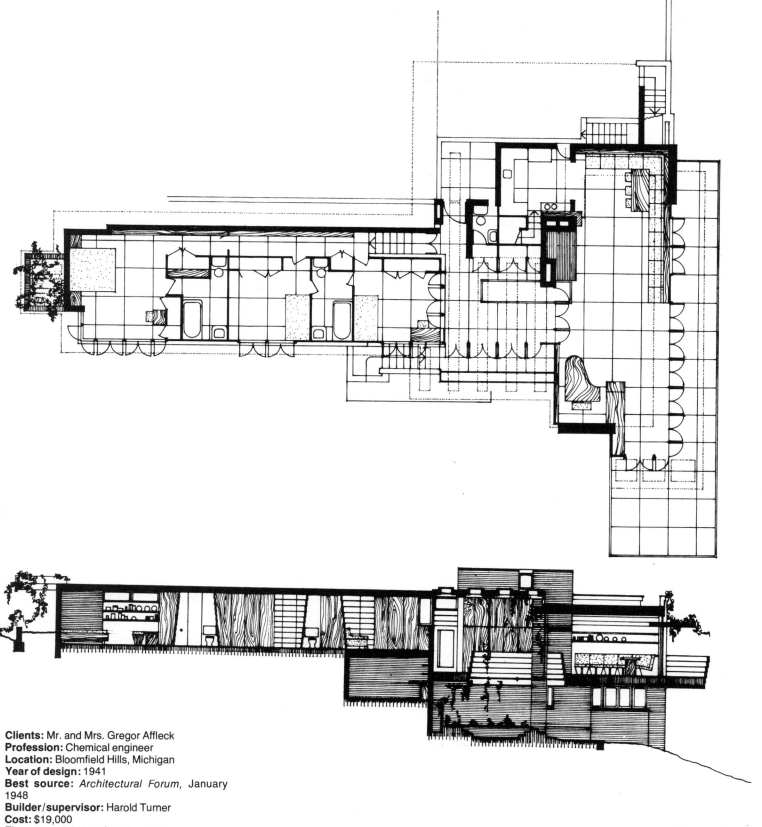

Clients: Mr. and Mrs. Gregor Affleck
Profession: Chemical engineer
Location: Bloomfield Hills, Michigan
Year of design: 1941
Best source: *Architectural Forum,* January
1948
Builder/supervisor: Harold Turner
Cost: $19,000
Floor area: 2,350 sq ft; 218.3 sq m

Affleck section.

The Quadruple Homes

In spite of his outpouring of creative work on individual homes through the late 1930s, Wright continued to propose new ideas for the community. The tight L plans of the archetypal Usonians — the Lusk, Jacobs, and Rosenbaum houses — sought to maximize the area of garden on a small lot. This search led to the "Quadruple homes." The first of these, and the only ones built, were the Suntop homes for the Todd Company in Ardmore, Pennsylvania, in 1939. Here the lot was divided into four gardens and the four houses placed into their adjoining corners. So far as the occupant was concerned, there was absolute privacy in each three-story mezzanine home, which was not overlooked by any other house. But by grouping the four buildings together, Wright was able to reduce external surface area and building and running costs. Only one of the intended four units was built, and the total building cost was $16,000.

The idea for the quadruple homes had precedents in Wright's work as far back as the residential land development plan he had formulated for the Chicago City Club competition of 1913. Similar plans had also accompanied the Broadacre City proposals.[50] The essence of the quadruple home plan lay in its clear zoning — which allowed for different activities on the ground floor and upper dining balcony — as well as affording the housewife a commanding position, with easy access from the kitchen to the children's bathroom and visual superintendance through clerestory windows of their play on the walled roof deck or in the garden below. The quadruple plan has received altogether insufficient attention for the important innovations in density and land use that it represented. With ½-acre lots, the density was eight to ten people per acre, but at Ardmore this was closer to thirty people per acre. Since 75 percent of each lot was not built on, the house type still suggests that it has clear potential in housing design.

72

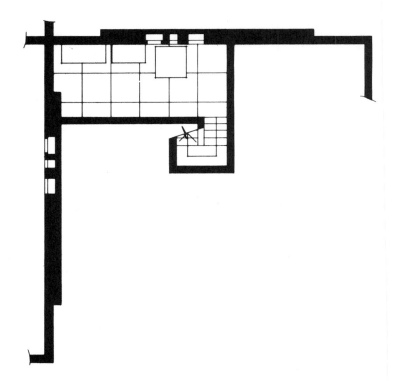

Suntop basement.

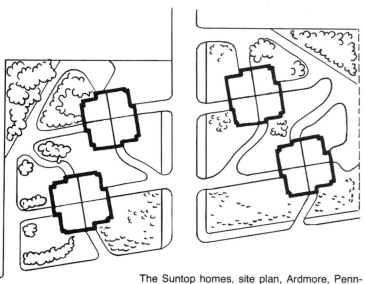

The Suntop homes, site plan, Ardmore, Pennsylvania, 1939. Four units were originally intended.

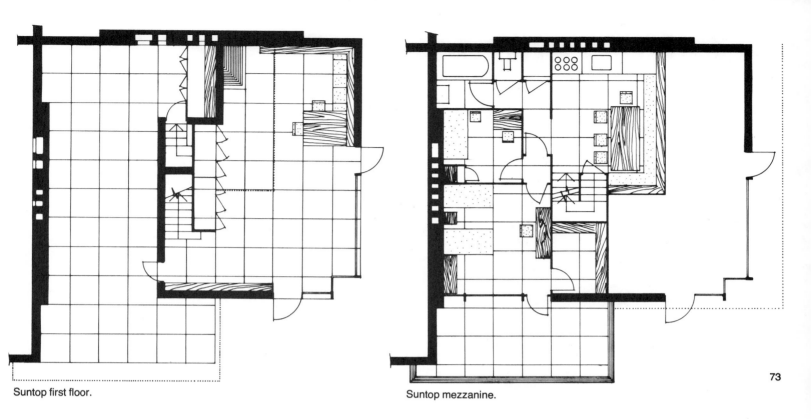

Suntop first floor.

Suntop mezzanine.

Suntop penthouse.

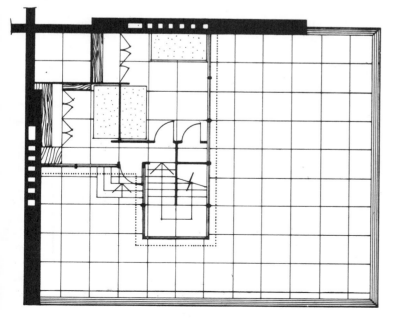

Client: Otto Mallory of the Todd Company (Suntop Homes)
Profession: Property developers
Location: Ardmore, Pennsylvania
Year of design: 1939
Best source: *Architectural Forum,* January 1948; Henry Russell Hitchcock, *In the Nature of Materials*
Builder/supervisor: Harold Turner
Cost: $16,000 for all four dwellings; approximately $4,000 for each unit
Floor area: 2,300 sq ft for each unit; 213.7 sq m

The driveway at left leads to the garage of the Suntop home at right. The home at left is entered in a corresponding way from the other boundary beyond view at left. Photograph by Robert Twombly.

Wright evidently regarded the quadruple dwelling unit as a model of its kind and described it in terms of the quality of lifestyle that it offered.[51]

Wright's 1942 housing project for 100 dwellings to be built for the U.S. government in Pittsfield, Massachusetts, developed both the plan and system of construction for such mass housing units. By pulling each unit away from the crosswalls and incorporating a 16-ft by 36-ft yard with light well above, the general lighting for the home was improved, especially for the one or two quadrants that might be relatively disadvantaged, no matter how the block was oriented. The livingroom area was increased from 405 to 432 sq ft, and a utility room was added. But mezzanine and upper bedroom plans were almost unchanged, with six bed places. The project was designed for standardized components, using precast concrete. While working on it, Curtis Besinger wrote, "This defense housing scheme is no snap to do drawings on: the whole thing is practically an invention in building technology, wall slabs in thick diatomaceous earth, floor slabs of 2½-in. thick concrete. Everything is precast. There are some wood walls that come near to being in the realm of the usual construction. . . ."[52]

Here is one of the four Suntop homes viewed over its boarded garden wall. The deep boarded fascia is a protective wall to the rooftop play deck behind. The mezzanine workspace (kitchen) at rear of the double-height, glazed livingroom overlooks this as well as the garden.

An aerial perspective of the project, however, does reveal a problem.[53] The aim of providing every dwelling with individual car access in the characteristic pinwheel fashion, resulted in each "cloverleaf" cluster being encircled by roads. Since Wright's ½-acre quads, discussed in *The Living City,* substituted perimeter car courts for pedestrian access to the house, a line of development was clearly open to shared car facilities and higher densities, yet with reduced road area and retention of 75 percent of the lot area for gardens.[54] But this design was not to be realized, since local Massachusetts architects pressed for the project to be given to an architect registered in the state and Wright was dismissed.[55] He did not allow the government to purchase his plans (the basis on which construction could have proceeded), since this would have meant a loss of control over execution. After this experience, Wright never returned to designing quadruple housing.

Cooperative Homesteads

The "cooperative homesteads" projected for autoworkers near Detroit, Michigan, was also designed in 1942. This low-cost housing venture was based upon the regime, proposed earlier for Broadacre City, of an industrial job plus self-supportive homesteading. For this project Wright designed the berm-type house. Earth was excavated from a surrounding sunken garden and rammed up against the house to form grassed banks. These deflected winds and provided lowcost, heavy insulation.

Each house was to stand upon 1 acre of land. The plan is economical, with grouped services, generous livingroom, and no wasted circulation space. The livingroom leads past the only floor-to-ceiling glazing to the entrance and carport, which includes, or doubles as, a porch. Beyond this, at a lower level, is located the workshop and dry food and vegetable storage area. This workshop was an esssential adjunct to the house's 1-acre plot for food production, and was part of the whole self-supporting nature of the coop.[56]

76

The Cooperative Homesteads project, typical house plan, Detroit, Michigan, 1942. The wing to right of the porch/carport contains a workshop and storage area for vegetables and dry food.

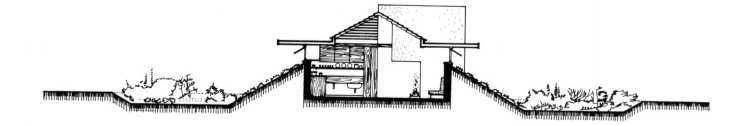

Wright's first use of low-cost berm insulation was planned for the Cooperative Homesteads.

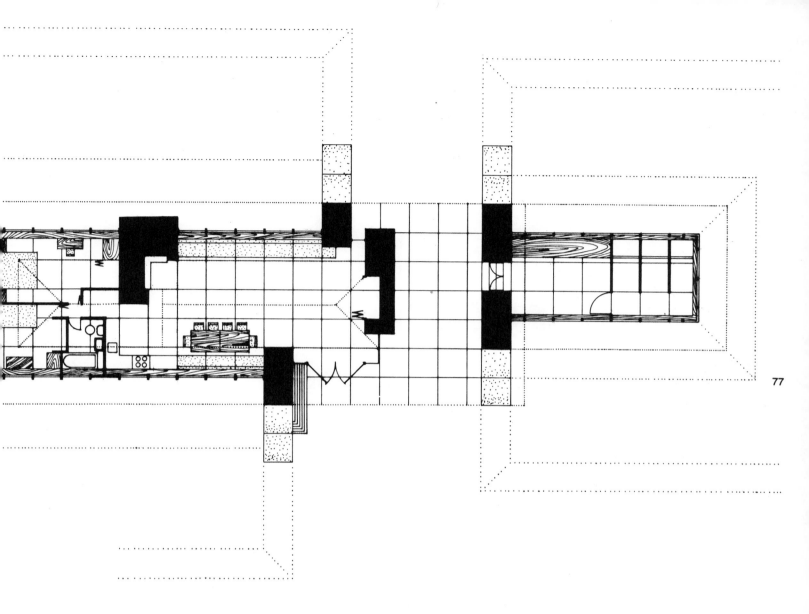

Usonia

One project did come Wright's way in 1939 that set the future pattern for his community design. On the inspiration of Professor Newman of the psychology department of Michigan State University at Lansing, seven faculty members formed a cooperative. After a period of operating a food coop, the group obtained an option on some land and then purchased it. At this point, Catherine Winkler and Alma Goetsch, both of whom were in the Michigan State art department, made contact with Wright, who proceeded with designs.

The project went through the stage of working drawings and was named Usonia I by Wright. In London in 1939 he both confused this and revealed plans for another group; he referred to Taliesin as Usonia I, Lansing as Usonia II and a project for Wheeling, West Virginia, as Usonia III.[57]

The Lansing cooperative was aborted when Harold Turner, the builder, was already on site and prepared to break ground. One of the group's sources of private financing had collapsed and application was made for a bank loan. This had to be made with Federal Housing Authority (FHA) approval. So important was the project to Wright by this time that he personally presented the application in Washington, D.C. Approval was turned down for familiar reasons—an ultraconservative view of construction.[58] The FHA claimed that "the walls will not support the roof; floor heating is impractical; the unusual design makes subsequent sales a hazard."[59]

The design may be regarded as the first practical demonstration of the principles of Broadacre City. The overall layout was for a tract of 40 acres, accompanied by detailed designs for the seven different homes and a cooperative farm unit with caretaker's house. Wright's suggestion for a farm was eagerly taken up by the group as a step toward self-sufficiency. Each lot had its own private garden, and the farm included small fields, an orchard, and a fishpond. Only the Winkler-Goetsch house was finally built on another site, while the Brauners built a new design after the war.[60]

Name: Usonia I project
Location: Lansing, Michigan
Date of design: 1939
Clients/founders: Professors Brauner, Garrison, Goetsch, Hause, Newman, Panshin, Van Dusen, and Winkler
Best source: *Architectural Forum,* January 1948

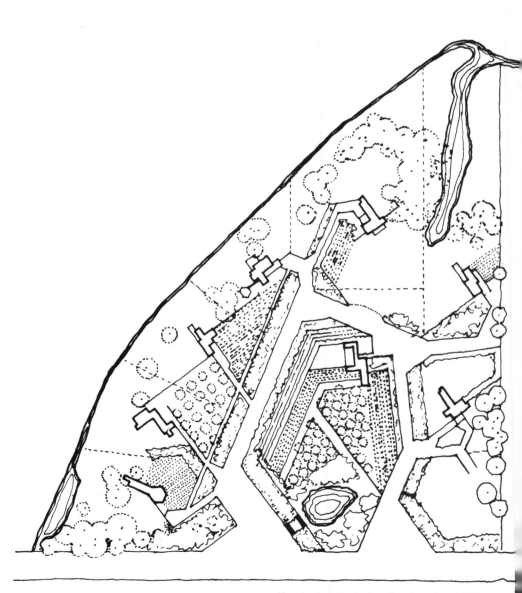

Usonia I project, site plan, Lansing, Michigan, 1939. The six Usonian homes were grouped around a shared farm unit.

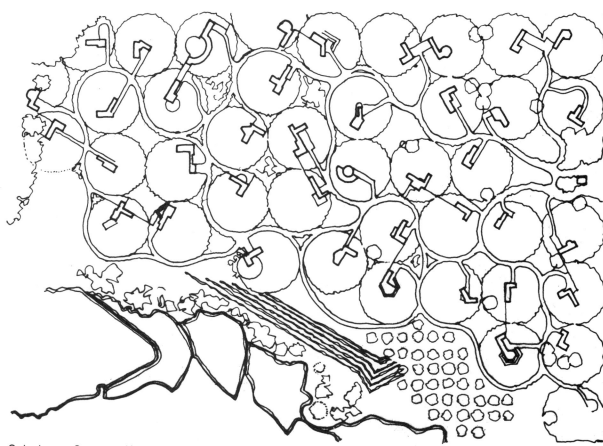

Galesburg Country Homes, site plan, Kalamazoo, Michigan, 1947. Each home was placed in a circular 1-acre lot.

Name: Galesburg Country Homes
Location: Near Kalamazoo, Michigan
Date of design: 1947
Clients/founders: Eppstein, Meyer, Pratt, Weisblatt
Best source: *Architectural Forum,* January 1948

Midwestern Communities

Following the war, in 1947, Wright designed the overall site plan for two other cooperative communities. At Galesburg Country Homes near Kalamazoo, Michigan, his four-house designs used concrete blocks to avoid postwar shortages of building materials.[61] The community members, a group of chemists from the Upjohn Institute, made the blocks themselves from a Taliesin mold, obtained materials in bulk and built their own homes. A second nonprofit organization at Parkwyn Village in Kalamazoo, Michigan, was built by similar self-help techniques. Contractors were called in to work on portions of, and in some cases, entire homes. The community has since grown, with some houses designed by other architects.[62] The site plans for both Michigan groups proposed a layout of serpentine roads meandering about the contours and servicing circular 1-acre lots.[63] For the most part, these lots touched only at their circumferences; open space between them was maintained as landscape held in common by the community.

Usonia Homes

The largest Wrightian cooperative is Usonia Homes in Pleasantville, New York. On 97 acres of virgin forest land, some fifty homes have now been built. David Henken, a young engineer, obtained Wright's help in planning this cooperative in 1940, with the express intention of realizing a section of Broadacre City, Wright's plan for urban decentralization.[64] First Henken and his wife moved to Taliesin for 2 years. He became an apprentice at Wright's combined home and architectural school. It had been Henken's original intention to have Wright design all the houses for the coop. However this was prevented by the postwar demand for the architect's services. Wright therefore designed the master plan for the site in 1947 as well as three homes.[65] He readily agreed to allow other architects and designers who were sympathetic to his ideas to carry out the remainder of the project, subject to his power of approval.[66] By 1953, nine architects had designed houses for the cooperative.[67]

The Pleasantville community plan again utilizes circular 1-acre lots, in this instance arranged in overlapping clusters of five. Each of these surround an open central area, intended as parkland for shared activities such as play, camping, and barbecues. These are untouched woodland, as are the triangular wedges at points in the plan.[68] The result is a development that largely realizes Wright's dictum that organic architecture improves its site. The design utilizes a particularly successful road plan whose serpentine form is closely related to the contours of the land. The community facilities include playgrounds, vegetable gardens, a children's farm, swimming pool, and community house. The members of the cooperative also laid out their own utilities, with well and storage tank.

80 Usonia Homes are a registered Rochdale cooperative, and the constitution has proved to be a successful answer to the social and financial problems of bringing it about. The principal difficulty lay in stringent postwar conditions: ". . . no bank would touch a cooperative mortgage because, they said: (a) the group might break up and the community assets would be dissipated; (b) because there was no racial or religious discrimination in the project which some of the banks regarded as detrimental to real estate values; (c) because the houses were of modern design and had no re-sale value."[69]

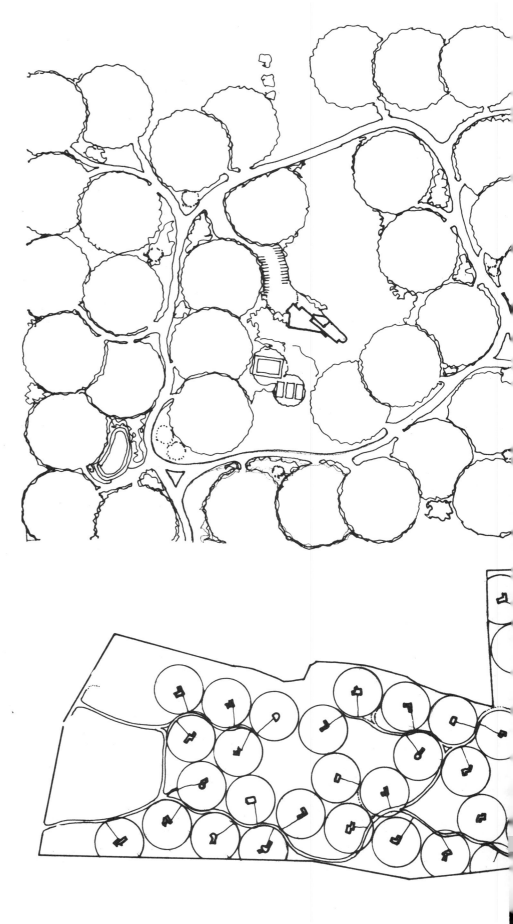

Three homes in the Pleasantville community are by Wright. Some fifty others are by other architects, the majority by David Henken.

Name: Usonia Homes, Inc.
Location: Pleasantville, New York
Date of design: 1947
Client: David Henken
Best source: *Architectural Forum,* October 1948; Priscilla Henken, "A Broadacre Project," *Town and Country Planning,* vol. 23, pp. 294 – 300, June 1954; "Usonia Homes," *Journal of Housing,* pp. 319, 320, 344, 345, October 1953.

Name: Parkwyn Village
Location: Near Kalamazoo, Michigan
Date of design: 1947
Clients/founders: Brown, Levin, McCartney, and others
Best source: *Architectural Forum*, January 1948

Parkwyn Village, site plan, Kalamazoo, Michigan, 1947. Wright designed four homes for this community; the rest are by other architects.

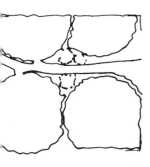

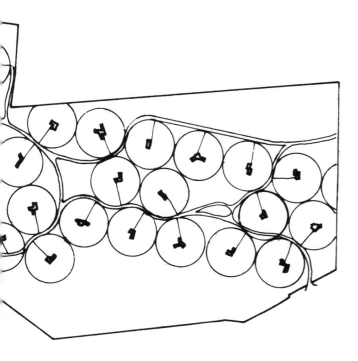

The Change from Kit to Architectural Portrait

After World War II, labor rates and building costs started to rise sharply. The skilled craftsmen who could execute Wright's demanding standards of brickwork and miter-cut millwork at low cost ceased to be cheap or readily available.[70] Moreover some of the materials themselves, such as cypress, became unobtainable. The Usonian kit ceased to be used in its pure form, and while Wright built in a similar way throughout the 1950s, many of his clients during the last decade of his life had large sites for which they required large homes. The designs that resulted could not be regarded as answers to "the small house problem." Wright himself had become a household word and his practice grew beyond all previous bounds.[71] He himself was in his eighties and concentrated his attention on the larger projects that had at last come his way, especially the Guggenheim Museum in New York City, built between 1956 and 1959.[72]

81

The bulk of Wright's domestic work fell to his assistants, although he retained overall control and personal contact with his clients. Whatever fresh interest Wright did bring to bear on domestic work in the last decade of his life was applied to two last attempts to achieve low-cost construction[73] and to unusual sites or clients who stood out sufficiently to capture his imagination. Increasingly he talked of organic design and the organic home. An organic building arose uniquely from its site, its climate, it client's needs, its budget, and the intent of the client/architect relationship. It became less a repetition of an architectural idea and more an interaction of architect and client's wishes and skills. Some houses began to realize Wright's ideal, formulated in the early years of the century, that there should be as many different types of houses as there are people.

Solar-Hemicycle Houses

A new type of plan-form appeared in Wright's work that linked the new development with the original kit Usonians. The ramped earth banks or insulating berms of the project for the autoworkers' cooperative homesteads of 1942 were combined in the same year with a curved form of house, which was glazed along its south side to receive sunlight. Wright called it the "solar-hemicycle."

The concept took shape in the second Jacobs house, designed in 1943 and built in 1948–1949.[74] The Jacobs family, now requiring five bedrooms, again provided Wright the opportunity for an architectural advance. The site at Middleton, Wisconsin, was to the west of Madison and the earlier Usonian. From the north, the direction of the coldest winds, the house appears to be a natural hillock, with outcropping native rock typical of the region. In reality it is a grassed bank against the curved rear wall of the house, which is built of stone, and capped by high-level bedroom windows and the roof. Entry is via a stone tunnel through the bank to the sunny interior garden. The fully glazed south facade of the house curves around this. The stair, chimney, and services are concentrated within a stone drum near the entrance and workspace. The interior contains a 40-ft livingroom visually linked through a curved double height to the bedrooms and their access gallery above.

Essentially the house forms one room, which is in turn an integral part of the sunken garden outside. This interpenetration is made complete by a circular pond placed beneath the glazed wall so that fish can swim inside or out. Construction is by daring use of wooden structure: 12- by 1-in. boards span from the north facade to the mullion posts of the glazed south wall, to which they are placed to form radiating double beams, bolted on either side. From these, the entire bedroom gallery is suspended on ¾-in. steel ties. The bedroom walls are made

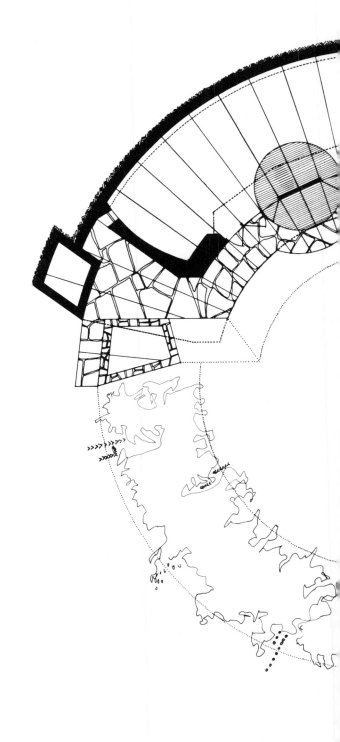

82

of lapped boards laid diagonally with no framing. The Jacobses did about half the construction, with Mr. Jacobs acting as "both contractor and supervisor."[75] Here, 30 years before the "energy crisis," was an instructive attempt to develop a "low-energy" architecture, deriving a lyrical form from the need to obtain maximum solar heat and protection from northern winds.[76]

A number of other houses were projected and built along hemicycle lines. These include the Marting house in Akron, Ohio, of 1947,[77] the Meyer house in Galesburg, Michigan, of 1948, the Laurent house in Rockford, Illinois, of 1949, and the Pearce house in Bradbury, California, of 1950. The Jacobs house realized some of the "bubble" planning concept of the Jester project of 1938 in the circular forms of its fireplace, service drum, and pool. The other solar-hemicycles demonstrate Wright's growing interest in a flowing architecture, free from the right angle. This development continued through the reflex curves of his 1953 design for his son, Robert Llewelyn, in Bethesda, Maryland, and the 1950 ramped spiral house for his other son, David, in Phoenix, Arizona, on to the Guggenheim Museum.

83

Second Jacobs house, ground floor plan, Middleton, Wisconsin, 1943. Entry is by a tunnel through the earth bank to the north. All spaces in the house overlook the circular sunken garden.

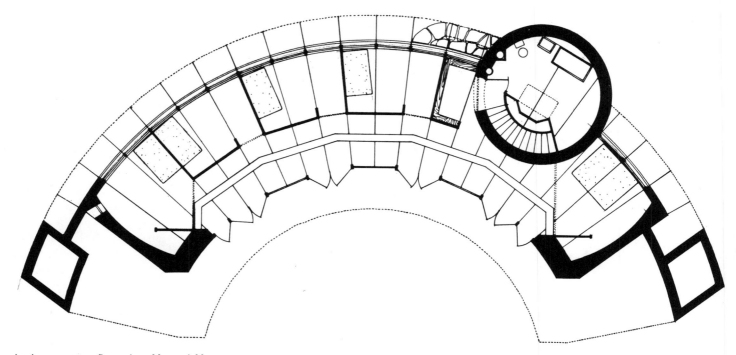

84 Jacobs house upper floor plan. Mr. and Mrs. Jacobs' bedroom was to the right of the stair and bathroom; the children's rooms were to the left. The upper floor is suspended by steel rods from the roof.

1

3

85

2

4

1 The entrance tunnel of the Jacobs house is shown here.
2 Here the Jacobs house is viewed from the north. Photograph by Robert Twombly.
3 The private facade of the Jacobs house faces south and its sunken garden.
4 This view of the Jacobs living area shows the integral relationship of interior and exterior space.
5 The David Wright house, exterior, Phoenix, Arizona, 1950.

5

Organic Houses

The postwar houses that chiefly attract attention are those that dramatize one or more of the determinents of Wright's organic architecture: client, climate and region, budget and site. No radical advance was made on the basic Usonian concept. The zoning of activities in the plan, polliwog form, service core, gravity heat, natural forms of climate modification such as roof overhangs, and use of differing geometric planning grids had all been stated during Wright's remarkably creative seventies. Close repeats of original Usonians, such as the Smith house of 1946 in Bloomfield Hills, Michigan, and the Weltzheimer house of 1948 in Oberlin, Ohio, illustrate what took place. The plan forms of the Jacobs or the Rosenbaum houses were executed in a construction technique that increasingly substituted masonry for board and batten walling. A decorated, notched fascia board made its appearance, and the intention of dry assembly or off-site frabrication was forgotten. The site strategy of the Wall house in 1941—of projecting a single-level house out from a hillside or slope, upon a massive and expensive masonry-retaining base — was increasingly utilized. Whenever simplicity survived the design process, handsome houses resulted. Otherwise, the "busy pencils of Taliesin," as one client termed them,[78] began to overwhelm the clarity of the Usonian house at a rate that corresponded with the reappearance of servants' quarters. Of some house designs of the last three years of Wright's life, nothing should be said.

There are however two beautiful California hexagonal houses that are worthy organic homes. The Walker house in Carmel of 1948 springs from its site, its terrace prow fused with a rocky promontory facing the Pacific Ocean. The 1950 Berger house in San Anselmo is integrated with its hillside in a particularly inevitable way, deriving its form from the successive stages in the owners' intended self-build process.

Two extremely elongated in-line plans stand out; the Zimmerman house in Manchester, New Hampshire, of 1950 and the Adelman house of 1948 in Fox Point, Wisconsin, which is also unusual because of its cedar shake roof and exposed ceiling rafters. The Palmer house in Ann Arbor, Michigan, of 1950, has a twin core, triangular plan that intimately relates to its site. A determined attempt to redefine modular construction was made in the cement asbestos-paneled Carlson house of 1950 in Phoenix, Arizona.[79] The form of the Hein project of 1943 for Chippewa Falls, Wisconsin, reflects the clients' lifestyle. It was to be built of coursed, battered, desert concrete,[80] with a linked "farm wing" required by the owner—including stabling, chicken run, and vegetable, hay, straw, and dry food storage.

The Grant house of 1945 in Cedar Rapids, Iowa, was built down the slope of a hillside in thin-layered stonework quarried on the site by the owner and his wife with a jackhammer.[81] The rooms of the house look along the contours, all reached by a stone-paved staircase that follows the slope of the hill. A horizontal roof lightly differentiates house from landscape. One project in Acapulco, Mexico, was to be cooled by chimney downdrafts directed through water sprays. In such very large homes as the Harold C. Price house of 1956 in Phoenix, Arizona, Wright caught the lifestyle of its occupants with consummate skill. Although all these late designs are radically different, their form was generated by different aspects of the concept of organic architecture, which they share.

The Palmer house, exterior, Ann Arbor,
Michigan, 1950.

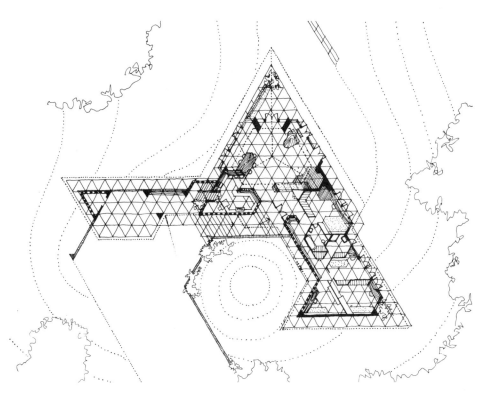

The Palmer house plan.

By 1950, Wright had reached the point of describing a house by the character or lifestyle of its clients. He called his design for Sol Friedman in Pleasantville, New York, "House for a Toymaker," and the building beautifully expresses an appropriate playfulness and light-heartedness. Intersecting circles in the planning geometry, a stone fireplace-grotto, mushroom-shaped carport, and round windows combine to achieve a happy, burrow-like atmosphere. Houses could have style, not a style. The point is important since it has been ignored by the critics who have lamented the lack of "followers" or "influence" of Wright. They are thinking visually, even superficially, seeking to categorize attributes. Is it not possible that a good organic architect might successively design buildings that are visually quite different? Wright sought to show at his Taliesin school that organic design was only a part of organic life, a manifestation of the balanced well-rounded person.

88

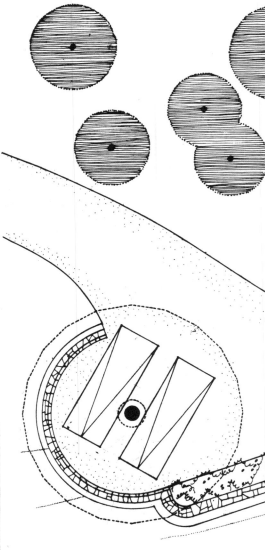

The Friedman carport is at left and the entry is reached along the retaining wall of masonry. The upper level contains bedrooms, bathroom, and a balcony overlooking the living room.

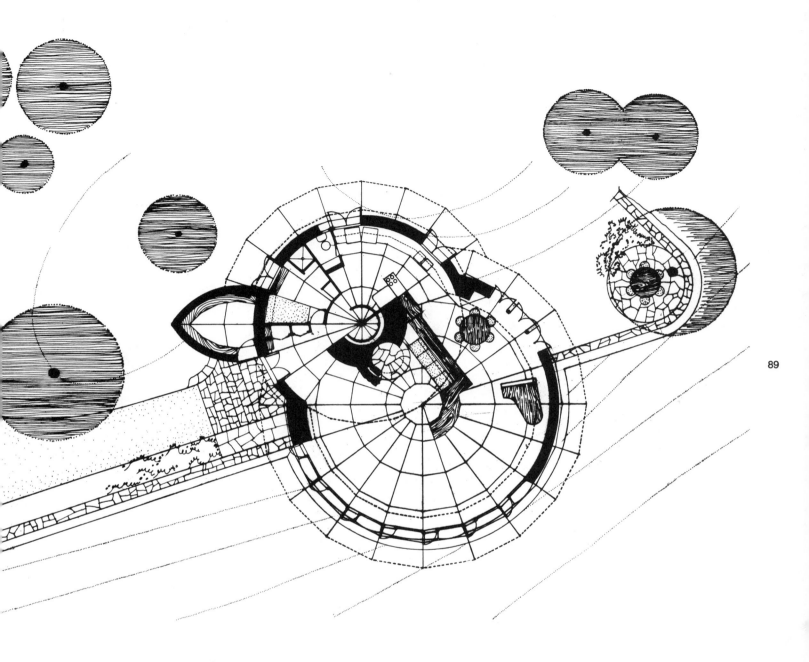

89

The Friedman house, exterior, Pleasantville, New York, 1950. The mushroom shape in concrete is the carport. The retaining wall at right of the Friedman house shields the private terrace at rear.

Close-up of Friedman exterior.

**Architectural Elements of
Usonian Houses**

Carports
1   The Affleck house.
2   The Rosenbaum house.
3   The Schwartz house.

91

2

3

Entrances
1   The Sturges house.
2   The Bazett house.

1

2

Assemblies

1 The typical stepback of soffit of roof overhang on the Rosenbaum house expresses the compound triple 2 by 4 in. joists behind. Rainwater chute is of an improved design to avoid splashback.

2 The junction of roof, clerestory, and cypress board and batten wall is illustrated in the Rosenbaum house.

3 The Affleck house has nonstandard lapped boarding without battens, and the mullion/sill junction is also different than most Usonians. Trellis at left, however, is typical.

4 The hexagonal discipline on the floormat of the Hanna house is reflected in the form of the glazed wall. The horizontal glazing muntins follow the 1 ft 1 in. vertical grid of the board and batten wall.

5 This view of the Winkler-Goetsch house shows the junction of the brickwork, glazing, floormat, roof.

6 This view of the Rosenbaum house shows typical interior elements, such as the clerestory lantern in the bedroom. The window light is broken by a fretted plywood pattern, which was different for each Usonian commissioned. The recessed light made by the builder is glazed here, but elsewhere it is shielded by a 1 by ½ in. cypress light baffle that is often pinned into a spiral. Bookshelves and desk are integral with the wall.

92

1

2

3

4

5

6

Fireplaces Wright's fireplaces, like every other element of the houses, are not symmetrical. A part of their design leads the eye away to points beyond view.
1 Bazett house.
2 Rosenbaum house.

Interior Lighting Where fretted plywood downlights were not used, cypress stripping was lined up to conceal bulbs and prevent glare.
3 Lloyd Lewis house.
4 Jacobs house (second).

Fixed Glazing Horizontal muntins visually continue the line of the battens. On the inside, the same line becomes a bookcase.
5 Rosenbaum house.
6 Rosenbaum house.

1

2

5

3

4

6

Detailing

1 This interior shows the junction of ceiling, clerestory windows with fretted plywood, and closet door on module in the Rosenbaum house.

2 Unusual detailing of linen closets built into the board and batten module is shown in this view of the Rosenbaum house. All the hardware is of high-quality brass.

3 The junction of the glass-to-glass corner window with brick base, rowlock course, planter, and glazed door is illustrated by the Rosenbaum house.

4 This view of the Rosenbaum house shows the reverse corner of the glazed wall, with the glazed door open and the screen door beyond closed. Note the module.

5 The soffit to the roof of the Rosenbaum house is shown here. The ventilation slot for the roof space is fitted with expanded metal mesh.

6 Note the junction of the door frame and the wall in opposite planes of the Rosenbaum house. The specifications of the Usonians normally called for all brass screws to be equally spaced, with slots horizontal.

7 This view of the Rosenbaum house shows the doors to the carport tool closet.

8 Here is an example of glazed doors centered on the module in the Rosenbaum house.

94

1

5

2

6

7

3

4

8

CHAPTER 3 Education, Design, and Construction

"Begin with a hoe."
Frank Lloyd Wright[1]

Wright's architectural practice during the period from the Depression to World War II was unusual. Not only did his practice become transcontinental in scope, but it was also a school of architectural design, with supervision of construction entrusted to members of the Taliesin school. This grew out of a working situation that was remarkable for both its sense of purpose and improvisation. Wright believed that organic design was an essential part of a well-rounded life, and the combined learning and designing activities of his architectural community were intended to bring about such a life. Just as the organic view affirmed integral change, the design and building of Usonian dwellings based on the two office-homes of Taliesin in Spring Green, Wisconsin, and Taliesin West at Scottsdale, Arizona, proceeded in a hurricane of activity.

The conventional professional office of Wright's early career in Oak Park, Chicago, was abandoned. Wright and his fellow communards physically built the extensions to Taliesin themselves as well as the winter camp at Scottsdale to house the school. They were quarrying, lime burning, wood cutting, and laying utilities and services. They were farming and raising their own food. They were carrying out an educational experiment. And they were formulating a social organization and methods of work.

Taliesin

If the classical loggia of his studio in Oak Park, Chicago, built in 1895, symbolized Wright's early career (in its relationship with the emerging suburbs that sustained it), the windmill and farm in Spring Green, Wisconsin, were the basis for the self-supporting community of Wright's late life. The first operated in conditions of economic growth, while the second started in the midst of the Depression. Wright's flight to Europe with Mrs. Cheyney in 1909, which combined his emotional needs with the necessity to work with his publishers on the monumental Wasmuth portfolio of his work up to that date, signaled the end of the "Prairie house career."

In a similar way, the foundation of an architectural school at Taliesin with his third wife Olgivanna, in the valley that his grandparents had settled, announced the second "Usonian career." Richard Neutra, Rudolph Schindler, and other architects from abroad had worked there on the concrete block-work designs of the twenties, a confused and personally agonizing period for Wright.[2] There had been an attempt in 1931 to set up a somewhat grandiose project for a School for the Allied Arts, which was envisaged as a pioneering design institution, based on the use of sophisticated machine shops. In conception it was distinctly analogous to the Bauhaus.[3] However, by October 25, 1932, this project had been dropped for lack of funds and forty charter applicants had been accepted for membership in the Taliesin Fellowship.

The Rural Location

The aim of the School for the Allied Arts had been "to establish and put into operation in private hands a 'style-center' or experiment station . . . ,"[4] and undoubtedly the same was true of Taliesin. Taliesin's location was the result of circumstances as well as Wright's emotional state upon returning from Europe with Mrs. Cheyney. Spring Green, Wisconsin, was chosen because Wright's mother had bought the Taliesin site for him there.[5] It met the need for security that he required in 1911, his feelings of rejection being so deep at the time that he described himself in *An Autobiography* as with his "back against the wall."[6] Norris Kelly Smith's observation that "architecture is the art of established institutions"[7] points to another strand in Wright's thinking at this time.

Although certainly the architecture of the "Prairie house career" was surely

Photograph on page 95
Taliesin during the 1930s includes a dairy herd in the foreground, with an intensively cultivated vegetable garden beyond. Photograph by Pedro E. Guerrero.

revolutionary, Wright himself was constrained to be conservative. He needed to attract clients. In another study, Leonard Eaton found that the only distinguishing feature between Wright's clients and those of a contemporary, fashionable Chicago architect was that Wright's clients tended to be self-made men and were more involved in spare time activities, such as hobbies and music.[8] Both groups of clients were likely to play golf and vote Republican. Wright's son John, in his book *My Father Who Is on Earth,* described a family lifestyle of constant luxuries and gaiety, both of which were funded on credit. He observed the opinions of Wright's fellow citizens, who concluded that Wright was an "eccentric visionary" who "didn't think, act, or dress like the fathers of the day, but was married like them and this, only, gave him the right to be at liberty."[9]

The private Wright, whose ideals were the self-reliance of Emerson and Thoreau, who galloped his black stallion over the prairie to read his pocket Whitman, had been increasingly intimidated by the settled nature of his practice and family. It was this bourgeois constraint that led him to find "failure in success" and to abandon a wife and six children, as well as a practice at its most successful point.[10] In choosing personal growth and a new life with a client's wife, Wright was, however, unprepared for the ferocity of public reaction. Taliesin helped him to weather this first scandal and restored his strength enough to weather even the tragedy of its burning in 1914. It gave him the land and buildings to sustain a community through the Depression and marked the transition from his early acceptance of the city to outright rejection and active work on proposals for urban decentralization.

Why the Fellowship?

It is impossible to divorce the Taliesin Fellowship from the grand old American tradition of flight from the city. This tradition is almost as old as the Republic, and its results can be seen in the foundation of alternative communities on an irregular cycle that continues to the present day. Wright must be seen against a historical background of lively cooperative experiments. The Shakers in New England, the Fourierist Wisconsin Phalanx, and the True Inspirationists at Amana, near Buffalo, New York, were all close to the time and place of his intellectual development. There were over one hundred cooperative or utopian communities with a combined population of some 100,000 in mid-19th century America, at a time when the national population was only 23 million. Owen's New Harmony experiment was the most publicized utopian failure, with its class divisions and lack of any workable organization, and Josiah Warren's anarchist Modern Times was the closest in many ways to contemporary thought in its emphasis on the liberty to differ and on individual before social happiness.[11]

Wright leading his apprentices to the desert of Arizona to build a winter camp, there to work on Broadacre City, was analogous to the new order of Brigham Young, the Mormon leader. Indeed the subsequent annual migration of the Taliesin Fellowship from Wisconsin to Arizona came to be as much a pioneering reenactment as a palliative for Wright's health.[12] At Taliesin, Wright's romantic outlook came into play. It was Kelly Smith's major contribution to the study of Wright to elucidate this.[13] In his book *Frank Lloyd Wright: A Study in Architectural Content,* Smith traces back the polarity and vacillation of Wright's thinking to Rousseau and points out its biblical origins. He cites Rousseau's championing of nature and *rus in urbe* and quotes *Emile,* "Men are not made to be crowded together in ant hills but scattered over the earth to till it."[14] Above all, Smith points out, Rousseau was aware of the problems inherent in his ideal society of free individualists.

Smith also correctly traces the origins of Taliesin to the arts and crafts movement in late 19th-century Europe, to the ideas of Ruskin and William Morris, "in general, to the ever-present tendency of romantic thought to exalt the virtues of a quasi-monastic brotherhood of craftsmen."[15] However, he develops this into a comparison of Taliesin with Camelot and the Arthurian Round Table. He compares Wright's belief in the "Cause of Architecture" with the search for the Holy Grail, which, while it has a certain plausibility, paints a picture of an altogether 19th-century Wright. It is likely that, like any intelligent man of his period, Wright would have read Tennyson, and it is undeniable that Taliesin projects the air of a bucolic royal court. However, a man may do something for more than one reason. It may be that Kelly Smith's analysis of a Camelot fantasy can be ascribed to the Taliesin Fellowship, but it would be wrong to ignore the conscious intellectual elements of Wright's behavior.

Organic Education

Wright saw life as a continual learning process. Attitude was an integral part of education, which was not a period of quarantine prior to life. His thinking goes back to the roots of his experience. It is also very modern in content. It was formed by his well-known exposure to the ideas of Froebel.[16]

Wright's interest in education was maintained throughout the struggle of the early Chicago practice by contact with educators through Jane Addams' Hull House, the settlement for poor and homeless immigrants. The pragmatist John Dewey at the University of Chicago and Alexander Meiklejohn, who became a professor of philosophy and head of the experimental college at the University of Wisconsin, were both known to Wright, and he shared their outlook. "The school itself shall be made a genuine form of active community life," wrote Dewey. "Society is a number of people held together because they are working along common lines, in a common spirit, and with reference to common aims. The common

needs and aims demand a growing interchange of thought and growing unity of sympathetic feeling."[17]

Wright refers to the community school of Meiklejohn in *An Autobiography*. However, he had direct contact with similar and earlier educational views when he designed Hillside Home School I and II for his two maiden aunts in 1887 and 1902, in Spring Green Wisconsin. This progressive school "antedated Dewey's ideas by ten years and Colonel Francis Parker's by fourteen."[18] Hillside was a country boarding school and emphasized experience rather than knowledge. "Character, said its teachers, is formed through one's experience of living."[19] Wright said of the school, "Woods, hills, and the river were supplementary classrooms always, and the teachers' knowledge of nature had to be first-hand."[20] There were few rules and "the first principle was to avoid behavior that made others uncomfortable, and fellow pupils as often as teachers rebuked offenders."[21] Mary Ellen Chase's description of Hillside in in *Goodly Fellowship*[22] suggests that Taliesin was in large part a continuation of the Lloyd-Jones' precepts.

Wright was a voracious reader, as attested to by the thirty-one names of his principal mentors carved on the theater wall at Taliesin and by all those who knew him. The influences on his educational ideas, and therefore on Taliesin, could be traced to numerous sources; however, one stands out. Wright affectionately mentions N. S. F. Gruntvig, the 19th-century Danish educator, in *An Autobiography*. Gruntvig brought home the old academic slogan "non scholae sed vitae" and sought to introduce a "school for life" for all, with such success that his influence on Danish education is still discernible.[23] Gruntvig " . . . received essential impulses for his crusade partly from the enterprising spirit of middle class England and partly from his experience in Trinity College, Cambridge where he stayed

in 1831. The free discussions between scholars and students in Hall inspired him to design schools for adults where the focal points are the community of teachers and students living and eating together and expressing themselves verbally. The *'Living Word'* being the slogan of the day" [italics supplied].[24] This was the essential aim that informed the early Taliesin Fellowship and clearly affected the choice of the name.

Finances and Apprenticeship

The word "Taliesin" — it has been tirelessly repeated—is Welsh for "shining brow."[25] It neatly symbolizes Wright's feelings for the ridge above the Wisconsin River where he made his home and for all he hoped to do there. It sits in a felicitous and pastoral landscape, near-alpine in winter, and in summer heavy with the sound of bees.

In 1932, "architectural commissions were almost non-existent," wrote John Howe.[26] The document, *"Charter Applicants for Fellowship,"* stated that "apprentices are sharing in the making of the fellowship plant and working on plans and models for [the] Broadacre City."[27] They busied themselves with the enlargement of Wright's home — where the studio of the 1920s had been located— and with extensions and repairs to the Hillside Home School, a quarter mile away, which had become dilapidated. And they started work on a permanent living and working quarters for the fellowship.

Tuition fees were paid by apprentices, as they were called until they graduated some years later as occasionally paid fellows. But the fees did not meet running expenses, and the venture relied on Wright's income from writing and lecturing. Many apprentices had dropped out of college as a result of hearing Wright's lectures "preaching rebellion to the point where he was often asked not to return."[28] In 1932 tuition cost $650, but within a year was raised to $1,100 annually.

This included food and accommodations, but these were of course produced largely by the apprentices' efforts.

The minimum period of stay was 1 year, with 3 months' probation, during which time both the apprentice and the fellowship could decide whether they were suited for each other. Apprentices had to provide their own bedding, T-square, drawing equipment, and box of tools — "at least hammer and saw."[29] An average stay might be 3 years, but after World War II an increasing proportion of apprentices were there for only 1 year. A period at Taliesin became a complement to completed conventional training elsewhere. Such disparate figures as Sean Kenny, Paolo Soleri, and Kevin Lynch passed through the community. For early members, however, the commitment was more total, for while it aimed to be an alternative to conventional society, it offered no ready-made qualification for life outside. On leaving, the apprentice could usually expect a letter of recommendation from Wright, but the Taliesin school was not recognized by the American Institute of Architects (AIA), nor was work carried out there negotiable for credits in the university system.

A select band of the charter members, as the founding group was called, stayed on and became fellows. Jack Howe, responsible for the drafting room, stayed 32 years until after Wright's death, and Wesley Peters remains to this day as chief architect to Taliesin Associates, a new organization set up in 1958. It was from this group of senior fellows that the superintendent clerks-of-works for carrying out construction of the architectural jobs all over the United States were chosen.

Each apprentice is expected to do his own share of maintenance work in the kitchen, laundry, and field as others do the same for him. All such routine maintenance duties are rotated among Fellowship members as we do not employ menials for any purpose. Inas-much as all live together as one big family those mutual offices are on a par with all others. Participating in building construction is obligatory and so is work in the drafting room. Each apprentice has his own drafting table there. Collateral work in music, cultural exercises, weaving and pottery are optional. In general work is divided equally into maintenance, drafting room, and building construction. The working day begins at 6:30 AM and ends at 4:30 PM. All lights are out at 10:30 PM.[30]

The flavor of early Taliesin is well caught by this statement in the prospectus. It speaks to many of the day-to-day problems upon which experimental communities have floundered, from New Harmony to the present day. It alludes to Wright's personal preference for early rising and to the probable need to conserve power. (Taliesin had its own generator and all other services, including transportation.)

Some "collateral work" was in the hands of Mrs. Wright, and occupied more or less time, depending on the pressure of architectural work. Wright stated in the Hillside prospectus of 1931: "Music would have to mean the fundamental study of sound and rhythm as emotional reaction both as to original character and present nature. Tone weaving in general . . . dancing in this school would be the actual cultivation of rhythms in the corelations of body and mind to make of both a perfect instrument."[31] Olgivanna Wright had attended Georgi Gurdjieff's Institute for the Harmonious Development of man at Fontainebleau and there were some similarities between the two institutions.[32] Gurdjieff was himself a guest at Taliesin a number of times, [33] and while his ideas may have had only an arguable effect on Wright's work, the seed of mysticism was planted with observable results.[34]

After her visit to Spring Green in 1934, Helen Beal wrote, "The school is really on the verge of a religious order, all of which I am gradually learning more about. . . . It takes some demonstra-

Frank Lloyd Wright surveys the 1930s reconstruction of the Hillside Home School to accommodate apprentices. Photograph by Pedro E. Guerrero.

tion to make it fully intelligible."[35] George Beal, a professor of architecture at the University of Kansas at Lawrence, and his wife became honorary members of the fellowship. They were a rare link with the architectural education establishment, and Wright was fond of referring to "our Professor." Helen Beal's correspondence with many members of the fellowship is a source of much information on the early days.

The Fellowship in Practice

"The aim of the Fellowship," wrote John Howe, "was the development of the complete man or woman and our lives were geared to creative work. Toward that aim Taliesin created its own life, its own rules and its own customs, without the usual categories. Mr. Wright was determined that Taliesin not be a part of the 'cash and carry system,' that work be done primarily for pleasure, rather than for monetary gain."[36] For variety, the apprentice could turn from mental to physical work. The routine was broken by tea with the Wrights in the tea circle in the hill garden and on weekends by picnics, films, in the theater, and supper and music in Wright's livingroom. Although Wright disliked institutions, these very events became part of the Taliesin ethos, and since his death, have become veritably liturgical.

The "rules" increasingly affected areas of private behavior, and as Wright aged, Olgivanna applied them more strictly. For many it was an experience close to the anarchist ideal of healthy mind and body, but it is not surprising that many others left. While surviving the Depression was challenging, and Wright himself was accessible, although in his seventies, the "one big family" inevitably lost some of its early camaraderie; a hierarchical atmosphere slowly developed. The "Chinese box" nature of Taliesin encouraged this, with its progressive courtyards and final master's living quarters strongly suggesting a holy of holies. Echelons developed, with master and mistress, inner family, senior fellows, fellows, and apprentices.

By the late thirties, an internal newsheet appeared containing an open letter to Wright requesting more contact with the master. "If you talked to us more often we would have more courage to tell our ideas [sic] and thus broaden our field of thought."[37] In the second newsheet, on October 8, 1938, it is claimed that "there has always been a feud between the older and younger apprentices." The former are called "supercilious" and the newsheet charged that they "brag of their past work, accomplishments, and sufferings." The older apprentices are asked to "condescend to carry out some very simple chores which they have sadly neglected and also step down from their self-made pedestals by letting the others work with them in the Drafting Room."[38] By the fifth edition, on November 5, 1938, there is satisfaction with a recent discussion with Wright, but still a request for regular Saturday evening discussions in the theater instead of films.[39]

There was also dissatisfaction among the senior fellows, some of whom were married. They felt financially insecure and overdependent on Wright's infrequent remuneration. To solve this problem they took on private architectural projects that they could work on at Taliesin. Wright allowed this but exacted a 25 percent share of their fee for the privilege. When he later "changed the rules and increased the percentage," according to Edgar Tafel, Tafel and some other charter members left the fellowship.[40]

It was also easy for Taliesin members who had generous temperaments to find themselves being exploited. One such person was Mabel Morgan, who gave unstintingly of herself in the Taliesin kitchen from 1933 to 1938. She corresponded throughout the period with Helen Beal, occasionally complaining that the others did not share in this labor. On August 17, 1938 she wrote: "Svet and I are cooking every other week. I'm getting very tired of it after five years."[41] She goes on to give some idea of the scale of work involved. "Just finished canning 163 quarts of tomatoes besides doing a week or two of house laundry. . . ." She feels that she must leave the fellowship since "I'm getting too old not to worry about the future."[42]

The self-sufficient nature of Taliesin unfortunately extended to its social life in a negative way. While the constant visits by eminent and famous people from all over the United States and the world were stimulating for apprentices, they became a substitute for meaningful contact with the local community. The impression was given of an easy superiority over Spring Green and its affairs.

Organization

The imperfections of Taliesin do not, however, overshadow its achievements. As a closed community it contained all the pressures, and more, of a marriage. On her stay there in 1934, Helen Beal described her considered impressions of the fellowship, saying that it was " . . . on the whole as fine a group as I have seen anywhere. Young fellows from high school, graduates on up to those who have college degrees and several years of travel or struggle for a livelihood behind them. Some are wealthy, some very poor, but all have a nice spirit."[43] She also described how the drafting room was run. "There are three bosses—all Fellows—one head, and two assistants who serve for a period of two weeks. Then the head boss is relieved, another assistant added, and the first assistant becomes head boss. Of course all work is directed by the Master, Mr. Wright."[44]

By 1939, when Curtis Besinger joined the fellowship, the situation had changed into one that was to continue until Wright's death. Only the war and the pacifist stance of some members caused disruption. Design and development of projects centered on the

100

The kitchen at Taliesin West. Photograph by
Pedro E. Guerrero.

drafting room. Jack Howe was responsible for the coordination of work there. Gene Masselink was Wright's indispensable secretary and he also periodically ran the Taliesin Press. Wesley Peters, Mrs. Wright's son-in-law, was generally responsible for assigning work and outside projects, such as farming. Svetlana Peters (Olgivanna's first daughter) was responsible for assignments in the kitchen, such as cook and helpers, after consultation with Mrs. Wright. Olgivanna, as has been seen, ran "collateral work" and putative summer schools, later aided by Iovanna, her other daughter.

According to Curtis Besinger, in 1939 "there was a Mrs. Schneider who seemed to exercise the role of housekeeper for the immediate living quarters of Mr. and Mrs. Wright."[45] Work assignments were made on a very informal basis and posted several days in advance. With the exception of the Sunday morning breakfast, Saturday evening dinner followed by a movie, and Sunday evening dinner followed by music, which all became traditions, Wright was opposed to institutions. "When anything got too organized he went out of his way to disrupt it."[46]

Squirrels in Hard Times

There was at Taliesin a feeling for good husbandry and harmony with nature that was unusual for the time. The U.S. Department of Agriculture had not yet learned the hard lessons of the dust storms and soil erosion.[47] Seen from the present perspective, with a realization of the harmful effects of indiscriminate use of insecticides, chemical fertilizers, and an energy-intensive exploitation of soil structure, the declarations of the fellowship are more central and realistic than romantic and agrarian, as they have sometimes been interpreted.[48] In this sense there is nothing exceptional in Wright's statement that manure is the "indispensible wealth that goes to bring the jaded soil to a greenness of the hills, bring fertility to life itself — for man"[49] This attitude was shared by one apprentice as the

"At Taliesin" article in the May 4, 1935, edition of the Madison *Capital Times* shows:

. . . you city folks, when you see the odious cow flop, you quickly hold your nose and jump gingerly aside. Perhaps I used to do the same . . . but now I proudly stand on a six-foot pile of it and pitch it into the spreader as if it were gold I was loading and then I drive the team over the fields and watch the stuff fly off the back and onto the hungry ground. . . . The landscape looks twice as good when viewed from the seat of a manure spreader because you mean something to it. Manure is an essential link in the great cycle of life. It is fundamental to all past civilizations. They have all been based on it. Perhaps the advent of the tractor on the farms will be the contributing cause to the decay of our modern city. . . .[50]

The use of what is now known as organic husbandry would be predictable for Wright, reinforced perhaps by Olgivanna's Gurdjieffian precepts and traditional Japanese practice, but surely based on his hard experience as a boy on his uncle's farm. It certainly gave him enormous delight to view the harvest and contemplate the independence that it gave him. It gives, perhaps, another meaning to his motto "Truth against the world."

The boys haul the provender into the root cellar at Taliesin and pile it up. We "put down" this year [1942] 1,000 quarts of tomatoes, besides many hundreds each of green peas, beans, and vegetables. But that isn't much. That underground reservoir of food can take several carloads and ask for more. A tunnel leads to it, and at the arched door in the masonry wall you switch on the light — the sight that meets the eye is a treasure-filled cave, not unlike Aladdin's. To the left are Olgivanna's wine casks: wild grape wine, elderberry wine, chokeberry, rhubarb, dandelion, potato wines, beet, tomato, true grape, wild grape, plum brandy, cider, chokeberry mead. Apples, cider, vinegar. Rows on rows of jams, fruits, marmalades, jellies, sauces, pickles, vegetables. Sauerkraut. To the right, on sand, are piles of potatoes, squash, beets, carrots, cabbage, onions, parsnips, and rutabagas. Melons in season. Hanging from the ceiling are dried herbs from the herb garden. If a barbed-wire entan-

Midway farm buildings, Spring Green, Wisconsin, 1938. Photograph by Pedro E. Guerrero.

Apprentices haymaking. Photograph by Pedro E. Guerrero.

glement were put around Taliesin for the winter we would all come out next spring with double chins.[51]

It is easy to understand the pleasure of Jimmy Drought, an apprentice who lost sympathy with Taliesin and left in 1935, when he returned on weekends in 1937 and 1938. "The dam had washed out for the eighth time in twelve years and Edgar [Tafel] came over from Racine and the two of us went out to repair the damage. It was good fun being there again—working hard and eating mightily of good solid food."[52]

Ad Hocism

The barrels of sauerkraut mentioned by Wright figure in the memories of many ex-members of the fellowship as an abiding element in a fast changing milieu. They were transported from the summer base in Wisconsin to the winter camp in Arizona. John Howe described these pilgrimages:

The caravan treks to and from Arizona were adventures in themselves. We took with us not only all our drawings and files, but also our personal belongings, sleeping bags, canned goods, produce and meat from the farm. . . . We usually departed either in a blizzard or moments before an expected blizzard. En route we met for gas (bought wholesale) and rolled out our sleeping bags in low-cost hotel rooms (bargained for by Mr. Wright) or, when the weather permitted in favorite campsites where we gathered round our "dinky diner" and a campfire for meals.[53]

These treks took the fellowship far afield, to the Badlands in South Dakota, to visit the Lusks, or once nearly over the north rim of the Grand Canyon, where Wright led them in darkness, by instinct, and without roads.

The extempore nature of the Wrightian environment is important. He himself never thought of his buildings as final statements; all were intended for growth or change, if needed. Both his homes were in a constant state of change, and the winter camp, which became Taliesin West and was a less ephemeral successor to Ocatillo, was always thought of as just a camp. In-deed Ocatillo, the breath-taking first camp of 1927, which was carried away by Indians to Wright's evident satisfaction, is probably one of his greatest creations.[54] An excellent description of their living conditions in the desert (where Taliesin West was established) was written by Mabel Morgan in 1938.

Mr. Wright and family were out here about two weeks earlier . . . and bought 160 acres of land where we are now, about 20 miles east of Phoenix, and we are living in the open except for a temporary shelter where we have a kitchen/dining room and some of the boys sleep and store their things. The married couples have small temporary cubicles and the rest of us sleep out and keep our things hanging on trees. A permanent camp will be started next week I guess . . . the Wrights are staying at Jokake Inn, but will move as soon as a cabin or some sort of shelter is made for them.[55]

When you realize that both presentation and working drawings were prepared in the open air and lit by the glaring desert sun, with dust blowing across the surface, the faded condition of the drawings as well as the improvisation of fellowship life can be understood.

Design

Wright himself might or might not develop his designs in the Taliesin drafting room. It is well known that he had an extraordinary capacity for developing designs in his mind, over a period of assimilation and analysis. He would then sit down and unhesitatingly draw site plan, plans, sections, elevations, and key working details, often on one sheet and in a form differing little from the finished building. This happened with the designs of La Miniatura, for Pasadena, California, in 1926 and Falling Water at Bear Run, Pennsylvania, in 1936.[56] At other times, a germinal drawing might be found at the drawing board when work started, or Wright would work at a board himself.

Production

Since Taliesin was a school of architecture, the central acitivty was consistent

The Taliesin caravan somewhere en route between Wisconsin and Arizona. Photograph by Pedro E. Guerrero.

Taliesin West under construction. Photograph by Pedro E. Guerrero.

The desert concrete is being finished off at Taliesin West, and the formwork has been removed. The apprentice at the upper right is Paolo Soleri. Photograph by Pedro E. Guerrero.

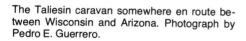

work in the drafting room. According to Besinger, "When a person was working in the studio, Mr. Wright probably showed up at their board at least once a day, looking for things that needed his attention."[57] Apprentices were assigned to work by Jack Howe, who was responsible for development of the designs. Howe was also the originator of some design work when he was a relatively free agent.[58] Besinger remembers: "There were some 'seniors,' most notably Allen 'Davy' Davison, who worked directly with Mr. Wright and somewhat independently of Jack's supervision."[59] Any set of drawings, preliminary or final working-drawings, once approved by Wright, received his signature, although "in the process of signing drawings he often made changes." [60]

106 Because Wright insisted that all changes be made to the actual drawing with no tracing or redrawing of the original, any record of changes was lost. Curtis Besinger wrily comments: "Architectural historians would suffer great pangs to know that all these records of changes, as made by Mr. Wright, were blithely erased as they were made."[61] Another result of this, according to Besinger, was that "Jack Howe had to keep two sets of drawings for each project—one for Mr. Wright to work on and one to be kept in a cleaner state for making prints, both to be kept current with each other."[62] This laborious practice became unnecessary once a better quality paper than the rag paper that Wright insisted on using became available, and draftsmanship and erasing became neater.[63]

A student working at the drawing board could expect Wright to "look over his shoulder, and if he saw something that he thought needed his attention he would ask to sit down—and proceed to study the drawing in progress — and make changes."[64] At times when Wright himself was working on a design, Howe discouraged younger apprentices from watching, otherwise Wright "would be inclined not to keep his mind on the project at hand and turn to a demonstration of cleverness."[65] Howe's role in this was clearly important since such demonstrations could lead to projects being changed or delayed. Besinger remembers an instance in the late 1940s when two apprentices working on final working drawings for a project were able to entice Wright to their boards every day for a week, with such effect that his "demonstration of cleverness" caused the house to be *redesigned daily,* "not as a process of developing this particular design, but of coming up with a different concept." The project was never built.[66]

The Client

Clients in the late thirties almost invariably came to Wright because they had read his books and were sympathetic with his views.[67] By 1940 they had often seen some Usonian houses or illustrations of them in magazines. They were quite aware of the type of house he was likely to give them; indeed they sought it.[68] Typically they did not imagine that this well-known figure would have the time or interest for their humble problems. Wright himself was at this time only too glad to receive commissions, however small, but this was not, of course, the impression created by the publicity given him. All his clients were surprised at the rapid and personal treatment they received. They experienced the attention, loyalty, and ultimately the mutual respect that characterized Wright's client relationships.

Jack Howe summarized this relationship, "He had the highest regard for each of his clients simply because they were *his* clients; he found virtues in them which were indiscernible to others and almost refused to acknowledge their shortcomings."[69] Their personal experience with Wright was the reverse of that gained by any reader of his tendentious, turgid books. Wright's business communications, on the other hand, were remarkably laconic and pithy. Howe described his letters

Wright is working with apprentices at their drawing boards in the Taliesin drafting room. Photograph by Pedro E. Guerrero.

The Taliesin West drafting room during the 1930s includes a model of Broadacre City in the foreground. Photograph by Pedro E. Guerrero.

as "generally limited to a few sentences and his telephone conversations to a minute or two on the farm line . . . He often said, 'One doesn't have to drink a tub of dye to know its color'"[70] For the man who trumpeted organic architecture it is at first surprising to learn that Wright rarely visited the sites of his Usonian clients; the scale of his practice forced him to rely on surveys. However, he invariably met his clients.

Bernard Schwartz's dealings with Wright might typify those of other clients. After an initial telephone call to Taliesin (Operator: "Is this call paid?"[71]), he was invited there as a guest. He found Wright supervising road construction and thought the setting to be "manorial." With reasonable leisure, architect and client grew to know each other and discussed their aims and intentions. Simultaneously Schwartz was welcomed into the fellowship and was able to observe its purpose first hand. He found it to be a "regular feudal estate."[72]

The client's visit to Taliesin was an important element in the process of finding a common purpose and was almost universal — it even continued with more numerous postwar commissions. Clients were provided with a brochure describing Wright's services and the fee arrangements. These were listed as "ten percent of the cost of the completed building which invariably includes the planting of the grounds and major furnishings." Details given on the supervision arrangements specified that an apprentice was to be "lodged and fed by the owner" together with a payment of $25 per week while he was on site. The client was requested to provide an accurate topographical survey of the site together with a complete list of requirements.[73]

Design Development

The visit to Taliesin was frequently the only personal contact that clients had with Wright. Subsequent communication was usually by letter. Many found that the act of building their houses introduced them into membership in a psychological club, and in later years they often visited each other and returned to Taliesin while traveling on vacation. According to a survey done by Eugene Streich, "Almost all owners reported that, to their surprise, Wright proved remarkably easy to get along with in negotiations over the design. There were a number of instances where Wright either extensively modified a design or created one or more schemes."[74]

According to Howe, "He never delegated conferences with his clients to his assistants and when the clients were in his study with him he would painstakingly work with them to make the necessary revisions on their plans."[75] But Streich also points out that "when Wright felt a client was ill-informed in requesting a particular feature, he could be extraordinarily persuasive."[76] It is notable that this was a long-standing feature of Wright's behavior with clients. A letter written by Wright in 1913 to Francis Little regarding Northome shows this.

Enclosed are glass designs according to your idea. It is not bad, of course, but rather sterile where something more is needed. I think the one I offered is much better — but if this one "suits them it's for" what can I do or say? The closing up of the ceiling lights deprives you of the room as I had got it in mind. I don't see it now at all but I will faithfully follow instructions. . . .[77]

In his "Reflections of Taliesin," Howe wrote of Wright, "He always, in imagination, inhabited the house, walking through and even performing the housewife's tasks, how she would entertain, look after small children. . . . When working on house plans he gave great attention to details, such as the arrangement of the workspace (kitchen), location of plumbing, and lighting fixtures."[78]

Working Drawings

Instructions to the builder were a crucial part of the Usonian "kit concept." As one Taliesin job supervisor wrote,

108

The central axis of Taliesin West in 1969. After Wright's death, the building was air conditioned and the canvas rooflighting replaced by fiberglass.

"Each house was planned to fit a particular site and to conform to the client's needs. What they had in common was the structural system — Mr. Wright called it the 'grammar' — which gave them a family resemblance despite their variety. . . . The plans for each house were accompanied by a Standard Detail sheet which was used over and over again."[79] These details were developed along with the concept, probably from the Hoult project of 1935. They were certainly fully developed in the Jacobs house in 1936. In later years, copying the sheet was one of the first assignments in drawing for a new apprentice. The information given on the sheet was as follows:

A cross section of the standard window and sash; the standard board and batten; the interior partition and the exterior wall; the full-scale detail of the perforated boards; connection of the roof with the outside brick wall; plate and cap for the outside wall; dimensions for the depth of concrete below grade and the depth of grade below the floor; the dimension of the mullion; and specifications for the hinges, the metal stripping and the floor coloring.[80]

Once on site the standard detail sheet required interpretation. Here the attendance of the apprentice on site was justified.

The Usonian plans were laid out in a two- by four-foot module but without detailed dimensions. Every time you got to a doorway, a corner or intersection where special conditions prevailed, the dimensions had to be modified one way or another. Builders always wanted to know why they couldn't have been just like any other plans, i.e., worked out dimensionally. I think Mr. Wright wanted to emphasize the system concept; and the plans certainly looked prettier without dimensions![81]

In practice the system probably slightly extended construction time because of the need to educate the contracting tradesmen. The living costs of an apprentice for constant on-site supervision seem to have been an acceptable expense. As a learning experience for a student architect, it is difficult to imagine a more ideal technique.

110

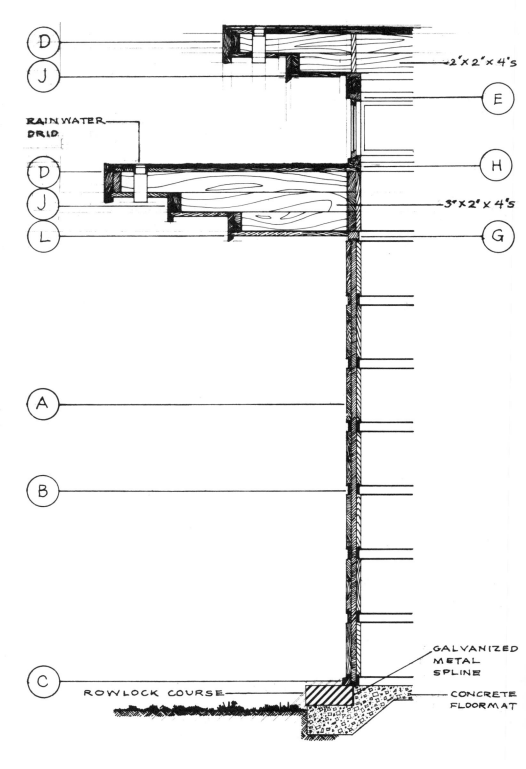

Typical section through the wall of a Usonian house.

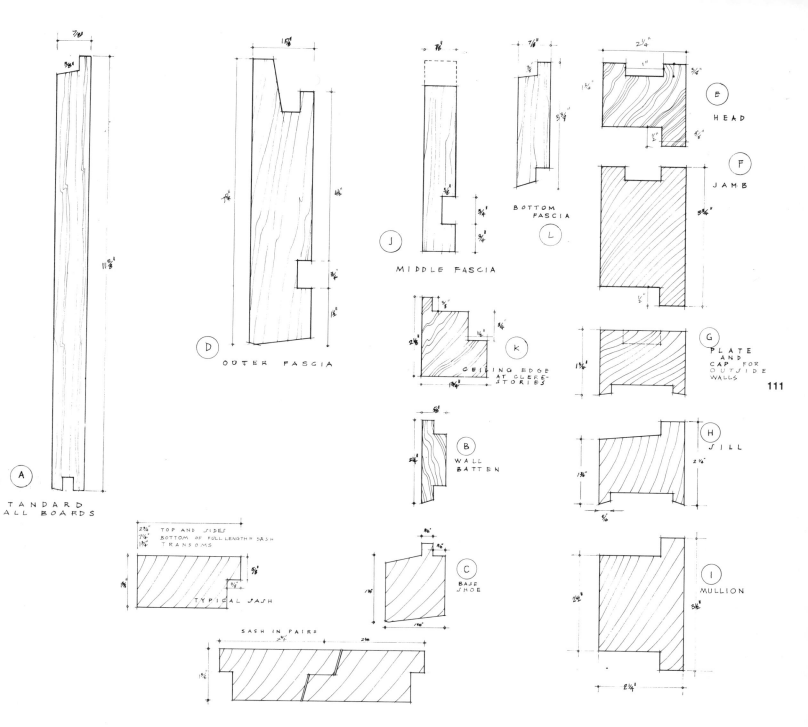

A
STANDARD
ALL BOARDS

7/8"
3/8"
11 5/8"

D
OUTER FASCIA

15 7/8"
7 1/4"
4 1/2"
3/4"
3/4"
1 1/2"

J
MIDDLE FASCIA

7/8"
3/8"
3/4"
3/4"

L
BOTTOM
FASCIA

7/8"
3/4"
3 3/8"

E HEAD

2 1/4"
1"
3/4"
1 3/8"
5/8"
1/2"

F JAMB

3 3/4"
1/2"

G
PLATE
AND
CAP FOR
OUTSIDE
WALLS

1 3/8"

K
CEILING EDGE
AT CLERE-
STORIES

3/4"
3/8"
1/4"
2 1/8"
1 3/4"

B
WALL
BATTEN

5/8"
2 1/4"

H SILL

1 3/8"
2 1/4"
5/8"

2 3/8"   TOP AND SIDES
7 1/4"   BOTTOM OF FULL LENGTH " SASH
1 3/4"   TRANSOMS

1 3/8"
5/8"
6/8"
TYPICAL SASH

C
BASE
SHOE

5/8"
5/8"
1 1/8"
1 5/8"

I MULLION

2 1/2"
3 1/2"
2 1/4"

SASH IN PAIRS
2 3/4"   2 3/4"
1 5/8"

111

Assembly drawings: some standard Usonian details.

Wright's Construction Methods

There were two methods of building used by Wright: one utilized apprentice clerks-of-works and the other, master builders. The first involved the apprentice running the job by direct contracting, or acting as a general contractor. The second involved master builders Harold Turner and Ben Wiltscheck. These two men were retained by Wright on successive projects and learned to interpret his intentions almost by a sixth sense, and always with superb craftsmanship. When they handled a job they were never supervised. Their work with Taliesin only terminated with World War II, as did the contracting nature of apprentice superintendence. After 1945, there were usually general contractors appointed, while the apprentice superintended the project in a conventional way.

Clerks-of-works

The prospect of a young Taliesin fellow setting off on some continental train journey, with six sets of drawings and six copies of the specifications for his project, is a romantic one. Once at his destination, after having made contact with Wright's client, he would proceed to the local bank manager and there find out who were the reliable (and solvent) tradesmen in the area to work with. He would normally appoint a chief carpenter and mason. He would then do the necessary shopping, check cost layouts, and hold the whole building operation together.

Taliesin handled the itemizing and bidding for millwork (machined joinery) and letting contracts for piecework. It will be seen that a practice like Wright's, which was on a continental scale in post-Depression America, needed to evolve practical methods of resolving local difficulties in the building industry. The apprentice often received substantial help from the active participation of the client. Both Affleck and Schwartz, for example, could remember the exact values of subcontracts they placed and the names of companies employed 30 years later.

Variations in Construction

It was necessary for all supervising apprentices to evolve variations from Wright's plans and to be occasionally inventive. The chief area of change was usually in the matter of assembly of the structure. Many apprentices found it difficult or impossible to comply fully with Wright's wishes in putting up the roof. He normally called for building the roof first, on temporary supports, to provide a workshop in which to construct the wall sections. These were supposed to be built on tables. At the Pope house in Falls Church, Virginia, built in 1940, Gordon Chadwick found that "it was impossible to make the mitered corners of the walls fit when they were built on tables. . . . Our solution was to build every other wall section on work tables and then to join them by a section built in place."[82]

Some apprentices needed considerable initiative. In the Schwartz house in Two Rivers, Wisconsin, built in 1940, Edgar Tafel protested to Wright that there was insufficient structure at the 30-ft span intersection of upper and lower roofs, which at that point were separated by continuous clerestory windows. Wright asserted that one cantilever roof would hold up the other (also in cantilever). Without permission, Tafel substituted steelwork for the timber specified, putting in a large I section in the upper roof with steel rods suspending the lower beam below. To this he added steel flitch plates.[83] He also substituted 2 x 4s for the plywood specified in the core of the ground floor bedroom, since both he and the client felt that the severe winter climate of northern Lake Michigan demanded greater insulation.

The Rosenbaum house, built in Florence, Alabama, in 1940, provides one example of the kind of problem caused by following Wright's plans too slavishly. Burton Goodrich encountered difficulties identical to those Tafel grappled with in the clerestory structure. But Goodrich endeavored to solve them as specified in wood. Only after an embarrassing sag had developed, with resultant setbacks and desperate consultation with Taliesin by telephone, was a solution adopted with steelwork. It is of interest that in the later, post-1943 houses, steel was incorporated in an entirely catholic way, concealed where necessary behind woodwork. Wright would no doubt argue that the spirit of the structure was revealed anyway and that the bad weathering qualities of steel were best avoided by encasing it. The property of steel that recommended itself to him was its strength in tension, and by using it for very long, thin spans and cantilevers he was working "in the nature of materials."

Technological Limitations

In a number of ways Wright was working at the limits of the technology of the day. This resulted in some problems of client acceptance as well as building and maintenance. The heated groundslab was a radically new concept requiring an imaginative leap from the conventional American timber house upon a basement. According to one of Wright's builders, Jimmy de Reuss, "Wright's use of crushed rock instead of standard footings saved about 20 percent on foundation costs."[84] Some owners were concerned about possible future problems with the buried heating loops. In fact in one case a leak did occur, in the iron piping in the Theodore Baird house built in Amherst, Massachusetts, in 1940. This required a section of the concrete floor to be cut out to make repairs. Chadwick described the normal procedure. The wrought iron pipes " . . . were tested for almost a week at approximately 120 pounds of pressure. The normal operating pressure of the system is only 11 pounds, so we had tested far above the maximum that would ever be required. Then we had crushed stone laid around the coils to prevent damage when the concrete

Stages of Typical Usonian Construction

The Richardson house, Glen Ridge, New Jersey, 1941 (built in 1951). Photographs by Stuart Richardson.

1   The drained footings and services connections are installed. The formwork is laid for the concrete floormat.

2   The gravel bed with heating pipes in position is shown here.

3   A worker welds the wrought iron piping.

4   The first concrete pour is completed here, and the second cement pour is started. It is red colored and steel troweled, with grid lines marked out.

5   A worker is troweling the final floor finish. The module was set out by taut lines, and a metal template formed into a hexagonal shape was used.

6   Next the building's brickwork is laid; the fireplace masonry is shown here.

1

4

2

5

3

6

7 The first stage of the board and batten walls are erected. Finished lumber of cypress is used and is included for the toe and head pieces of the wall and window units. The Richardson house differed from other Usonians in that it had a core built of pine boards, instead of plywood.

8 Shown is the carcasing joinery. Notched joists, which receive the cypress-boarded soffits are of pine. Just visible at a high level are two of the three main-span steel girders.

9 The exterior cypress boards and battens are fitted to the wall core. The roof is waterproofed.

114

7

8

9

10 This is a detail of the board and batten walling. Note how the nail holes are stopped, the screw fixings of battens are regularly spaced, and the screws turned in the horizontal position (left). The notched underside of the roof joists is ready for the lapped cypress beneath.

11 The exterior joinery is finished. The roof has been waterproofed, the soffits boarded, and the interior is ready for board ceilings.

12 Shown here is the internal joinery in the livingroom, which is being used as a workshop for the finished lumber.

10

11

12

115

13　The ceiling of the master bedroom shows another example of the internal joinery. The lapping of the cypress boards and the miter cutting of the junctions are visible.

14　The first waterproof layer is laid on the roof.

15　The final waterproof layer is dressed into the cypress fascia board. The openings are ready for the skylights, and the last brickwork is being done on the chimney, which is nearing its completed height.

16　The joinery is completed, and the windows are ready for glazing. Rainwater spouts are visible.

116

13

14

15

16

Expanding the L plan: The Smith house, Bloomfield Hills, Michigan, 1946. The brick edge to the
floorslab, electric conduit, and gravel base are in
position ready for the heating pipes to be installed and the concrete floorslab to be poured.

was being poured. From a design point of view, radiant heating was marvelous because getting rid of radiators—then almost universal—reduced visual disturbance."[85]

Needless to say, the Wrightian gravity heat groundslab was looked at with disfavor by the writers of America's many building codes. A good indication of the backward state of the rural science of building was given when the piping in one Usonian was welded together by an operator who did not realize that he should wear goggles. Later copper piping was routinely used.

The severity of continental weather conditions caused differential expansion and leaks in the flat roofs of some early Usonians. Flashing the roof waterproofing membrane was the weakness, and the problem was worked on for a number of years at Taliesin before being solved by the present canvas, fiberglass, and metal flashing treatment.

The ubiquitous board and batten walls of the Usonians were thin to the point of structural and insulating limits. Where possible, they were stengthened by frequent folding (characteristic of hexagonal Usonians) or even by bookcases. Chadwick cites an amusing instance of building inspectors' reaction to this information.[86] In the case of the Rosenbaum house, the long, 48-ft north wall could be made to bow by hand pressure until the growth of the book collection solved the problem. Mrs. Rosenbaum was concerned, on watching the battens being screwed together, that her children "might undo the house."

The large number and variety of window openings also caused problems in a period before the availability of efficient, low-cost screens and door closure hardware. After a snake entered the Rosenbaum home, and before simple modifications, Stanley Rosenbaum remarked that this was no doubt "what Wright meant by the outside coming inside." He summarized the situation by observing that "if you commissioned a Usonian you were going against conventional social wisdom."[87]

Master Builders

Wright once quoted his old chief, Dankmar Adler, the business partner of Louis Sullivan for whom he worked in Chicago, as saying that "he would rather give work to a crook who does know how to build than to an honest man who does not. . . . 'I can police a crook, but if a man doesn't know good work, how am I to get it out of him?'"[88] Neither Ben Wiltscheck nor Harold Turner were crooks, but both built superlatively. Wiltscheck was responsible for both stages of the Johnson Wax buildings in Racine, Wisconsin, built during the years 1936 to 1939 and 1947 to 1950. He also built Johnson's home, called "Wingspread," in Racine in 1937 and the Community Church in Kansas City, Missouri, in 1940.[89] Howe said of Wiltscheck, "Mr. Wright had great respect for him and wanted him to build more, but a bad heart forced him to decline."[90]

Harold Turner traveled the country for 6 years, building some of the largest and most complex Usonians—Hanna in 1937 in California; Rebhuhn in 1938 on Long Island, New York; Suntop Homes quadruple housing in 1939 in Pennsylvania; Winkler-Goetsch in 1939 in Michigan; Armstrong in 1939 at Ogden Dunes, Indiana; Christie in 1940 in New Jersey; Affleck in 1941 near Detroit, Michigan; and Wall in 1941 in Michigan. Turner was Danish and had no experience in building when Wright took him on to rescue the Hanna house after difficulties in finding contractors. There, and in the subsequent homes, Turner conjured up the quality of fine cabinet work out of designs that few builders would have taken on. Wright himself frequently complained that just the sight of his name at the bottom of a drawing was enough to make most builders roll it up.

The Hanna and Wall houses required 60° and 120° mitered corners with their hexagonal plans, and the Affleck house called for virtuoso work at corners and door jambs because of the inclined walls and overlapping boards. Turner therefore searched out craftsmen. He said he would "prefer old men for four days a week to young fellows full time."[91] His considered opinion was that the chief problem with Usonians was one of expansion and contraction. This tended to show up at junctions of different materials, especially where the roof membrane, which was the element most exposed to the extremes of climate, was pierced by masonry. He found cypress to be a moist board, requiring particular care in detailing and benefiting from the moisture of house plants or an internal flower garden.

In 1942, Turner built his own home in Bloomfield Hills, Michigan, with a small farm, which he ran along Wrightian lines, canning his own produce, running a cold and a freezer room, and ultimately employing Japanese prisoners of war. He became a "designer-builder" and completed a number of homes in the Detroit area before his death in 1974.

Summary

Construction of Usonian houses and the activities at Taliesin during the thirties proceeded against a background of public indifference, which was only followed by a very slow acceptance of modern architecture. General acceptance of modern design in housing did not occur until after the war. In 1925, a French building exposition was held in Paris, whose rules were that entries should be of contemporary style. No American exhibit appeared because President Hoover and his advisers knew of no architect able to design buildings that were free of classical orders.[92] Architectural education in the United States was academic and architectural schools were the repository of formidable piles of classical plaster casts. In 1928, George Beal obtained permission to operate a nonclassical course at the University of Kansas. It was 1935 before Columbia University followed suit, under Dean Hodnut, who then went on to Harvard, where he invited Walter Gropius, and the international style, to America.

Criticism has been made that Taliesin failed because it did not produce another architectural superstar to succeed Wright. This view, however, seems to depend on a narrow definition of success. Taliesin's effect can be seen in the work of many unassuming architects, working all over the United States to realize their clients' needs. Its influence is discernible in the work of the National Parks Division of the Department of the Interior, where many ex-Taliesin fellows worked in the thirties. It can be seen in the Los Angeles, San Francisco Bay, and California coastal areas and in much good, human housing across the country.

Wright felt that the acquisition of a skill, without relationship to experience was valueless. His abhorrence of impersonal fact-feeding was strong enough to move him to turn down work when he most needed it, as a letter of the mid-thirties to the superintendant of public schools in Kansas City, Missouri, shows:

Mass production in education appeals to us as prostitution we are not inclined to encourage. And the shopping for an architect in the manner to which you subscribe is a worthy attribute to such mass-production methods. Not only do I regard the thing miscalled education which such a building as you propose is intended to serve as murder, but a worse form of murder than war, because war disposes of the carcass while so-called education murders the soul and leaves the dead to walk for a lifetime.[93]

For Wright the experience of nature was the most enduring and meaningful element in all education. The "little experiment station" of Taliesin was not an escape from an industrial society, but a bold step toward the way all society should go. If nature could not be brought to the schools, then the schools could go to nature. Decentralization would be the result.

CHAPTER 4 Broadacre City

Human planning never reaches its goal in the sense that no further planning is needed, as life goes on.
Alexander Meiklejohn [1]

The chief work of Wright's mature life was his plan for Broadacre City. This was a program for cultural as well as physical change and contained his views on social and economic matters. All of Wright's late architectural achievements reflect the ideology of this project. As a piece of city planning it was totally outside the holistic approaches of both immediate prewar and postwar thinking. Its open-ended philosophy was illustrated by the well-known "Model," which unfortunately encouraged the plan itself to be regarded literally. The fact that Wright committed himself to a modeled illustration of how his view of democracy might look made it easier to dismiss. It also detracted the attention of commentators from Wright's written work. Although his writings collectively trace the origins of his social and economic ideas to highly regarded figures of American radical thought, they are obscure and repetitive and therefore have not attracted serious study. His buildings have been taken seriously, but his views on society have not, and little account has been taken of the formative nature of his early career. The critics of late Wright have treated him "inorganically."

Broadacre City has been regarded either as an enigma or simply as irrelevant. Most American architectural commentators have chosen to set Wright in the intellectual cast of either the 19th century of abstruse ideologies, as a mystic or a seeker of some Judaic paradise. His outlook has been variously traced to the English romantics and arts and crafts movement, to Rousseau and the French utopian socialists Fourier and Proudhon or to Biblical and anti-Hellenic modes of thought. Some have seen Wright as a Marxist; others have called him a fascist. Only Mumford and the Goodmans have in their time perceived the strength of influence of Wright's

American cultural background. Mumford recognized in Wright the transcendentalist strain of Jefferson, Emerson, Thoreau, and Whitman, while the Goodmans saw in him the influence of Henry George, Ralph Borsodi and the economic remedies of the New Deal. Like Mumford and the Goodmans, European critics have also felt less impelled to remove Wright from his immediate milieu. Herbert Read saw similarities in his work with the anarchist program of Kropotkin for an agrarian-industrial society. (Kropotkin had visited Hull House 4 years after Wright's arrival in Chicago.) And Lionel March has demonstrated most clearly the turbulent social background of Wright's period of development at the turn of the century, as well as his relationship with 20th-century American radicalism.[2]

The way in which the ideas of Wright have been misunderstood is remarkably similar to the reception given to those of Ebenezer Howard, that other heretic of city planning. Howard's chief work took place in England, but he was in the western United States as a young man and visited Chicago, the "garden city" as it was then known, while Wright was there. Wright's social and political aims are exactly summarized by the title of Howard's book, Tomorrow: A Peaceful Path to Real Reform, in which the argument for the Garden City was first put forward. Both Wright's Broadacre City and Howard's Garden City were based on pragmatic social reform, and both realized their principles by their own direct action. Although this was on a small scale, it meant the founding of Letchworth and Welwyn for Howard and the whole of his subsequent work for Wright. Both correctly foresaw needs and trends, which took the form of decentralized urban sprawl in the United States and the New Towns in Britain, but these occurred without the social and economic principles that the two men envisioned.[3] Their ideas were similarly dismissed by the political left of their day — Wright by Meyer Schapiro in the

Partisan Review and Howard in the *Fabian News*.[4]

Wright and Howard share a decentralist vision and belief in the future, which was put forward in a number of widely read books during the 1890s; Edward Bellamy's *Equality* and *Looking Backward: 2000–1887*, Peter Kropotkin's *Fields Factories and Workshops* and William Morris's *News from Nowhere*. Their thinking on the land problem springs from the common source of the writings of Henry George. The English writer H. G. Wells was converted to Howard's views of the urban future and evoked them with prophetic clarity in 1901:

The same reasoning that leads to the expectation that the city will diffuse itself until it has taken up considerable areas and many of the characteristics, the greenness, the fresh air, of what is now the country [implies that the country] will take to itself many of the qualities of the city. The old antithesis will altogether disappear; it will become merely a question of more or less populous.[5]

As the *corpus* of knowledge thought necessary to carry out the activity of city planning became more complex, it became more specialized. Wright and Howard shared the fatal error of being amateur.

Wright's Plan for Decentralization

Wright started work on proposals for urban decentralization in 1930, when the Depression destroyed his growing practice.[6] Elements of Broadacre City appeared in his *Kahn Lectures* of that year[7] and were brought together in the book, *Disappearing City,* published in 1932.[8] The concept was firmly enough developed in March 1932 in a *New York Times* magazine article entitled, "Broadacre City: An Architect's Vision," to combat an earlier piece by Le Corbusier advocating his vision of the city as an efficient machine, entitled "Green City" (Ville Radieuse).[9]

By 1935 the Taliesin Fellowship had completed models of a typical section of how the city might appear. These were exhibited, together with a statement of its aims, at Rockefeller Center in New York. The exhibit was accompanied by an article "Broadacre City: A New Community Plan," in *Architectural Record* in April 1935. Wright then developed his proposals in a series of books: *Architecture and Modern Life* in 1938, with Baker Brownell; in *When Democracy Builds* in 1945; and finally in *The Living City* in 1958.[10]

The Model

Since Broadacre City was to be a continuum, and nothing less than the nation urbanized, its presentation by a small, local area modeled in great detail introduced an immediate problem. As Wright described it, Broadacres was to be "the entire country, and predicated on the basis that every woman, man, and child in America is entitled to own an acre of ground so long as they live on it or use it, and every man at least owning his own car. . . . This design presupposes that the city is going to the country, and assumes the country to be a characteristic four square miles of some future American county where the hills come down to the plains and a river flows down and across the plain."[11]

The model that the apprentices built by much desperate labor was financed by Edgar Kaufmann and seen by 40,000 people at Radio City Music Hall.[12] It thereafter went on tour around the United States and Europe.[13] It depicted a post-scarcity society that employed technical and mechanical aids, but one which chose to live in a close relationship with nature. The model gave a prevision of the physical situation now enjoyed in almost every suburban part of America. It differs from this environment of the majority of present-day Americans only in its greater space-scale and visual beauty and in the fact that no section of the population would be excluded from it.[14] As will be seen, Wright's preconditional political principles for such communities have not been realized.

123

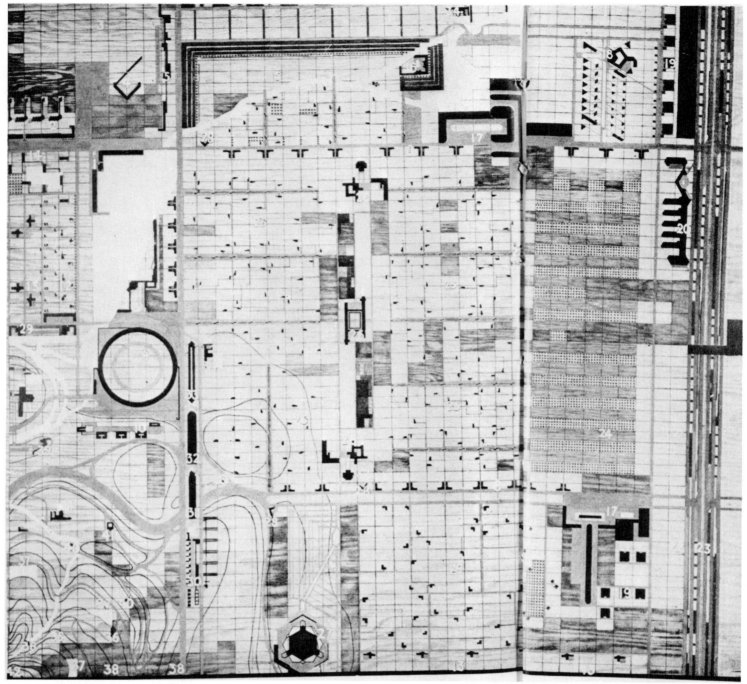

Plan of Broadacre City model: When this was
photographed for *Architectural Record* in 1935,
the one-acre module was visible. (*Architectural
Record,* April 1935, pp. 250–251.)

The Broadacres model represents a 4-sq mile area depicted by Wright as "a typical countryside developed on the acre as a unit [a 1-acre module] according to conditions in the temperate zone and accommodating some 1,400 families. It would swing north or swing south in type as conditions, climate, and topography of the region changed."[15] Entry was by the main arterial road, or intercounty highway, of ten car lanes above and two truck lanes and continuous warehousing below. Above the median ran a high-speed monorail. This bordered the west boundary of the model and attracted roadside businesses, markets, industry, and decentralized hotels (motels)—anticipating what has since occurred. Next removed were owner-occupied light industrial units, workers' homes, and vineyards and orchards. The central area consisted of small homes, with three schools at its heart.

Elements that would have only appeared irregularly in Broadacres were also illustrated in the New York exhibit. Workshops, offices, and the county administrative seat overlooked a lake, and around them were arranged an airport, games and sports areas, professional offices and clinics, arboretum, zoo and aquarium, hotel, county arena, health and religious facilities, and small industrial units. Recreational facilities were scattered along the river and an "automobile objective"[16] located on the hill to the northeast. Elsewhere on the hill were a "Taliesin equivalent," or commune, and commodious homes for wealthier citizens. Wherever necessary, filling stations (which were also community centers) and landing fields for "aerotors" (helicopters) were located.

The service infrastructure consisted of a hierarchy of arterial highways to local distributors at a 1-mile grid, with ½-mile intermediaries and dead end streets as needed. On the hill, topography forced a characteristic contour layout. Power and water supply would be under-

Broadacre City: collateral models. The Inter-County Highway interchange with a major secondary road is shown here. The high-speed monorail and low-level warehousing can also be seen. (*Architectural Record,* April 1935, p. 246.)

Broadacre City: collateral models. Some of the different types of homes that were modeled are shown here: a two-car house, a minimum house, and a medium house. (*Architectural Record,* April 1935, p. 247.)

125

ground, and roads could incorporate lighting in the design of the curbs. "Electricity, oil, and gas are the only popular fuels. Each land allotment has a pit near the public lighting fixture where access to the three and to water and sewer may be had without tearing up the pavements."[17] Overlaid on the length and breadth of the decentralized city was a three-dimensional grid of spaced air corridors for the "aerotors," bee-like crafts, which would rise automatically to a pre-set destination. Wrightian vehicles also included an energy-conserving car designed around a 6-ft flywheel.

In arguing as he did that rebuilding high-rise urban housing merely perpetuated slum conditions of exploitation, Wright maintained that it was preferable to subsidize transportation, to enable people to find independence on their own land.[18] "The space scale therefore has changed throughout. Changed "in the ground allotments as in the dwellings themselves . . . space can be reckoned by time rather than feet and inches."[19] Wright postulates, "On this basis, the whole population of the U.S. could be accommodated in Texas alone."[20] Visual form was given to a way of life designed to allow a dual mode of working — on the land and in the office or factory — where the individual might attain dignity and realize his potential. To this end, government, the means of exchange, and intermediary and regulatory institutions were reintegrated and made local.

Wright expected his decentralized city to grow organically, that is gradually, away from existing concentrations of population. Such centers would slowly wither as their citizens took the opportunity to have their own house and garden. Wright quite specifically indicated that ports of entry and centers of mining and mineral extraction would continue so long as they were needed: "The new Broadacres will absorb all needless cities and towns where they stand."[21] He declared in a radio broadcast in 1935, "I do not say

Broadacre City is *the* form, but I see it as one that might well be our own if we are to go forward. . . . (Broadacres) goes forward with nature broadly based upon enlightened human egoism."[22] Wright summarized his proposals:

In the models may now be seen in actual form all the elemental units of our social structure: the co-related farm, the factory (its smoke and gases eliminated by using coal at the mines): the decentralized school: the various conditions of residence: the home offices: safe traffic: simplified government: all common interests taking place in a single coordination wherein all are employed: *little* farms, *little* homes for industry, *little* factories, *little* schools, a *little* university, going to the people mostly by way of their interest in the ground, *little* laboratories on the ground for professional men.

Broadacres as conceived here would automatically end unemployment and its evils forever. There would never be labor enough, nor would there be under-consumption. Whatever a man did would be well done—obviously and directly — because done mostly by himself in his own interest. . . . Economic independence would be near every man who worked; a subsistence certain. A life varied and interesting is the natural consequence. Nothing too good for anybody — and no substitute for quality.[23]

The Significance of Broadacre City in Wright's Work

Why should Usonia or "Organic America," which is what Broadacre City amounts to, contain one-car and five-car homes yet be based on "some form of universal social credit"?[24] An unexploitative capitalism operating within what would now be called "ecological limits" was of central importance to Wright.[25] Clearly it is imperative to understand what he meant by "enlightened human egoism." So important was Broadacre City to him that Wright indicated at the end of *An Autobiography* that the project would form its sixth and final book. This book was written in 1943, but dropped on the insistence of his publishers because they felt it contained material likely to be prejudicial to the conduct of the war.[26] It was published privately on the Taliesin press in the spring of 1944, and includes Wright's clearest elaboration of his ideas, sources, and rebuttal of criticisms of him made since 1935. In this work, the idea of direct Usonian democracy was developed in detail in subjects such as defense. Wright held that "A Conscript is a slave subject to his ruler: his own conscience is destroyed so far as his own acts toward his fellow men are concerned."[27] Wright's solution was that ". . . war may be declared in circumstances other than actual invasion only by a two-thirds popular vote so instructing Congress. Everyone voting for war is thereby self-enlisted regardless of age, occupation, or authority."[28]

In Broadacre City, Wright was endeavoring to give physical form to his concept of democracy. For him good architecture arose from a deep understanding by its architect of his life and times. Broadacre City was thus Wright's scenario for a city plan to realize the most common good. Among his commentators, Norris Kelly Smith and Lionel March, in their very different interpretations, are agreed on the importance of Broadacre City. Smith wrote:

There is an underlying principle which establishes the unity of Wright's work, and that principle is best expressed in Broadacre City. To judge Broadacres is to judge everything he created—and vice versa.[29]

March said of Broadacre City:

To my mind, there can be no doubt of the central significance of Broadacres to the last thirty years of Wright's architectural output. No proper understanding of his architectural contribution during those years can be made until his aspirations for the emergent city are appreciated.[30]

Of the whole critical reception that it received,[31] no writer has so intentionally caricatured Broadacre City as has Smith:

To the practical and ordinary citizen Broadacres has meant less than no-

thing. Judged by the pragmatic standards of the workaday world, it is so irrelevant that it has simply been ignored—for the realization of Broadacre City would require the abrogation of the Constitution of the United States, the elimination of thousands of governmental bodies from the make-up of the state, the confiscation of all lands by right of eminent domain but without compensation, the demolition of all cities and therewith the obliteration of every evidence of the country's history, the rehousing of the entire population, the retraining of millions of persons so as to enable them to be self-sustaining farmers, and other difficulties too numerous to mention.[32]

It was March's achievement to "test this critical assessment by setting Wright's views against those held within society at large" and to investigate the extent to which they were upheld and by whom. He showed that "many of these views, contrary to the impression given by Wright's critics, were shared by some of the most notable intellectuals and practicing politicians of his day."[33] In a series of broadcasts over the BBC, March also sought to demonstrate that the strength of conviction of Wright's proposals in the 1930s grew from his direct observation of the excesses of the American system in the 1890s and 1920s.

The Unacceptable Face of Capitalism

Wright was always far from the conservative strands of American development. His formative background was closer to Populism, the Grangers, and the International Workers of the World (IWW) than to the settled outlook of his later clients, and he took no part in the "Coolidge prosperity" of the 1920s.

Chicago

Growing up in rural Wisconsin exposed Wright to the exploitation of farmers by the banks and railroads through the direct sufferings of the Lloyd-Jones family. In 1887, Wright dropped out of college at Madison and arrived in Chicago. Cities were in a tumultuous state, with strikes and urban unrest everywhere. At

this time, seven anarchists were hanged, in spite of a complete lack of evidence, for their supposed part in the death of policemen engaged in breaking up a labor rally. William Morris, the 19th-century English designer and socialist, was one of a flood of worldwide protestors, and 20,000 people, March wrote, "marched to the burial ground singing the Marseillaise and Internationale."[34] It was this event, the death of the Haymarket martyrs as they were known, that propelled Emma Goldman, the American anarchist and women's liberationist, to abandon her marriage and take up politics.

As Wright became a successful architect, it would have been easy for him to have adopted conservative friends and joined establishment institutions. Instead, through his uncle Jenkin Lloyd-Jones, who was deeply involved in welfare work, he was introduced to Jane Addams and became active in the affairs of Hull House. This center of reform and radicalism was connected with John Dewey and the new University of Chicago. Jane Addams herself later became the first American woman to be awarded the Nobel Peace Prize. In his BBC broadcasts Lionel March drew attention to events over a period of three years in Chicago that illuminated Wright's experiences at this time:

In 1891 a Mrs. Kelly came to Hull House. She has been described as "the toughest customer in the reform riot, the finest rough-and-tumble fighter for the good life for others, that Hull House ever knew." She was a divorced woman with three children who boarded out with Frank Lloyd Wright's mother, now living close to her son in Oak Park. . . . Mrs. Kelly was a doctrinaire socialist who had translated Engel's *Condition of the Working Class in England* into English, and she investigated Chicago slum and labor conditions as searchingly as Engels had done for Manchester earlier in the century.[35]

In 1893 the World's Fair or Columbian Exposition took place in Chicago, commemorating the 400th anniversary of the discovery of America. For countless Americans its "White City" of plaster classical architecture represented the arrival of "culture," albeit dead and imported. They flocked to see it.[36] For Sullivan and Wright it meant that modern architecture in America would be set back 50 years. For Wright the exposition also meant his first encounter with Eastern culture in the Japanese pavilion. For Burnham and other Chicago architects it meant the end of one way of building and the start of another.[37] For architectural historians it marked the arrival of electric appliances on the domestic scene, and more importantly for this discussion, the start of the City Beautiful movement, as well as the application of a classical renaissance style to public buildings and the homes of the rich. March observed:

What was going on behind the white facades of the Exposition? It generally was not the democracy that spoke of justice, domestic tranquility, general welfare, and liberty for all. Huge numbers of workers who had been needed to complete the exhibition on time were summarily dismissed, adding to an already acute unemployment problem. The homeless and out-of-work occupied the damp, cold corridors and stairways of the old City Hall. Workmen smashed windows and insulted policemen in order to be jailed, fed, and warmed. Great demonstrations were made on the lakeshore and the chief of police ordered his men to "club and brutally maltreat all unemployed who gathered there." At a vast meeting a veteran socialist leader declared, "Your laboring men may assemble peacefully on the lake front, begging work, and with the strong arm of the law are driven back into their tenement houses, so that visitors who come to see the White City might not see the misery of the Garden City which built it." The white facades were lies masking social realities.[38]

In 1894 the railway coach workers at the paternalist new town of Pullman, 10 minutes south of the Chicago Loop, went on strike against high rents and low wages. The bloody clashes with federal troops confounded the hopes of those who, 10 years earlier, had praised this supposed solution of social problems by the imposition of a visually harmonious order. March commented, ". . . the economist Richard Ely could see, while the town was 'so pleasing to the eye that a woman's first exclamation is certain to be "perfectly lovely,' " that the idea of Pullman was un-American — everything is done *for* the people and nothing *by* them."[39] Jane Addams was called in to arbitrate and found that although Pullman's aims were liberal, his method was restrictive. March showed that this facadism, which Wright despised, was derived from an imported and autocratic culture, from the Paris that Haussman built for Napoleon III.

Engels, in his book *The Housing Problem* had, many years before, coined the word Haussmanism for this cosmetic treatment covering up the ugly social realities behind the facades of urban reconstruction. I think it is certain that Mrs. Kelly and other Chicago radicals recognized the Haussmanism of the White City and the City Beautiful movement which grew out of it. The countless classical domes of the public buildings which followed contrasted with the corruption, or "militarism" as Jane Addams called it, of city government, to which Wright gave the name "militocracy."[40]

The topology of Chicago itself, and its intellectual stimulus, were formative influences on Wright's outlook at this time. The city he knew was the fastest growing metropolis in the world and the dynamic force behind the humanization — as the pragmatists James and Dewey called it — of a wilderness. It was simultaneously what has been called the "City as Energy System"[41] — a city of skyscrapers and the Loop, multilayered, and the nexus of a boulevard, streetcar, and railroad matrix extending further than any city before it. Chicago was also the "Garden City" of circling leafy suburbs, of which Oak Park was a small part, and the morphological archetype of the sociologists Park and Burgess.

It was in this city that Wright formed his generally optimistic view of technology and his conviction, in common with the pragmatist philosophers, that the purpose of democracy was to aid the individual to reach the "full stature of his possibility."[42] The pragmatists' flexibility in reaching social reform by piecemeal steps — as occurred in Wisconsin[43] — and without resorting to a fixed "Grand Design," gave Wright a philosophical stance that echoed his observations of the social scene in Chicago. This inclination to see democracy as a process and not a form is fundamental to Wright's thinking, and found its sharpest expression in his reading and action in the 1930s. He believed that the citizen must participate in formulating society's values and that the technology of industry and communication would facilitate this. Wright's address to Hull House, *The Art and Craft of the Machine,* of 1901,[44] is an example of this stance, and goes together with his youthful vision of seething Chicago, with its industry and blast furnaces. The pragmatists' views were confirmed for Wright by the analysis of the economic historian Charles A. Beard, whose interpretation of American political history traced the continuing conflict of economic interests. This was the origin of Wright's "vehement attacks on big business and bankers," according to March, "and his conviction that the credit system leads to over-production and consequently to either unemployment or militarism and imperialism."[45]

The roots of another Wrightian conviction are to be found in this turn-of-the-century period. Rent and the rentier class became for him synonymous with the inability of capitalism to prevent poverty in the midst of progress. Here the work of Henry George and Thorstein Veblen took hold in his thinking. The pragmatist's open-ended readiness to find means toward general social welfare anywhere at hand attracted Wright because of his profound belief in nature and its law of change. He wrote, "Karl Marx never appealed to me because he seemed to see the world as a factory for factory workers and his view of society, with all its reality, seemed to me the worm's eye-view. After all the industrial revolution was a passing phase."[46] On the other hand, Henry George felt that the struggle was not between labor and capital but between laborers and the owners of land.

The reason why, in spite of the increase of productive power, wages constantly tend to a minimum . . . is that with the increase in productive power, rent tends to an even greater increase thus producing a constant tendency to the forcing down of wages.[47]

Veblen, like Wright, believed that capital controlled industry to the detriment of the consumer, and in his *Theory of the Leisure Class* he pilloried the rentiers. March pointed out the similarities between Veblen and Wright:

Both believed that modern industrial resources could release men from drudgery but for usury and the price spiral, both argued that a community which lived close to the soil could surpass the most advanced technical nations controlled by absentee ownership and finance, both despised speculation in real estate, both pointed to the conspicuous waste of salesmanship.[48]

Veblen, like Wright, came from Wisconsin farming stock and was in Chicago in the 1890s when George and his "single tax" on the ownership of land were being widely discussed. Wright's *lieber meister,* the architect Louis Sullivan, was a member of a Georgist group.

Wisconsin

When he left Chicago for rural Spring Green, Wright was returning to the most politically progressive state in the union. Emma Goldman lectured in Madison in 1909 and found there the most advanced social consciousness and receptive audience of her American career.[49] First as senator, then as governor of Wisconsin, Robert La Follette had tamed the railroad monopoly and brought about a long course of progressive reform.[50] Eventually, when

the Progressive party was past its peak and he himself was sick and old, "Battling Bob" ran as the Progressive candidate for the presidency in 1924. He, and the policies he had formulated in Wisconsin, polled five million votes. While governor, he brought in a number of distinguished academics as advisers to his administration. Chief among these was the institutional economist, John R. Commons, a lifelong friend of Wright's, whom he describes in *An Autobiography* as "the grand old man of the University of Wisconsin."

These men, commented March, ". . . eschewed holistic systems and theories for practical engagement and experience, for piecemeal amelioration wherever and whenever men were ready to be persuaded to take a step forward. This slow but sure method of reform, in which all parties could see the reasonableness of the measures enacted had established the Wisconsin administration by the late twenties as the most enlightened and humane in the whole of the United States. Such was the 'Wisconsin idea.' Not a credo, but a manner of working with people."[51] During the thirties, under the younger La Follettes, this process was developed in the Progressive program into social advances that presaged much of Wright's discussion of society to be found in *The Living City.*

The Southwest and Technical and Economic Change

By 1920 Wright had made a number of trips to Los Angeles, but had been geographically isolated in Japan for 5 years and was emotionally isolated by the long, drawn-out affair with Miriam Noel. In southern California he was witnessing the birth of what he came to call "automobilization," over an area that dwarfed even the spread of Chicago. By 1923 the Los Angeles basin was united by the Pacific Electric Railroad, 50 mi from San Fernando in the north to Balboa in the south, and 70 mi from Santa Monica in the east to a point west of San Bernardino.[51] The

Chicago motto, *urbs in horto,* was eclipsed by an urban network that encompassed not only parks and gardens, but a port, movie center, and extensive farming and horticulture. Here Wright could observe the emergent phenomena of two-way commuting and the free-ranging potential of the automobile.

Wright was always an enthusiastic motorist himself. His son John wrote in *My Father Who Is on Earth,* "Papa was a handsome figure in the driving seat with linen duster, goggles, and his wavy hair dancing in the breeze."[53] From 1910 on, Wright drove his way through a succession of roadsters, Packards, the ubiquitous Auburn Cords of the thirties, and the later Lincoln Continentals. He understood at first hand the nature of the agent of change. He witnessed a period in the ad hoc development of the Miracle Mile of Wilshire Boulevard, and everywhere he saw the humble filling station, then only emerging from its origin in the blacksmith's shop. Wright wrote:

Watch the little gas station. . . . In our present gasoline service station you may see a crude beginning to such important advance decentralization; also see the beginning of the future humane establishment we are now calling the free city. Wherever service stations are located naturally these so often ugly and seemingly insignificant features will survive and expand. [The new city] . . . is all around us in the haphazard making, the apparent forces to the contrary notwithstanding. All about us and no plan. The old order is breaking up.[54]

It is easy to underestimate the speed of change taking place in Wright's mature years. Between 1913 and 1930 automobile registrations had increased twenty-fold. Telephone installation had kept pace. The first grade-separated highway intersections had been built. By 1920 a registered continental airmail service had been established, and between 1928 and 1930 there was a 360 percent increase in air passengers. The efficiency of power generation was so improved between 1920 and 1929 that a 25 percent increase in the quantity of coal burned gave a 100 percent increase in kilowatt hours generated. In 1914, 30 percent of American factories were electrically powered, and by 1929 the figure was 70 percent. Factory location was freed from primary energy sources, meaning that industry could be near its markets. In 1913 the assembly of a Model T Ford required 14 hours. One year later this had been reduced by electric conveyor belts to 98 minutes. Little wonder that Wright could declare in 1935:

The three major inventions at work building Broadacres, whether the powers that over-built the old cities like it or not, are: (1) The motor car: general mobilization of the human being; (2) Radio, telephone and telegraph: electrical intercommunication becoming complete; and (3) Standardized machine shop production: machine invention plus scientific discovery.[55]

His statement that "it is in the nature of universal electrification that the city should not exist"[56] is not, when taken in context, so outrageous.

Phoenix, Arizona, near which Wright built Taliesin West, was developing toward a density in parts quite as low as that projected for Broadacre City. There, in the desert, his early social and political attitudes coalesced under a new influence to form the basis for Broadacres. Through Owen D. Young, a client of the twenties and near neighbor, who ran for the presidency, Wright was introduced to the ideas of the German economist, Silvio Gesell.[57] Wright subsequently heartily recommended Gesell's work, *The Natural Economic Order,* and especially its preface, to his followers. John Maynard Keynes wrote that Gesell's work "may be described as an establishment of anti-Marxian socialism, a reaction against laissez-faire built on theoretical foundations totally unlike those of Marx in being based on an unfettering of competition rather than its abolition. . . . I believe that the future will learn more from the spirit of Gesell than from that of Marx."[58]

130

Taliesin West from the air during the 1930s. The drafting room, desert garden, and main buildings can be seen in the foreground. Beyond are the apprentices' shelters. Photograph by Pedro E. Guerrero.

The Broadacre City model is viewed "from the air." Community-held tree belts separate and delineate private self-supporting holdings of 1 to 10 acres.

This airview of Phoenix, Arizona, shows the David Wright house, 1952, in the foreground amid citrus groves. Photograph by Pedro E. Guerrero.

Gesell aimed to bring about an equitable distribution of land and medium of exchange by means of a compensated land nationalization and redistribution of rent, along with a form of money that constantly depreciated at 5 percent. Since goods were the foundation of economic structure and money only represented their value, and since goods rot and deteriorate, then why should money not deteriorate also? His currency, which lost value with time, encouraged holders to exchange it, and could not be capitalized. The terms "free-land" and "free-money" used by Wright in *The Living City* originate with Gesell. "During the thirties free-money was realized in a number of local situations in America, and in 1933 a bill was presented to both Houses of Congress directing the Federal Treasury to issue a billion dollars worth of free-money. Thus this idea, which Wright accepted for his Broadacres proposal, was in its time and place a practical political and economic proposition."[59] Gesell's philosophy crystalized Wright's ideas and represented, along with Progressive political reform, some definition of his "enlightened human egoism". Wright's inclinations must have been echoed in Gesell's words:

A man must be something not appear something; he must be able to stride though life with head erect . . . to speak the truth without incurring the risk of hardship or injury. . . . An economic order . . . founded on egoism is in no way opposed to the higher impulses which preserve the species. . . . The Natural Economic Order stands by itself and requires no legal enactments: it makes officials, the State itself, and other tutelage superfluous.[60]

It was self-interest that was to make the economy self-regulating by the free play of economic forces. It would also make altruism possible. For Wright "the choice lies between private control and state control of economic life" and "democracy is a way of living, not a form."[61]

The Depression

Following 1929, Wright lectured at Princeton and traveled the country, absorbing the many economic remedies proposed and the varied solutions of the New Deal.

The degree of desperation and flavor of reaction to events, as national politics became chaotic and the Depression deepened, is shown by the rise of the Technocracy movement. This movement, which burst upon the American public in 1932, had its origins in the Technical Alliance, of which Veblen and Howard Scott, the leader of Technocracy Incorporated, were members. It provides a contemporary contrast with Wright's proposals, and was discussed at Taliesin.[62] Technocracy was chiefly remarkable for its *Energy Survey* and *Plan of Plenty,* — formulae for solving the nation's problems by cool deployment of white-hot technology, as well as for its proposal for a two-level money system. A central cooperative would direct and plan for the necessities of life, and in return for his work each citizen would receive a guaranteed income for life, with choice of work, hours of work reduced, and leisure increased. Luxury or scarce articles such as paintings and antiques were to be subject to barter or the old money system.

In the early thirties Wright was lecturing at the New School in New York at the same time as Veblen, and probably had the opportunity to acquaint himself with other precedents for his proposals of decentralization. In 1918 Veblen had submitted his *Memorandum for Food Administration* to Congress, proposing a distributive system with features of parcel post, mail order, and chain stores. All food would be handled through post offices, and since these would also be banking units, there would be no transfer of funds, certainly in rural areas, and therefore less paperwork.[63]

In 1921 Veblen published *Engineers and the Price System,* the work that became the manifesto for Technocracy. In it he analyzed the nature of previous revolutions to have been military and political. He predicted that an American revolution would be industrial and technological. Under the phrase "disallowance of absentee ownership" Veblen predicted that there would be "no ownership of an industrially useful article by persons not habitually employed on it,"[64] a position similar to that of Henry George. Reference to this monograph is also made by C. H. Douglas in *Social Credit.*[65] Wright concurred with Major Douglas's attack on centralized monopoly capitalism and adopted the general elements of his proposals, as developed in his draft for Scotland and applied in parts of Canada. These were not seen as a panacea but rather as a principle and were incorporated into Broadacre City's three inherent rights of man:

1   His social right to a *direct* medium of exchange in place of gold as a commodity: some form of social credit.
2   His social right to his place on the ground as he has had it in the sun and air: land to be held only by use and improvements.
3   His social right to the ideas by which and for which he lives: public ownership of invention and scientific discoveries that concern the life of the people.[66]

These are Wright's prerequisites for Usonian democracy, which are expanded on but not essentially altered in his many books. The currency proposals of Gesell and Douglas are linked with the homesteading and pioneer tradition, the land tenure ideas of Veblen and George and a proposal of his own that owes something to Thomas Jefferson, Edward Bellamy, and Veblen. Wright's books never had the clarity of his buildings. He regarded himself as a member of a group of men of ideas who were better able than he to express them. All those who have been discussed here were his friends, or else their works were "respected" and "consulted" by him, as he confesses in *An Autobiography.* The strands of Wright's thinking go far back, as the names of his philosophical heroes carved on the wall of the Taliesin theater show. The basic right of land

tenure, for example, is traceable to one of these men, John Ruskin.

Land, by whomsoever held, is to be made the most of, by human strength, and not defiled,[67] nor left waste. But since we live in an epoch assuredly of change, and too probably of revolution, I affirm the one principle that each man shall possess the ground he can use— and no more — USE I say, either for food, beauty, exercise, science, or any other sacred purpose. . . . That each man shall possess for his own, no more than such portion. . . .[68]

Wright's concept of decentralization won support from planning administrations and as a result of the events of his time. Dean Malcolm A. Willey, the Minneapolis client for Wright's prototype Usonian house in 1932, had published the paper *Communication Agencies and Social Life.*[69] This was an expert report to President Hoover's Research Committee on Social Trends and according to March, "recognized the overwhelming personal advantages of 'automoblization,' and gave evidence —contrary to what might be expected— that 'localism' was being fostered by the new mobility.[70] It urged the integration of public modes of transport and use of containers in a manner similar to that of Wright's intercounty highways, and "discussed the impact that mail, telephone, radio, and television would have on, what it calls, mass impression.[71] These ideas were seminal to the ideas for use of the media put forward in Wright's *The Living City.*

Lionel March pointed out that other reports to the president's committee backed up Wright's work. R. C. McKenzie's *Metropolitan Community*[72] recognized the emergence of spread supercities, as did J. H. Kolb's *Rural Life.* The research director to the committee, William Ogburn, put forward a concept of social trends that is quite crucial to Wright's view of the impending death of the old cities and their inevitable replacement by decentralized forms. March described Ogburn's ideas in one of his BBC broadcasts.

To slow the trend of the movement of city dwellers out of the city, city chambers of commerce will have a very hard time of it and are not likely to be successful for long.

Success is more likely to come to those who work for and with a social trend than those who work against. But should our principles dictate that we work against social trends we would do well to appraise the size of the effort needed, unless we wish to be martyrs. This should be heeded by city and national planners. They should not start with a Utopian urge and a clean slate. Rather they should see what the trends are. Only then can they approach realistically the task of planning.[73]

Wright was familiar with Henry Ford's proposals in 1921 for the integrative linear planning of Muscle Shoals, and he followed its development into the Tennessee Valley Authority.[74] If confirmation of his correctness was needed, he received it from the many decentralist measures of the New Deal and two government agencies. One agency, the National Resources Planning Board, recommended in 1935:

The integration of agricultural and industrial employment by the establishment of homes for workers employed in non-agricultrual occupations, where they may produce part of their living, to become a permanent national policy; and that this policy be broadened to include: Encouraging the location of industries in rural areas now seriously deficient in sources of income. . . . Encouraging the location of industries in definite relation to rapid transit facilities in the countryside.[75]

In 1944, the second agency, the Special Committee to Investigate Industrial Centralization, submitted its report to Congress entitled, "A Graphic Guide to Decentralization." This report proposed that industries be developed in the West to create jobs for the 3 million people then working on war contracts in new plants. When the war boom ended, these people, supplemented by 2 million demobilized men, would otherwise find their homes threatened and the potential economy of the area undermined. "Our workers must not be reduced to nomads," it declared. Decentralization was put forward as being

synonymous with freedom, and the centralized urban system "with an emphasis on control" and totalitarianism.[76]

Many practical and individual demonstrations of Wright's ideas, or of very similar ones, were also evident at the time. Ralph Borsodi had left New York in 1920 for a life of homesteading. From the experience of his family's use of electric home appliances to achieve economic independence, he developed the theories that he put forward in *Flight from the City,* published in 1933.[77] These had two premises: (1) that as the cost of production falls, the cost of distribution rises; and (2) that social and economic security required a large number of diversified farmers. To this end, a number of Borsodian communities were founded — one at Suffern, New York, another in Dayton, Ohio, and elsewhere — which put into practice home production and mutual self-sufficiency. One of these, Bryn Gweled Homesteads near Philadelphia, was reviewed in detail in *Pencil Points* and exhibited many similarities with Usonian homes and Wrightian communities.[78] Wright's diagnosis of the ills of society and the city was also echoed in the intellectual rationalization for the actions of such individuals as Scott and Helen Nearing, who left New York during the Depression to go to live and farm in Vermont.

Achieving Broadacres

What we need is the wedding of the city and the country. I designed Broadacre City on that idea and modeled it in 1933. There you have all the advantages of the city, without the city. And the country is not spoiled, because quality in building comes into the picture to save it from destruction. You can build an organic house anywhere and it will not spoil anything; so you could build an organic city out in the country and not harm the country. But you cannot take the country into the city; the city has to go to the country. It certainly is proceeding now. It is nothing that I have invented. The little gas station was the first sign . . . then the produce markets and the merchants going out. The best people are already gone and the city is a kind of gregarious hangover at the present time.[79]

Since 1930, Wright had indicted modern city life as overcentralized and congested, polluted and dehumanized. Such events as the erosion of the tax base of most western cities and the near-bankruptcy of New York 45 years later have borne out his diagnosis of the forces and strength of change. He was, in his time, working within a body of knowledge for social and urban reform. He was attempting to give architectural form to what he believed to be the most humane and progressive thought of his generation. His outstanding talent was to show how this could be achieved by enhancing the landscape; he looked for young people to "go again, enlightened now, to native ground making their land and buildings and way of life there homely and surpassingly beautiful."[80]

In the great scale of Broadacres, Wright's concern was with the careful design of highways integrated with landscape. This is illustrated in the matter of tree planting. "Certain specific acres . . . are, in every generation, planted to useful trees" in such a way that they define and enrich the countryside and provide fruit, nuts, building materials, and fuel. The suggestion showed awareness of both economic and spiritual needs.[81]

The community decided all matters affecting it. Democratic planning was for Wright experimental and tolerant as well as a continuous and cooperative process, what Dewey had termed "an operative method of activity, not a pre-determined set of final truths."[82] And here was perhaps the central concept of Broadacres — life as learning. Through the educative process, starting with the hoe of the kindergarten and with guidance from Wright's "experimental design-centers" (which were linked with universities and the media), individuals could join in formulating the growth and maintenance of their community.

Nothing to my mind could be worse imposition than to have some individual, even temporarily, deliberately fix the outward forms of his concept of beauty upon the future of a free people or even of a growing city. A tentative, advantageous forecast of probable future utilitarian development goes far enough in this direction.[83]

Yet 21 years after that statement, Wright expected that "every kind of builder would be likely to have a jealous eye to the harmony of the whole within broad limits fixed by the county architect, an architect chosen by the county itself."[84]

As will be seen, the relationship between client and architect was for Wright a thing of joint intent. However, the change that occurred once that client was no longer a single individual became his chief problem. In large projects he always sought out one person and never a committee, to represent the client. The tendency was therefore to build paternally. Essentially what was at issue was no less than the architect's right to and use of, his skill. Wright had no doubt; Broadacres was to be permissive but led — a "unity in variety."

Democracy stood in my mind for the *growth* and *protection of individuality*. . . . Thoreau's "That government is best government which governs not at all," I accepted as a truism. . . . I saw cooperation all around us as the natural thing, and not selfishness and violence. The anarchist's ideal, faith in the common-wealth based on voluntary instinctive respect for the other fellow's rights, I saw as the normal thing and could never understand why it was not recognized as ideal even though unattainable in present day society.[85]

There should be as many kinds of houses as there are kinds of people and as many differentiations as there are different individuals. A man who has individuality (and what man lacks it?) has a right to its expression in his enviroment.[86]

135

These ideas are a total challenge to planning orthodoxy. The dilemma of the individual in relation to society is expressed in Wright's tangled attitude to this problem. It is also a current problem of architecture. His solution was instinctive and has been denounced 40 years later as elitist. Yet, in fact, his county architect was to be elected, and was not the dictator that Wright's critics made him out to be. His role was educative. In Wright's greater sense all human endeavor was "architecture," and he saw the Wisconsin Progressives and Roosevelt himself as "social architects." Such leaders would bring about the social reality of Broadacres, just as the county architect would set up the varying tone of its environment. They would guide or advise the community through the televised "fireside chat" or by means of popular social experimentation carried out through universities and the media. These proposals are developed in Wright's work, *The Living City.*[87]

Why must Revolution be only partial and then start all over again the other way? Is it because Revolution is either regardless of organic law or is it an explosion under too great pressure?[88]

Wright looked to Jefferson's natural aristocracy, those men of ideas who could renew democracy as he knew it. His intention was not revolution but evolution. It was to these men that he appealed for the realization of Broadacre City in his radio broadcast in 1935.

So here in the forum of Rockefeller Center are these models based upon the actual American concept of freedom that founded this country. A new success ideal. . . . It is high time for some fundamental radicals among us to gather together the loose ends of opportunity, and out of a sense of the whole as organic, project with feeling . . . a sensible plan for the future our Forefathers believed would be ours.[89]

When, by the time World War II had broken out, this did not occur, he made a last attempt to put forward Broadacre City as the organic, broad-based capitalism for the peace to follow. In 1943 he organized a *Citizens' Petition* asking the government administration, through Frederick Delano of the National Resources and Planning Board, to authorize Wright to develop his "search for democratic form." The petition was signed by many eminent "architects, artists, capitalists [sic], civil authorities, directors of institutions, editors ,educators, lawyers, landscape architects, preachers, and writers." These included Thurman Arnold, John Dewey, Albert Einstein, Clark Foreman, Buckminster Fuller, Archibald MacLeish, Robert Moses, Nelson Rockefeller, Ferdinand Schevill, William Allen White, and Mies van der Rohe.[90] In all, Wright gathered the names of 64 men important to his development and sympathetic with his aim.

I do not believe in a "back to the land" movement; I think that any backward movement would be folly; but if we can go forward to large scale practical application with all that science has provided us . . . to the new forms which *must* be made for the accommodation of life so that men may live more generously. . . . Inevitably, there will develop a new form of community life, but just what it will be except as Broadacre City tentatively outlines it as free to grow, who can say? Not I. Who is going to say how humanity will eventually be modified by all these spiritual changes and physical advantages, sound and vision coming through solid walls to men, each aware of anything in or of the world he lives in without lifting a finger, making it unnecessary to go anywhere unless it is a pleasure to go. The whole psyche of humanity is changing and what that change will ultimately bring as future community I will not prophecy. It *is* already greatly changed.[91]

Wright was an architect, never a politician. His urban plan was an earnest and instructive attempt to integrate all the forces of society into a liberating form. It was a scenario for change.

136

CHAPTER 5 Popularizing Organic Architecture

"THE CREW AND I are proud of this Frank Lloyd Wright house. Here we are on the gravel court leading up to the entrance. That's me in front. Behind me, from left to right: three masons, tender, concrete finisher, driver, apprentice, and three carpenters."

The Usonian career grew out of circumstances that Wright deplored. Before the Depression and after the war, the housing economy was dominated by land booms and land speculation. Wright felt that this situation was predatory. His ultimate solution to this problem, and to the "money-interest," which he was convinced encouraged nonproductive exploitation, was, as has been seen, cultural and political change. However, as an architect, Wright was impelled to improve standards in the existing housing market in any way open to him. He sought to initiate change in the status quo through his house design, with its attendant architect-client relationship, and through his increasingly challenging public statements. His success can readily be seen in the American housing field.

Methods of Achieving Organic Housing

The Usonian house, designed in 1934, quickly increased in price. It was extremely difficult to achieve a built cost of $5,500 for the Jacobs house in 1937, $7,000 for the Pope house and $8,500 for the Pew house in 1940. Wright found his solution to the "small house problem" was beyond the means of those aspiring to it. To continue to reach lower income homebuilders, he devised new forms of construction, designed for an increasing amount of client "do-it-yourself" activity, and proposed self-build homes that had only an initial and remote connection with an architect. Gradually the home finance situation changed from active opposition to modern design on the part of prewar banks and the Federal Housing Authority, into one of guarded acceptance.

Wright's Architect–Client Relationship

No man can build a building for another man who does not believe in him, who does not believe in what he believes in, and who has not chosen him because of his faith, knowing what he can do. That is the nature of architect and client as I see it.[1]

Wright and his clients shared a common *intent.* This applied to more than the spatial and organizational characteristics that both sought. It included an attitude toward lifestyle and the integration of building with site, which was largely Wright's invention. Most significantly, this common intent often originated in similar expectations for the freedom of the individual in society and for a just society. Although not all Wright's early Usonian clients shared the *details* of his political beliefs, most were drawn to the man through reading his autobiography and were fundamentally sympathetic to the message of Broadacre City. Indeed, most were supporters of the New Deal.[2] In Wright's view, he and his clients were building Broadacres whenever they came together. His buildings were intended to be points of excellence and influence for each region in which they were located. They were inserting fragments of Usonian society into the existing built environment. This has been called by March "perhaps the most audacious of Wright's attitudes towards Planning."[3]

Spreading the Organic Idea

Wright had always been concerned with proselytizing his ideas. The "quadruple block" housing scheme of 1901 was intended to illustrate the principles stated in "The Art and Craft of the Machine," a lecture delivered at Hull House in that year. His concept of "a simple mode of living" was made explicit and understandable to laymen by articles in the February and July editions of *Ladies Home Journal* of 1901, entitled, "A Home in a Prairie Town," and "A Small House with Lots of Room in It." However, this was a mere hint at Wright's thorough use of popular journals to disseminate his Usonian concept. Through Howard Myers at *Architectural Forum,* and later through Elizabeth Gordon at *House Beautiful,* he spoke to other architects and the expanding population of homebuild-ers. Most consistently, he sounded out the theory and practice of building the Usonian dwelling through the 1950s in *House and Home* magazine. Wright tried to bend the psychological demand for the American dream house to organic, and therefore real, purposes. Indeed, it is not fanciful to suggest that the tangible models of Broadacre City were intended to flesh out an American "Dream City."

Both the spotlike realization of Broadacres by Wright and his clients and the use of publicity had a theoretical basis. It has been pointed out by March that this basis is to be found in three concepts put forward by William Ogburn, the distinguished Chicago sociologist who was Director of Research to President Hoover's Committee on Social Trends.[4] These concepts were "social trend" itself, which has been shown to have formed an important operative adjunct to pragmatic philosophy, "cultural lag," and "diffusion of inventions." The second is brought about when society cannot adapt sufficiently fast to keep pace with technical change, and Wright made constant use of the phrase. The third refers to the slow but inevitable acceptance of innovation that answers a social need—precisely Wright's activity. This idea is reinforced by Talcott Parsons' designation of one of the roots of social change. "The pattern of acceptance of a potential change starts with the deviate and proceeds to embrace larger sections of the population."[5]

The Housing Context

In America immediately after the war the new house was changing for three reasons: (1) there emerged a freer attitude toward children;[6] (2) there was a new woman's role with more activity outside the home; and (3) with a proliferation of external functions, less time was spent in the home.[7] All these changes meant that people needed dwellings that worked more efficiently at an operative level, were easy to maintain, and called for minimal housekeeping. The financial situation was dominated by the FHA and tended to frustrate a fresh expression of this need. According to a study done by Irving Rosow, loan-giving officials disapproved of houses that "did not conform to their neighborhood in architectural style." Furthermore, wrote Rosow, they tended to "establish the value of a house according to its cubic footage. This rough formula frequently undervalues modern houses. Seldom is there an accurate reflection of intrinsic facilities such as built-in furniture or features of convenience."[8]

Loan policies and current financing practice have fixed a fairly stable range in the ratio between annual income and house costs. According to the credit directors of seven major Detroit banks and the local FHA office, sound financing would generally limit house cost to twice annual income. But as annual income rises and individual resources warrant, this ratio may be allowed to reach 1 to 1½. In the discretionary judgment of loaning officials, highly unusual cases may be permitted to reach 1 to 3. Under no circumstances do bankers advise a higher ratio.[9]

Rosow's study shows that the effect of financing policy was to put a premium on prudence and conservatism. "Traditional homes are standard market commodities whose resale value is stable and predictable within the given market situation. Bankers and FHA officials have felt insecure about the resale possibilities of a modern house."[10] The uncertainties of the situation were nowhere so clearly shown as in the dilemma of architectural schools.

Put yourself in my place; it's such a responsibility, I assure you, to prepare these young men for the world they will enter when they leave college. If I emphasize the Modern too much, where will they find employment? Most of the architectural firms, and the largest ones, are still doing period or eclectic work. If I stress too much the period style, what will become of them if everyone does Modern tomorrow?[11]

This is, of course, what Wright would call miseducation.

Irving Rosow's thesis, "Modern Architecture and Social Change," compared a number of clients commissioning new homes during the 1940s.[12] He sampled thirty-three households, twenty of which were classified as modern clients and thirteen as semimodern (these were largely traditional homes with superficial modern features). He found the modern clients to be better educated, in professions rather than in business, to have more interests and leisure activities, to be more active in political or community service, and most significantly, to have a professional or working wife. Rosow's study confirms the observations of Parsons and Ogburn, on the pattern of acceptance of change and social trend, which is not at all surprising.

The clearest comparison that can be made between Wright's domestic design and other housing of the period was provided by a popular journal. In September 1938, *Life* magazine presented a feature entitled, "Eight Houses Especially Designed by Famous American Architects."[13] Pairs of houses appeared, one modern and the other traditional, for increasing income brackets. The architects included were Stone and Koch for the $2,000 to $3,000 range, Worster and Kelley for $3,000 to $4,000, Wright and Wills for $5,000 to $6,000, and Harrison & Fouilhoux and Embury for $10,000 to $12,000. The styles represented varied from Cape Cod saltbox to colonial to full curved-corner international style. Significantly, where the other architects merely addressed themselves to satisfying the requirements of the clients selected by *Life,* Wright accompanied his designs for the Blackbourns with a letter explaining their purpose and initiating a dialogue with his client. Readers could write to *Life* requesting a knock-down cardboard model of the house of their choice. Wright's contribution in *Life* was seen by Bernard Schwartz and is similar to the house he built in Two Rivers, Wisconsin. It used Usonian construction, efficient planning, and small bedrooms to provide a spacious and varied livingroom, with loggia and swimming pool.

As the Depression eased into the war boom, and again after the war, home building picked up and more modern houses were built. The postwar public was ready for change and welcomed the more efficient planning that modern houses provided. Single-story houses making optimal use of the surrounding site became popular. The family patio rather than the porch, cleanly planned and detailed kitchens, carports, dens, rumpus rooms and the open plan all entered the general imagination. Emphasis was on immediate family life rather than the remote, tuxedo-clad lifestyle projected by the escapist movies of the thirties.

It would be idle to speculate on Wright's hand in all this. Certainly his own attitude toward Usonian innovations would render such speculation unrewarding. Like Jefferson, who anonymously published his own inventions, Wright never attempted to patent the carport, the cantilever toilet, or any of his other architectural innovations. A study of postwar home-building magazines merely chronicles their greater acceptance. Such a book as *Tomorrow's House,* written by George Nelson and Henry Wright in 1945, demonstrates attitudes that Wright would have approved of, in addition to using photographs of his designs to illustrate them.[14] The "great tradition" of the home was reviewed as a technical, social, and psychological fact, and its sections were organized to test this proposition. Activity areas were analyzed in terms of their performance: dining and entertainment, the work center (Wright's kitchen), bathrooms, organized storage, and "sound conditioning." Even if its form was debased into the ranch house, the Usonian concept entered the American subconscious. Wright's response was to try to lift the level of awareness, to propagate the sense of space that he had found described by Lao-Tse,

and to show people how they could make their homes more natural.

The Small House Amidst Rising Prices

As postwar home construction gathered pace, it also became more constrained. Regulatory agencies grew in number, zoning laws became tighter, and union power and practice became more restrictive. Prices rose, but Wright was deluged with work. He was a personal celebrity and *The Fountainhead* whose architect-hero was based on a thinly disguised life of Wright was a best-selling novel.[15] In commissioning a Wright house, you were no longer "going against conventional social wisdom," to use Stanley Rosenbaum's phrase.[16] The clients were increasingly not Parsons' "deviates," but established middle class citizens availing themselves of a proven artifact.

The Usonian home became more akin to a consumer durable. One client admitted "I wanted one of the old boy's masterpieces before he died. I figured it couldn't help go up in value after his death — like an art work."[17] This is not to slight those clients who had "chosen Wright for their faith." It is merely to say that the situation had changed. Wright himself always gave exacting and personal attention to his clients, but they were more likely to get, indeed to request, a variation on a published or cancelled previous project.[18] Those most likely to inspire him in his old, but incisive, age were those for whom the building would be a financial sacrifice, a continuing lifetime project, or a personal building activity.

Do-It-Yourself

The degree of owner participation in building Wright's houses varied. Herbert Jacobs built the joinery in his first home and was both contractor and superviser for his second. Carl Wall, in Plymouth, Michigan, in 1941, designed and fitted out his basement and installed electrical wiring. This was a

140

common do-it-yourself activity. Engineers, like Dudley Spencer in Wilmington, Delaware, in 1956, designed and made their own steelwork; Spencer even built his home with the aid of a gang from the local penitentiary.[19] The Berger, Grant, and Loveness homes were all built from the ground up by their owners. Although these were all beautifully made, some other do-it-yourself projects, especially some concrete block houses, were badly built. Mrs. Grant described her experiences engagingly in the journal *Northwest Architect.*[20]

The Grants bought their site in Cedar Rapids, Iowa, during the Depression, contacted Wright in 1945, and started work a year later. They went to him because of the fine limestone available on the site and because they thought that Wright was the architect to help them best use it. The house is inserted easily into a slope under a sweeping 127-ft-long roof. The interior is, in effect, a series of events upon the contours. They are connected by a flowing walkway, "one of the grandest and most dramatic stairways ever invented, straight as an arrow between two steeply rising walls of stone, for over forty feet."[21] The Grants first dug, then blasted the stone with rented equipment and evolved a method of laying it up in boxes, with concrete to the rear, in a way not dissimilar to that used by the Nearings in Vermont.[22] The walls incorporate an air gap and are faced in stone on both sides, giving a "tweedy" effect. Mrs. Grant described her husband, who worked for local radio and television, as "contractor, carpenter, electrician, quarry worker, stone mason, ditch digger and any other task that came along."[23] She herself was taken for an employed worker by visiting architectural students while she was arc-welding high in the scaffolding. After 9 years of building they still looked forward to making extra furniture and working outside.

Bob and Gloria Berger knew that they could not afford a normal Wright house

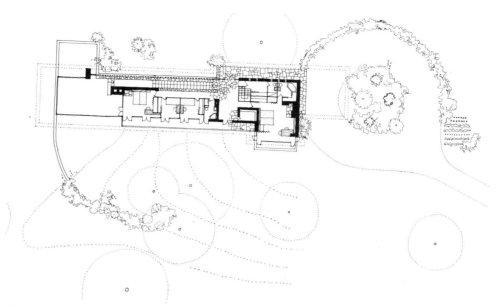

The Grant house, upper floor plan, Cedar Rapids, Iowa, 1945. The limestone stair runs down the contours to a double-height livingroom; the end bedroom gallery overlooks this.

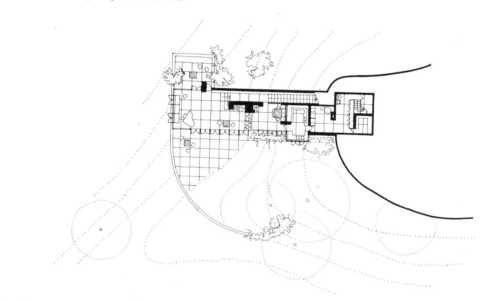

The Grant house lower floor plan shows that the livingroom leads directly out to terraces on the slope.

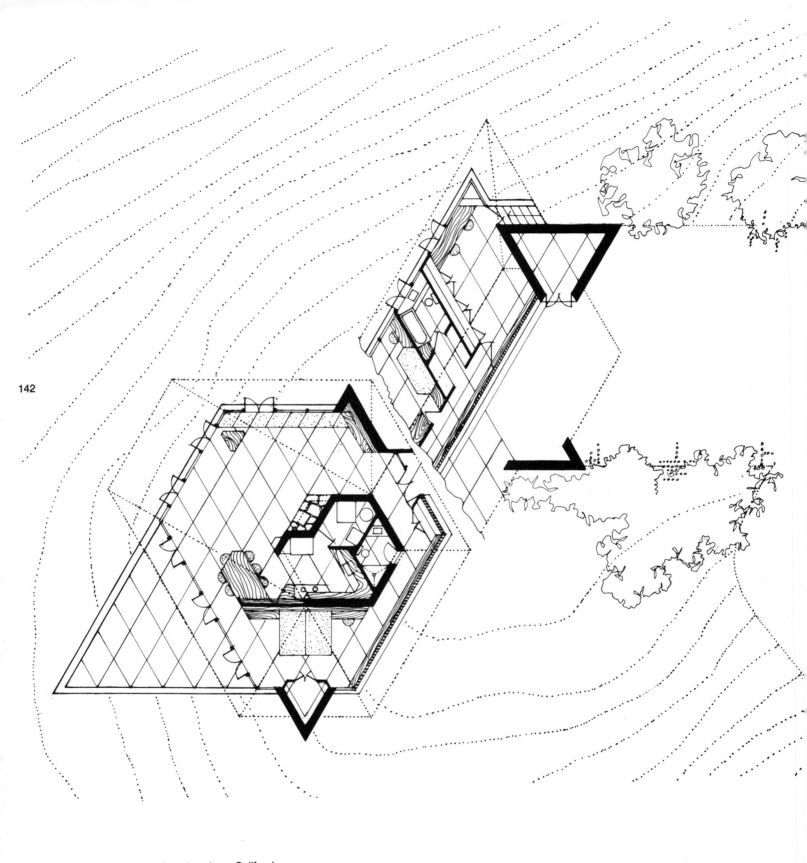

The Berger house, San Anselmo, California, 1950. Wright designed this house to be built by its owners in stages.

All joinery in the Berger house is beautifully made in mahogany.

The masonry in the Berger house is desert concrete.

for their site in San Anselmo, north of San Francisco. They were therefore surprised to find that their circumstances interested him for the fee involved. In fact, Wright felt tested enough to produce a design that was not only exactly what their program of building required, but which amounted to an archetypal statement of the do-it-yourself Usonian. The house was planned hexagonally, on a diamond module, to be built in stages. The first, and key, element at the center of the design was the service core. This, like all the masonry, was built of desert concrete,[24] and contained fireplace, kitchen, utilities, and bathroom. At this stage the Berger family could live on site in tents if they wished.

Stage two in the building process involved surrounding the core with the beautiful living area. This took the form of a tepee and placed the core off-center, causing an asymmetrical division of the space — encouraging continuously varied use and uniquely including the parents' bedroom. At this point the great built-in seats could provide beds for the three children. The last stage, the children's wing, or the tail of the polliwog, contained a second bathroom, a bedroom, and a playroom. It would have been possible, however, to build the masonry workshop earlier if necessary. The workshop terminates the plan and supports one side of the carport. The house is immaculately built. The lumber is solid mahogany throughout and put together with a sense for the material, its grain, and figure, which is of the order of traditional Japanese architecture.[25]

Berger had trained as an engineer, but taught high school and night school during the period of building, so that work on the house was confined to weekends and vacations. It took over 17 years to complete, from 1950 to 1969. During this time his wife raised the family and budgeted the money to continually buy building materials. She even sold her set of Spode dishes to buy concrete.[26] A retaining wall of des-

144

The Adelman house, exterior, Scottsdale, Arizona, 1953. Usonian automatic construction.

ert concrete on the lower road announces a house that, even for Wright, grows in a peculiarly inevitable way from the ground in which it is set. The interior, floating inexplicably in the trees, is a revelation.

The Usonian Automatic

In the early 1950s Wright revived his textile block building system of the 1920s in an effort to simplify construction for the self-builder and to circumvent the unions. A metal mold could be used to cast hollow concrete blocks. These were formed with grooves around their edges so that they could be threaded into a mesh of light, reinforcing steel bars. In one operation a final finish was formed — the system working like giant children's building blocks. It could span openings, contain servicing, and incorporate glass. Wright called it the "Usonian Automatic." The best-known example of this was the Adelman house near Phoenix Arizona, built in 1953 for $25,000 and published in *The Natural House.*[27]

However, eight self-build houses in Galesburg and Parkwyn Villages, near Kalamazoo, Michigan, preceded it in 1951, and numerous others of increasing expense followed, such as the Tonkens house built in 1954 near Cincinnati, Ohio,[28] and the Turkel house built in 1955 in Detroit, Michigan. Wright stated his intentions in an address to the Detroit chapter of the American Institute of Architects (AIA) on May 27, 1954. He was asked: "What do you have to offer those people who . . . have only $15,000 to invest and who believe in you and need you?" Wright answered:

I have given it to him and he doesn't know it . . . in what I call the Usonian Automatic, where the union has been eliminated; where masonry at $29.00 a day is out; where there are no plasterers at the same rate; where there are no carpenters at all. It is a block house. I did it for the G.I.'s. The G.I. can go in his back road . . . he's got sand there . . . get himself some steel rods and cement, make the blocks, and put the blocks together . . . I have done that

The McCartney house, Parkwyn Village, Kalamazoo, Michigan, 1951.

thing . . . you can build your own house!"[29]

The block system was usually planned on a 2 by 4 ft module, although this varied. In those homes with little or no wood trim, the house was somewhat utilitarian in appearance. However, in such examples as the McCartney house of 1951 in Parkwyn Village, Michigan, with wooden shelving and hardwood-faced plywood ceilings there is a fine contrast with the regular blockwork. However, the cost exceeded $25,000 unless those houses were owner built. Great care had to be taken in construction to ensure that block joints occurred on module, otherwise an incremental error soon built up, and the necessary fine tolerance was difficult to achieve in homemade blocks. Wright continued to use blockwork in such fine designs as the Adelman House of 1948 at Fox Point, Wisconsin, and the Wilson house of 1954 in Millstone, New Jersey. For his son David, who ran a con-

crete block-making company, he designed the virtuoso spiral ramped house in Phoenix, Arizona, in 1952. However these last houses were conventional, unreinforced blockwork.

Prefabricated Houses

In 1951 Wright built the Raymond Carlson house in Phoenix, Arizona, for the editor of *Arizona Highways.*[30] This design made use of wood frame and panel construction, reminiscent of the earlier project for the all-steel houses for Los Angeles in 1937. He claimed a construction cost of only $16,000. Prefabricated construction was familiar to Wright. The designs for the American system ready-cut houses of 1911 were realized in a number of locations.[31]

In the last decade of his life he returned to standardized techniques in order to lower costs. Between 1956 and 1958 he designed four types of prefabricated homes, which were manufactured by the Marshall Erdman Company in Madison, Wisconsin. The first was heralded in *House and Home*.[32] It contrived to obtain a horizontal Usonian appearance from externally boarded studwork panels. The later types used synthetic fiber wall panels and concrete blockwork, and could be varied to suit individual needs by rearranging standard modular elements. The perspective of an interior in *The Living City* shows the second of these, a two-story "one-room" house.[33] According to Erdman, although at least twenty prefabs were built in a number of states, shipping and assembling doubled costs, and final prices were in the $30,000 to $50,000 range.[34] Thus the late prefabs failed to realize a new, low cost version of the small Usonians.

Self-Build Methods

Most of Wright's clients were from what he called the "middle third of American life." He claimed, "I wouldn't build for the rich and I don't build for the poor."[35] If he was under no illusions that one-third of the population could afford his services, or indeed any house, Wright did have a program for them. He was not confident that this could be achieved without the Broadacre City reforms, but he was clear as to the method.

The poor man? Yes. . . . Usually he is now wage-slave at some machine. . . . He ought to be able soon, *even as things are,* to buy a standardized privy, cheap. That "privy" civilized is now a bathroom, manufactured complete and delivered to him as a single unit (his car or his refrigerator the same as the privy) all ready to use when connected to the city water system and a fifteen dollar septic tank or a forty dollar cesspool. *Well advised,* he will plant this first unit wherever it belongs to start his home. The other necessary units similarly cheap; bedrooms designed for beneficial living added. As months go by, the rent he saved may buy other standardized units; a comfortable living-room and as many more bedrooms as he needs.[36]

According to Wright's plan for Broadacre City, such good advice would come, most likely, from the local experiment station or county architect, by televised "fireside chat."

These and other well designed prerequisites may be added as soon as he earns them by his work or the work of his family, in nearby agriculture, crafts, or mechanized industries. His family, meanwhile, are helping to maintain themselves free on their own ground.[37]

The economic situation has evolved, as Wright sees it, from "even as things are" into one of Gesellian free land and free money. The technical idea behind this is older and has an architectural pedigree. Like other architects of the modern movement, Wright assumed the imminent arrival of cheap, mass-produced service elements. The nearest any designer came to this was his friend, Buckminster Fuller, in his second Dymaxion house at Wichita, Kansas, which lost both him and the Beech Aircraft Company much effort and money.[38] In 1932, Wright spelled out his intentions more clearly, in a speech to the convention of the National Association of Real Estate Boards, when he used the analogy of the Model T Ford.

I shall call the thing the "assembled house". . . . Now in working out this "assembled house" we already have the bathroom as a single unit to draw upon. We will call it Unit number one. . . . Now, your kitchen has been worked out in many different ways. I think there are at least five now available where you can get a complete, and more practical, and more beautiful kitchen than almost any architect could design himself. Unit number two. And in connection with that unit you have the heating of the house . . . all that needs is a single connection, screwing it up and putting it together. The appurtenance systems in any house are more than one-third of the cost of the house. As the cost of building comes down, the proportion rises. . . . The bedroom unit can be in various sizes: it can be assembled in various ways with other units. Then we can have a living room unit of two or three sizes. In fact, all the features which are characteristic of modern life . . . we can now buy on some standardized scheme of arrangement. Those can be laid out on a unit system so that they all come together in an organic style, and the design of these things in the first place can be of such a character that in the

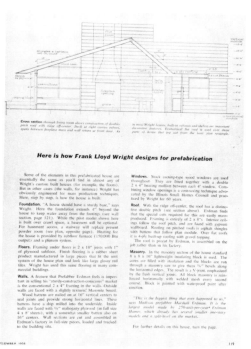

The Erdman prefab shows the studwork, boarded component wall unit.

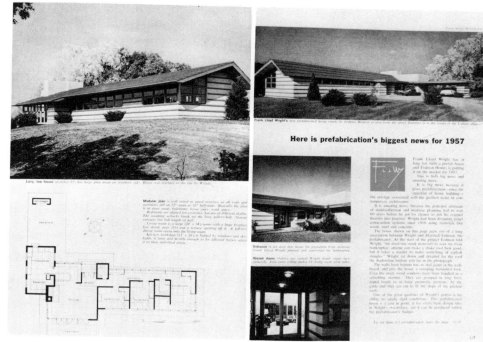

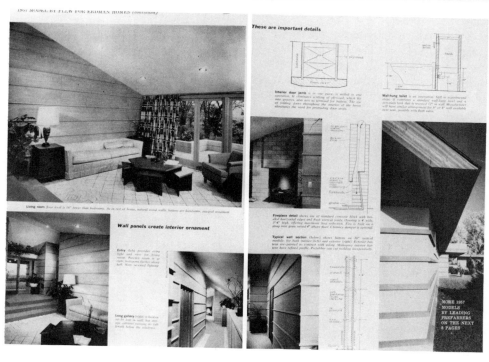

(*House and Home,* December 1956, pp. 117 – 121.)

final assembly no wrong or bad thing can happen.[39]

In the same speech Wright went on to describe the minimal three-unit house and the knock-down metal construction he envisaged. His house assembler "will not have to encourage the mortgage banker to quite such an extent. As his means grow and his family grows, his house can grow."

Popularizing by Magazine

In the celebrated editions of *Architectural Forum* of January 1938 and 1948, Wright confronted his profession with a grand slam of renewed activity. He demonstrated a new tradition for the American dwelling within the broad sweep of Usonian design, which included the Administration Building for the Johnson Wax Company, built between 1936 and 1939, at Racine, Wisconsin, and other designs for public buildings. A Usonian dwelling was formulated for the varied conditions of continental climate. There was a house of the north, a house called "Below Zero," a desert house, and a house for the Texas prairie. In the 1950s *House Beautiful* took up his work, and published it in color. It was possible for Wright to reach a predominatly female public with sophisticated and individual ideas about homemaking and communicate to them the total experience of the organic home (so far as this is possible through photographs and drawings). Color plates caught the tones and texture of materials and the quality of interior light. Both *Architectural Forum* and *House Beautiful* published periodic collections of houses — for the most part spectacular solutions to local site conditions — for example, a home by the Pacific with the prow of a boat to shatter the surf from storms, or homes dug into hillsides and buried in woods.

House and Home was by contrast a more hard-headed proposition. It was a "magazine for homebuilders" but contained sections on real estate development, mortgages, and FHA financing. In the early 1950s it addressed itself to the entrepreneurial builder and his market. It provided clear evidence that Ogburn's theory of "diffusion" and Wright's use of it worked.

In March 1958, *House and Home* surveyed homebuilding in Oskaloosa, Iowa. They found that "here everybody's trading up . . . seven out of ten new houses are built because people want better housing, not because they need shelter. . . . Here trade-up works like a game of musical chairs — each new house means a better old house for someone else."[40] Two Wright houses that were completed in 1951 in Oskaloosa, one for Carrol Alsop and the other for Jack Lamberson, were viewed by over 9,000 people. The article stated that "more than a third of the visitors went back for a second look and what they saw started a home-building revolution in Oskaloosa." Because people had experienced homes that fulfilled many of their unarticulated dissatisfactions with traditional houses, they were fired by a new conception of "home." "I'm not afraid to build a 'different-looking' house now," everybody said. The survey found that more than 40 percent of the new houses built since 1951 broke with conventional design.

"What really impressed us was how you can put a house on the rolling hills around here," says one new-house owner who insisted his new house be designed to snuggle into its hillside site just as the Wright houses do. "I don't think any of us realized that we were literally shaving off the beauty of our town by grading down the sites."[41]

(*House and Home,* March 1958, pp. 90–104.)

Frank Lloyd Wright midcentury prairie house built in Oskaloosa, 1951

On the rolling prairie...

OSKALOOSA, IOWA

...Here everybody's trading up

...Here 7 out of 10 new houses are built because people want better houses, not because they need shelter

...Here trade-up works like a game of musical chairs — each new house means a better old house for someone else

...Here in Oskaloosa new houses like the one above helped set off a chain reaction that is still going on.

They sparked a demand for better housing in a community where there was no shortage of adequate housing.

Better new houses often inspired the remodeling of older houses and started a series of family trade-ups, each move better than the last.

In Oskaloosa 443 new houses have been built in the last 11 years. They dot the seven new "additions" in the town and stand across the boxwood hedges from their older neighbors along the maple- and elm-lined avenues leading out from the business center.

These new houses have prompted over 900 trading-up moves and are indirectly responsible for the 135 bottom-of-the-heap houses now slated for demolition.

Why did Oskaloosans want *better* houses? And what does a *better* house mean? The answers come from 310 families who told House & Home why they bought a new house and from 591 families who gave their reasons for moving up to better older houses.

For these answers, turn the page

In Oskaloosa...   GEORGE JOHNSON

FIRST FLLW HOUSE looks like "a ship riding the waves," Oskaloosans say in describing way house sits on hillside among alfalfa fields.

People trade up because they see houses like these

Over 9,000 people trekked out to look at these two Frank Lloyd Wright custom houses when they were built in 1951. Even though they were private homes—and not builders' models—more than a third of the visitors went back for a second look and what they saw started a homebuilding revolution in Oskaloosa.

"I'm not afraid to build a 'different-looking' house now," everybody said. And they meant it. More than 40% of the new houses built since 1951 "break with conventional design." As one new owner put it: "We didn't worry about what the neighbors would say—they ended up by liking our house."

"What really impressed us was how you can put a house on the rolling hills around here," says one new-house owner who insisted his new house be designed to snuggle into its hillside site just as the Wright houses do. "I don't think any of us realized that we were literally shaving off the beauty of our town by grading down the sites."

What else did Oskaloosans find in the Wright houses? "Intrinsic value—something so important it can't be measured," says their builder Jim DeReus. "People who came out of curiosity went home with a longing: they, too, wanted a house with all that the word stands for."

SECOND FLLW HOUSE has "enough ideas in it to inspire 50 other houses." Old house (left) was bought by another family trading up.

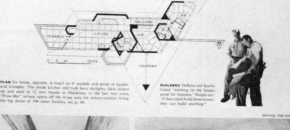

PLAN for house, opposite, is based on 4' module and series of equilateral triangles. The inside kitchen and bath have skylights, ideas picked up and used in 12 new houses in Oskaloosa in the last two years. "Prow-like" terrace opens off the living area for indoor-outdoor living, the big desire of 306 other families, see p. 98.

BUILDERS DeReus and Sparks found "working on the houses good for business." People say: "if they could build those houses, they can build anything!"

PHOTOS: THE IOWAN

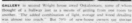

GALLERY in second Wright house awed Oskaloosans, some of whom thought of a hallway just as a means of getting from one room to another. The added combination of light, storage and wood detailing was almost too much. But 70% of new-home owners say similar halls and passageways in their new houses were inspired by ideas like this.

LIVING ROOM of same house impressed Oskaloosans with its sweeping ceiling lines, mammoth brick fireplace, built-in seating. Almost all families with growing children (see p. 102) say they built to get built-ins because "there's nothing to get out of line and the house always looks presentable."

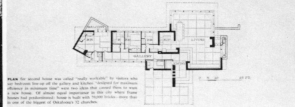
PLAN for second house was called "really workable" by visitors who say bedroom line-up off the gallery and kitchen "designed for maximum efficiency in minimum time" were two ideas that caused them to want a new house. Of almost equal importance in this city where frame houses had predominated: house is built with 70,000 bricks—more than in one of the biggest of Oskaloosa's 32 churches.

A ROOM WITH A VIEW worth looking at symbolizes one family's trade-up from old house to new house (see below).

People trade up because they want something new

PHOTOS: HAH STAFF

DESIRE FOR LIGHT, air and privacy helped to sway one family toward a new house. Their older home was too small, too close to neighbors. New house has view from every side to rolling hills and shade trees. Fireplace in living room (top) also serves screened-in patio. "The new house soothes all our wants," owners say. "The children's rooms are light and sunny and they've got more room to move around in." Children can play in family room without disturbing parents in living room. Architect: Wm. Nielson; Builder: Sparks.

"My old kitchen had everything wrong—too many corners, too poorly lighted, too little storage too high or too low." The old house was dingy, drafty and dark. We wanted more light, an open plan and a weather-tight house."

"I was so tired of clutter. We wanted lots of built-ins."

Eighty Oskaloosa families (owners of 18% of the new houses) give reasons like these to explain why, when they wanted something new, they decided to build everything new. What did Oskaloosans want to see changed?

Thirty-nine families ranked the kitchen first and every Oskaloosa builder agrees that it's the most important room in the house today—judging from attention buyers give it. Sixteen families wanted more and better bathrooms. "We are a 1½ to 2 bath-per-house town," says builder Jim Sedrel, "and new-house buyers are really specific about what they want. They want more colored tile and plumbing fixtures, linen storage under counter or on the wall."

Fifteen families call built-ins "the most important single thing in the house," and say that "once we knew we wanted built-ins we found other things we'd change so we decided on a brand-new house."

Ten families found their old houses too awkward in plan. "By the time we knocked out partitions and opened up rooms remodeling would cost as much as the new house—so why not have the new house?"

DESIRE FOR UP-TO-DATE KITCHEN in up-to-date house caused one family to switch from rented house (like rental units in picture left) to a new house. Brick wall at right backs living-room fireplace, includes a built-in barbecue on kitchen side. Oven, under-counter dishwasher, 4-burner cook tops are all built-in, so are wall storage cabinets. Ceiling has exposed mahogany beams. Adjoining breakfast room, which opens out to a patio has built-in benches, ceiling-high windows. Architect: Carl Winkler; Builder: McKee-Fansher Co.

PHOTOS: HAH STAFF   THE IOWAN

DESIRE FOR PLANNED PRIVACY helped to spark this trade-up. New house gave owners a zoned plan with clear separation of living, entertaining and sleeping areas—all on one floor. Parents' bedroom has its own private bath-dressing area, its own view with windows placed high enough to allow varied furniture arrangements. Baths for both parents and children in this house are compartmented to avoid clutter and crowding. Family room—non-existent in older house—opens to playyard. Architect: Gerald Watland; Builder: McKey-Fansher Co.

PHOTOS: HAH STAFF   OSKALOOSA DAILY HERALD

DESIRE FOR BUILT-INS helped prompt this family's trade-up from rented house (now vacant) to new house. Built-in wall in living room houses TV, hooks, has sliding storage cases underneath which allows family to store more items in less space than in older house. Some seating in living room is also built-in. House, although custom built, was opened for inspection during one week in winter and 1500 people went through it. "If it had been built in summer, probably 3,000 people would have come," says the builder, Jim Sedrel.

150

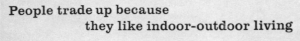

OUTDOOR ENTERTAINING in new houses takes place on suspended deck off family room. House sits in glade, has view of trees and pond.

People trade up because they like indoor-outdoor living

PHOTOS: HAH STAFF

PLAN of new house opens family room and living room to the outdoors. Architect: George Russell; Builder: Sparks Construction Co. Old house (above plan) concentrated most of its outdoor living on front porch, as many older houses here still do.

Three hundred and six families consider indoor-outdoor living of such prime importance that it is often mentioned even when another reason is given for trading up to the new house. (So the desire for indoor-outdoor living is a factor in 69% of the new houses built.)

What makes indoor-outdoor living so important in Oskaloosa? "The old 60' x 120' lots we lived on before new developments were opened up," many families say. "There was no room outdoors and no privacy. Without privacy, there's really no such thing as indoor-outdoor living."

One new owner says: "We bought a house with an acre of land and we feel as though we've got an acre of house, too, because we've got room outdoors to move around in. That's how important it is to us."

House planning enters the picture, too, say Oskaloowans. "Our old house had a fair-sized front lawn and only enough room to hang out the clothes in the back. Our new house stretches out and leaves plenty of room in back."

Many new house buyers came from apartments and one of these families said: "You can't imagine how it felt to get a new house with a nice big patio out back. We are outside whenever weather permits and we have twice as much company as before because we can entertain outdoors without fear of disturbing anyone else."

Outdoor living became twice as important after the two FLLW houses were built. "Those houses did more to make people want something better than anything that ever happened in this town," says Realtor Walter Reasoner.

OLD HOUSE has less space for the kind of activities family wanted: room to garden, privacy to entertain. New house (above and right) is well back from street, has plenty of space for a picnic table, flagged terrace, flowers. Architect: Gerald Watland; Builder: McKey-Fansher.

GEORGE JOHNSON   GEORGE JOHNSON

105-YEAR-OLD HOUSE (above) uses outdoors merely as a handsome setting. New house (right and below) uses the outdoors "as another room" and gives owners extra space, extra view. Stone fireplace was on lot; house was built onto it. Architect: Aaron Emery; Builder: Sparks.

In Oskaloosa...

PHOTOS: H&H STAFF

GOOD HOUSEKEEPING magazine house inspired real-life house in Oskaloosa. Owners got help of Des Moines architect George Russell in adapting plan to their needs. Since children no longer live at home, second story was left as attic space. Builders: McKey-Fansher Co.

People trade up because they get ideas from magazines

"The minute we saw this magazine house we decided to build," reports the owner of the barn-red house above. "Our older house was too large for two, but the magazine house looked just about right. We saw the house in the January '56 issue of *Good Housekeeping*, moved into our version of it that fall."

That's how 39 families traded up in Oskaloosa. Each told H&H that a magazine inspired their new home. (This accounts for 9% of the houses built.)

One typical case-study family explained the trade-up this way: "There are five in our family and we were completely happy in our older house. But one day we saw a house plan in a magazine that seemed to change our whole outlook. Before we knew it we were making plans of our own—for the new house. We think we gained a lot. Thanks to the magazine house we've got a built-in hi-fi, my husband has a workshop and most important, we gained a fourth bedroom."

Another Oskaloosan is so sold on the good ideas he finds in magazines houses that he says: "We built our house in 1951 from a picture in a magazine and now that our kids are married I'm getting that old feeling again. I'm looking over magazines to find a house that's just a little smaller . . . perhaps a house with no basement but with a large utility room."

MAGAZINE HOUSE started a chain reaction of trading up in town. When banker and his wife moved from 11-room house (1) into magazine-inspired house (top), lawyer and his family left their smaller house (2) and traded-up to 11-roomer. Druggist and family moved up to house 2 from rented house (3), and rented house was re-occupied by original owners, railroad employee and wife who had been living in Illinois.

100

The *House and Home* survey also found that

The 443 houses built since 1947 were not built to meet a shortage (there was practically no doubling up) nor to house a growing population (according to Federal Census estimates, population in 1957 was only 100 more than 1950's 11,024). The 443 houses were built to satisfy what Lumber Dealer Porter calls "the urge for the best."[42]

The Wright houses started a chain reaction of "trading up," causing new homes to be built, old homes to be exchanged, and "bottom-of-the-heap" homes to be demolished. The new houses were, according to the survey, "very different from their neighbors. Almost all are one-story ranches with open plans and outdoor patios. They include built-ins in kitchens, baths, and living rooms: they cut down on steps and are easy to heat and cool." And the survey summarized why Oskaloosans traded up. They did so, according to the report, because "they see houses like these [the Wright exemplars], because they want something new, they like indoor-outdoor living, *they get ideas from magazines,* because neighborhoods change, families get bigger, children grow up, and because they are moving up."

A follow-up article on Oskaloosa articulated the builder's point of view. In the February 1959 *House and Home,* builder Jim de Reuss told readers "What We Learned from Frank Lloyd Wright": "Before we built our first Wright house, you couldn't have sold a slab house or contemporary styling or walls of glass in Oskaloosa, people were afraid to be different. They were also afraid their builders couldn't build anything new or different without running up costs."[43]

He found that building for Wright taught him and his crew that good craftsmanship was what good building was all about. "A builder must believe that; otherwise his work doesn't have much meaning." And he found the Wright house good for business. "People say, 'if they could build those houses,

151

About the story
that begins
on the opposite page:

This is a story about a house that changed a town.

The town is Oskaloosa, Iowa; the house is a Frank Lloyd Wright house. The town was conservative; the house was not—and the house started a homebuilding revolution.

It sparked a demand for better new houses and started a series of trading-up moves to better older houses. That part of the story was reported in March 1958.

This part of the story is about the local builder who worked on the Frank Lloyd Wright house, and his account (as told to Associate Editor Kathryn Morgan-Ryan) of what he and his crew learned on the job.

The builder's name is Jim De Reus. He first began to study the work of Frank Lloyd Wright when he was an architectural engineering student at Iowa State College. After college De Reus came to Oskaloosa and got a job as carpenter with the Sparks Construction Co. He worked his way up from carpenter to partner in the firm.

Not long after De Reus was made a partner he heard that a local merchant was having a new house designed for himself and his family. The architect: Frank Lloyd Wright.

De Reus wasted no time going after the building contract. "It meant a lot to me," he said. "How often does a small town builder get a chance like this?"

Jim De Reus got his chance—and the contract. Although he did not

LIFE: Alfred Eisenstaedt

FRANK LLOYD WRIGHT

know it then, this was the start of the homebuilding revolution in Oskaloosa.

"Before we built our first Wright house you couldn't have sold a slab house or contemporary styling or walls of glass in Oskaloosa," says Jim De Reus. "People were afraid to be different. They were also afraid their

builders couldn't build anything new or different without running up costs."

That attitude doesn't exist any more in Oskaloosa. There are still plenty of big, old two-story houses with wide front porches and graceful, tree-sheltered lawns. But there are also plenty

of new, architect-designed slab houses, with contemporary styling and walls of glass.

Oskaloosans aren't afraid to be different any more; and they aren't afraid to trust local builders with their new houses. They've found out that men like Jim De Reus can build modern houses with modern methods and still keep prices down.

Because of this new attitude in town, Jim De Reus is busy all year round. His company does a yearly gross volume of from $200,000 to $400,000 and he has a staff of about 20 men. They build about ten houses a year, usually two or three on spec, the rest on contract. They take some trade-ins, and also do a lot of remodeling work. That's because all the older houses are constantly being upgraded to keep pace with their newer neighbors.

The architect who started the home building revolution in Oskaloosa and the builder who helped keep it going have never met. The construction of this house (and a second FLLW house built the same year) was supervised by John deKoven Hill, now editorial director of *House Beautiful*, then an assistant to Mr Wright in Wisconsin.

But Jim De Reus attributes much of his success today to what he learned from Frank Lloyd Wright. "His houses taught me that good handcrafted work is what good building is all about," says De Reus. "A builder must believe his work can't have much meaning."

Let Jim De Reus continue his story . . .

Hedrich-Blessing

"THE CREW AND I are proud of this Frank Lloyd Wright house. Here we are on the gravel court leading up to the entrance. That's me in front. Behind me, from left to right: three masons, tender, concrete finisher, driver, apprentice, and three carpenters."

Builder Jim De Reus tells you:

"What we learned from Frank Lloyd Wright"

"The minute I saw the blueprints I knew that we were in for a completely new experience—new for us and new for our community. For the blueprints showed that:

"This was a new kind of house.

"This was a new way to site a house.

"This was a new way to build a house.

"The custom house that Mr. Wright designed and we built was different in every way from the kind of houses we had been building in Oskaloosa.

"When I was preparing my bid on the contract for this house and taking off quantities for my estimates, I figured that even if I didn't make a dime out of the job, the

experience for my crew and for me would be well worth it.

"Well, we got the contract, we didn't lose money, and we learned things no money could buy.

"For instance: We had built only one slab house before. We had never worked with so much glass before. We had never carpentered such intricate built-ins. We had never done such fine finishing work on walls, floors, and masonry.

"So this house was more than just another job to us. It was a lesson in the art of homebuilding. I think what we learned from this house has given us a new perspective on our jobs and on every house we have built since. I think every one of us is a better workman today because of this house."

continued

152

(*House and Home,* February 1959, pp. 126 – 133.)

"This new kind of house got us out of the rut of always building in the same old way"

"So we're not afraid to build differently any more.

1) "We found out how important the land is to the look of the house. We used to level our sites and bulldoze scenery right out of the way. But Mr Wright designed this house to suit its site. He didn't change the site to suit the house.

2) "We learned you cut costs by not having a basement. We pared excavation time and work down to almost nothing, and the owners of this house got more storage above ground than they ever could have got with a basement.

3) "We discovered the foundation for the house is about 20% cheaper and about 90% better than any other we'd seen. It's a simple trench—20" wide, 3½' deep. You put drain tile down the middle and fill up the trench with crushed rock. We used a certain amount of fines so the rock would stay firm. Then you pour a 9" reinforced pad on top of the rock —so the foundation is simply a 9" beam floating on a crushed rock sub base. With Mr Wright's trench, the moisture finds the tile so the foundation stays dry.

4) "We saw that the use of gravel for the motor court saved money, as compared to a conventional hard surface. It also gives you a better turn-around for cars, and I think the gravel drive makes the approach to the house a lot more inviting than rigid paving would."

"We learned it saves time to work in masses

5) "The house is divided into four distinct components: the slab, the masonry mass, the window mass, the roof mass [see detail, right]. You have only the men you need for each section on the job at any given time, which means the other trades can be off on other jobs. Here's how it works:

"My masons finished the slab and the brickwork, moved their equipment off the job and onto another. When they left, the rough carpenters moved in, set the structural mullions and put on the roof. Then they went on to another job. They were followed by the finish carpenters who did the interior work. We didn't tie up a single bit of equipment or a single man unnecessarily—and that certainly means as much to a builder like me as it does to a much bigger builder."

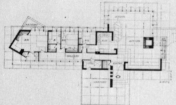

ROOF

SET-IN DOORS

STRIP WINDOWS

MASONRY WALLS

SLAB

153

they could build anything.'"[44] The article displays an understanding of the advantages of the planning and features of the Wright house—corner windows, cantilevered fireplace, and built-in furniture. It also shows an understanding of Wright's sequence of practical building in a remarkable way. De Reuss wrote, "Exposed materials let you eliminate trades and cut down on job time," however, "here everything is seen, so your crew has to do good work. Any mistake would show . . . better materials encouraged better handling. . . . Unusual techniques intrigued the crew. It's a challenge for a man to learn to do something differently." De Reuss discovered that "the foundation for the house is about 20% cheaper and 90% better than any we'd seen."[45] The job lost him no money, and he said, "we learned things money can't buy." In particular he found that there was a clear correlation between the design of the elements of the house and its construction.

The house is divided into four distinct components: the slab, the masonry mass, the window mass, the roof mass. You have only the men you need for each section on the job at any given time, which means the other trades can be off on other jobs. Here's how it works:

My masons finished off the slab and the brickwork, moved their equipment off the job and onto another. When they left the rough carpenters moved in, set the structural mullions, and put on the roof. Then they went on to another job. They were followed by the finish carpenters who did the interior work. We didn't tie up a single bit of equipment or a single man unnecessarily—and that certainly means as much to a builder like me as it does to a much bigger builder.[46]

Direct Instruction

A number of instructional articles appeared in *House and Home* during the mid-1950s aimed at disseminating the skills, indeed the secrets, of the organic home.[47] The most important of these articles, "This Rich and Rhythmic House Expresses 32 Simple and

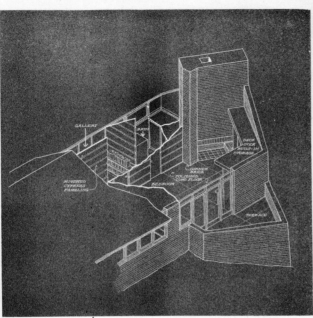

"**EVERY DETAIL** of the workmanship is always on view—brickwork, built-ins, paneling—so it must be right. There's no margin for error."

"This new kind of interior treatment brings out the best in your crew"

"In conventional building you can cover up mistakes with plaster, paper or paint. But here everything is seen, so your crew has to do good work. Any mistake would show.

1) "Better materials encouraged better handling. Materials like cypress and redwood, corner bricks and rectangular T's of glass just naturally encourage a crew to handle them more carefully. We all learned a lot about why Mr. Wright uses the materials he does, and it helped us understand and appreciate our work more. The brick, cypress and glass in this house all contributed to the spirit of the building. The brick gave it line and color; the cypress gave it tone and character; the glass gave it light and a feeling of airiness.

2) "Mitering took time and patience. A good carpenter needs both. I think it is a rather esthetic point that the carpenter is trying for when he miters. Maybe no one else will appreciate it, but he knows it is there. [See detail, right.]

3) "Solid partitions demanded skilled work. We milled ours in the shop which took time, but was worth the effort. You save room space because these partitions are only 2¼" thick, compared to 5½" with plaster, 4⅜" with drywall.

4) "Unusual techniques intrigued the crew. It's a challenge for a man to learn to do something differently. Mr Wright specified red cement for all vertical joints in the brickwork, white cement for the horizontal joints. At first the masons complained about using two mortar boards. Now they say brick houses two-years-old don't look new as this house."

Photos: Hedrich Blessing

"**MITERED CORNERS** give you a tighter fit and make the paneling look as though it is all out of the same wood mass. Each cut takes a lot of fitting. It took four cuts on the machine to get this paneling."

"**WOOD INTO PLASTER** gives a nice texture contrast. Casing trim was mitered just like the paneling and here the wood was handled differently to give wood contrasts. The door is hung on piano hinges."

© Ezra Stoller

"**POLISHED CONCRETE FLOOR** is integrally colored red. You must use care to get a uniform color and a smooth trowel job. We used a special sealer and hardener. Floor is marked with V joint."

"**CORNER BRICK** had to be specially made because the corners were 60° angles so we couldn't cut bricks. I got a mold made up so we could run the bricks as long as we needed."

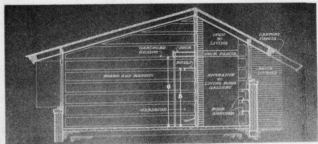

"**VERTICAL UNIT SYSTEM** is based on the number of brick courses and on the number of boards and battens. For instance, in the master bedroom, wardrobe height is based on six boards and battens, shelf on five. Once walls are up, carpenters don't have to measure; they simply position their work along board and batten or brick modules. Decks in house maintain room scale, despite pitched ceiling."   /END

155

Basic Design Ideas," gives an illustration of what the fireside chat of the Broadacre City county architect or experiment station's advice might have contained.[48] It communicates all the fundamental ingredients of house design and spatial skill that took Wright a lifetime to learn. The ideas are presented lucidly and are freely offered as advice.

The exemplar for the *House and Home* article was the Zimmerman house built in 1951 in Manchester, New Hampshire. "It was designed for a doctor and his wife, whose children have grown up and moved away. It is a cold-country house, farthest east of all Wright's houses."[49] The propositions that this house illustrates still have much to teach architects. The lessons into which the article is organized summarize hard-won advice: "To make a small house look bigger — inside and outside" and "To make a small house work better — inside and outside." The advice given includes such things as: "stress the horizontals" and "keep the roof line low"; or "the plate line here is 6'9". People are so used to higher walls they will assume the 6'9" is really 8' or more so the building must be longer." Pragmatic design is encouraged. "Don't waste a big overhang on the north, and don't feel you must use the same roof pitch on both sides."

The whole key to Wrightian interior space is revealed in the article: "Dramatize a high ceiling by emphasizing a below-standard 'ceiling' line to fool the eye. Use a dropped ceiling in the hall to make the living room ceiling higher by contrast." Surprise and time-scale can also give lyrical qualities: "Use a glass gable without an overhang to let the sun play changing patterns on the ceiling." A hint of the journey that led Wright to Lao-Tse is also reflected in the article: "Break up the open plan by letting it flow around corners, so you can't see all the dining area from the living room or all the open kitchen from the dining room." Practical planning and reduced work are encouraged: "Don't landscape the grounds for expensive maintenance. . . . Put everything in the kitchen within reach of the housewife. . . . Use natural materials that call for little maintenance."[50]

The Ubiquitous Influence of Organic Architecture

It did not matter that the *whole* message of Wright's popularizing activity was rarely communicated. North Americans all over a continent encountered it in one garbled form or another, through magazines and radio, often locally produced or syndicated, or by the example of a local Wrightian design. Advances were made, and the American home of the late 1950s and early 1960s does represent a distinct architectural achievement. Wright himself was carried along in a clamor of publicity. He needed no one so far as domestic clients were concerned, and indulged in such effrontery as informing the inhabitants of Chevy Chase, a fashionable suburb of Washington, D.C., that they lived in a "blighted area."

Beneath the need for adulation, however, ran a serious intent to demonstrate a better way of living for the mass of people. "There should be as many kinds of houses as there are kinds of people" was a liberating, anarchic proposal. It meant that people might perhaps express themselves directly, without an architect. The implication was that architecture might be best advanced by educated laypeople, rather than by professionals operating in their behalf. Certainly decentralization would generate few large, complex buildings, and this would tend to subvert the profession. The traditional architect's role might become more experimental and advisory. With greater awareness and education, people would express *themselves* out of their direct need and the means and site at hand. Such expression might scorn superficial outside influence. A house might be "a poor thing but my own."[51] In other words, it might be organic, even though the result might differ considerably from organic architecture as designed by Wright. Such an attitude leads to a way of building that fulfills all that Wright meant by organic, while resulting in a radically different built form.

(*House and Home,* September 1956, pp. 136–141.)

156

Ezra Stoller

This rich and rhythmic house expresses 32 simple and basic design ideas

This is the Zimmerman house in Manchester, N. H., built on a one-acre lot in 1951. It was designed for a doctor and his wife, whose children have grown up and moved away. It is a cold-country house, farthest east of all Wright's houses.

At first glance, it belongs to Wright's prairie period, but it reflects the continuing evolution of the architect's thought, with many features not found in his early work—like the inside kitchen; the asymmetrical roof pitch; and the large sheets of glass (instead of his earlier mosaic of small panes to break up the reflection on the glass).

As you can see, this house is a lot more than the sum of its ideas, but each idea is worth remembering.

of Frank Lloyd Wright

LIFE—Alfred Eisenstaedt

To make a small house look **bigger—outside**

1 Stress the horizontals. (a) Stretch the roof line. *This 1,547 sq. ft. house has a 2,917 sq. ft. tile roof.* (b) Keep the fascia in one straight line, except for a good reason. *The little line at the dear corner (c) is needed to let light reach the gable and window (see 10).* (d) Define a strong middle line. *Wright used a horizontal strip of white concrete block to carry your eye along the house length.*

2 (a) Don't waste a big overhang on the north, and (b) don't feel you must use the same roof pitch on both sides. *On the south, the big overhang needed a low pitch, but the living room inside needed a high ceiling. Solution: a one to four pitch on the south, a three to five pitch on the north.*

3 Keep the roof line low. *The plate line here is 6'9". People are so used to higher walls they will assume the 6'9" is really 8' or more so the building must be larger.*

4 Don't build a whole wall, and punch holes in it for your windows. Build your wall only to sill height, then rest your windows in structural courses above it.

5 Scale an entrance to its wall. Don't put a dinky, too small doorway in a big surface.

6 Don't stick a toy chimney in a big expanse of roof or it will look like an afterthought.

To make a small house look **bigger—inside**

7 Dramatize a high ceiling by emphasizing a below-standard "ceiling" line to fool the eye.

8 Use a dropped ceiling in the hall to make the living room ceiling seem higher by contrast.

9 Make the room seem wider by placing an important design element—like these brick window columns—at right angles to the room.

10 Use a glass gable without an overhang to let the sun play changing patterns on the ceiling.

11 Plan built-ins around the walls to free center space, and make a narrow room work like a wider one.

12 Break up the open plan by letting it flow around corners, so you can't see all the dining area from the living room or all the open kitchen from the dining room.

13 Make the terrace seem a part of the living room. For example: (a) Carry your planting through the glass. (b) Carry your floor line through the wall. (c) Use ceiling-high glass to let people see your ceiling run right past the wall. (d) Continue the ceiling pattern out onto the overhang.

14 Miter the glass in corner windows to make the corner disappear.

To make a small house **work better—outside**

15 Provide a driveway big enough for off-street parking.

16 Don't landscape the grounds for expensive maintenance.

17 Give the house privacy from the street—by planting, by facing glass areas toward the rear, by setting the house back.

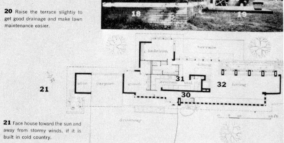

18 Raise the planting boxes so the gardener won't have to bend; provide hose bibs in each box.

19 Make the terrace big enough to serve as an outdoor room, or it becomes merely a path.

20 Raise the terrace slightly to get good drainage and make lawn maintenance easier.

21 Face house toward the sun and away from stormy winds, if it is built in cold country.

To make a small house **work better—inside**

22 Put everything in the kitchen within reach of the housewife. Store utensils and dishes used every day on open shelves so she doesn't have to open cupboard doors over and over.

23 Make the kitchen tall so cooking odors can rise.

24 Keep the mess of the open kitchen out of sight.

25 Punch a hole in the roof of an inside bath; light it from above.

26 Give the owner a huge bathroom mirror, and light it evenly all around the border.

27 Make the low "ceiling line" (in this house, actually a plate line) do double duty as a lighting trough.

28 Use natural materials that call for little maintenance.

29 Use shelves for decoration.

30 Make even a small entrance hall long enough to give the living room some privacy. And make the coat closet big enough.

31 Put your kitchen at the heart of the house, even if it has to be an inside kitchen.

32 Pivot rooms around a huge fireplace—and hide the heater room behind it.

158

140

Friedman house, Pleasantville, New York.

CHAPTER 6

Implications of Organic Design

Broadacre City expressed a developing local and individualistic culture. Wright attempted to lead a way to its realization through his work and trusted other architects to do the same. He thought it "unlikely that any such effort should ever greatly succeed until changes are effected in our so-called 'system' by more intelligent education."[1] Such small changes as have occurred, however, have come about through those who have turned their backs on formal education. And those political leaders to whom Wright looked for change have not brought it about. But his forecast that "little by little people are going to become more and more dissatisfied with increasing urban pressures" would not be disputed.[2]

Those who could afford it have left the city and have taken with them the urban tax base. Those who cannot leave are increasingly without resource. Therefore it is necessary to look at the fringes of established society to find those changes of an organic nature that have come about since Wright's death. It is only lately, with the ecological critique and the energy crisis, that this minority action has become a central issue. Wrightian "organic design" covers a wide spectrum, and its implications are best observed separately — at the individual level of the dwelling and at the social level of Broadacres.

The Organic Dwelling

In an organic architecture the ground itself predetermines all features; the climate modifies them; available means limit them; function shapes them.[3]

It is difficult to imagine a more antithetical statement to what has recently happened in modern building. Wright's definition looks to a recognition of nature, rather than its subjection. It recognizes variation and the need for the building to react to its environment, rather than to repudiate both by air conditioning and massive energy inputs. Wright's attitude welcomes in-termediate technology and the use of indigenous materials, rather than being reliant on the increasingly distant, impersonal products of centralized technology. Like agriculture, architecture is a modification of the natural order. Organic design is the conscious selection of techniques enabling the designer to achieve a desired quality of life. It negates technology for its own sake. The continued existence of the wayside flower is no less important than technical innovation.

The Organic Architect

There are contradictions inherent in Wright's view of organic architecture. These do not so much involve the architecture, the purpose of which is clear, but rather the role of the architect. The proposition that homes should be unique to their owners becomes threatening to the architect when it is combined with the Broadacres program, which will enable citizens to design and build their own dwellings. At the same time, Wright is adamant that the architect is essential to bring the form of the new city about. The clue to this tangle is perhaps to be found in his fundamental belief in democracy and the self-reliant individual.[4] In The Living City he envisaged that " 'professionalism' would diminish, wherever recognized as a depreciation of form, regarded as gangsterism properly refined."[5] This would be easy to digest if it were not for Wright's conviction of the need for, and usefulness of, his own ability and unique skill. Architecture for him had to be poetry; romance was the "new reality," and the architect was the "master of know-how" who could interpret for the building owner his individual needs.

Clearly, not everyone is going to have sufficient interest or skill to build his own home. Those who can afford it will approach an architect. Wright never had any doubt that his skills and those of any other organic architect would continue to be in demand, and he never considered the possibility that he might go against the client. That would have violated the nature of their joint intent. He gives the impression that the five-car homes of Broadacres, or the house on the mesa,[6] would be built by architects, while the masses built for themselves or even perhaps bought homes from others. However, he also advocated the demolition of buildings of the past that stood in the way of the present, unless they were needed as museums.[7]

Architects, like Wright's political leaders — his "social architects" — would help bring Broadacres about, thought Wright. Once established and equipped with research "style centers," the architects would abdicate in favor of the citizens, who would themselves take over. The situation is complex, but it is perhaps analogous to that of the state for Marxists, who hold that once the state has achieved communism, it will itself wither away. Wright held that architecture as a profession would wither away, to be replaced by organic architecture. Through the county architect ". . . each county would naturally develop an individuality of its own. Architecture — in the broad sense."[8] What is clearly proposed here is a new vernacular. The "style center group stations" would work with the universities, and through

. . . television and radio, owned by the people, broadcast cultural programs illustrating pertinent phases of government, of city life . . . agrarian practices as well as the practice of art and architecture, philosophy, archeology, and ecology.[9]

Wright, however, could not personally accept the implications of his own proposals. He declared:

Without hesitation or equivocation let's say that architecture would, necessarily, again become the natural backbone (and architects the broad essential leaders) of such cultural endeavor.[10]

As can be seen from this, he had no intention of withering away.

Bruce Goff

Although Wright formulated the concept that organic houses should be as different as their owners, he only rarely realized this intention toward the end of his life. The architect who has developed this idea most strongly is Bruce Goff. His work could hardly be more visually different from Wright's, yet at its root, it achieves the intentions of the architecture envisaged by him. Wright's house for Sol Friedman at Pleasantville, New York, had traveled a long way from the kit approach of the family of Usonians, and Goff logically continued this development. The result has been a career already 50 years old, which is close to the American psyche, yet which has been largely ignored by American architectural writers. This failure is the result of Goff's success. So completely does he immerse himself in his clients' needs that the resulting building bears little similarity to those he has designed for others. To recognize is to categorize, and Goff eludes categorization.

Goff is a plainsman. He has always worked in the Midwest and Southwest. The epicenter of his activity is Oklahoma. As a result, some of the most audacious houses of this century have been built in a region far from the sophistication of the East and West coasts. Like Wright, Goff suffered little academic prelude to practice, and was already building before he was twenty. But unlike Wright, Goff has addressed himself solely to the private home and has never written on the social basis of his work. Nor has he made proposals for the city.[11] His one-time assistant, Herb Greene, has described Goff's attitude to design:

There are the particular conditions of the site, climate and context, the life experiences of the client or user; the building program, the limitations of materials and construction techniques, and there are the notions of order and art influenced by the life experiences of the architect.[12]

The Goff houses are not variations of a repeated concept; they are descriptive of their uses — for example, a "house for a musician" or a "house for a lover of plants." They are the result of freshness of approach, not polemics. Joe Price, the client for a celebrated design, has written:

Bruce Goff has no concept which describes a "wall," or distinguishes a "floor" or a "ceiling." He begins a home (even the word "home" is preconceived and should not really apply) by eliminating from his thoughts every known impression of a home, as if in his mind never before had a house even been constructed.[13]

A home can therefore be a starfish-like tent containing a pool bridged by ramps that lead to antennae bedroom-arms; a shimmering crystalline pentangle of blue aluminum and pale green marble; or a shambling game of looping stone buried in woods.[14]

Price's own house was originally a bachelor's retreat.[15] It was based on a requirement for informal entertainment, with guests sitting on the floor. To encourage this, Goff formed an interior of total softness. A padded white carpet sweeps over both floor and sloping walls, and toplight falls across a ceiling covered in goosefeathers. The exterior is harshly pristine; a gold-anodized aluminum roof upon walls of shining coal, capped by jagged cullets of splintered blue glass. All these apparently diverse approaches spring from an understanding of the needs and occasion of building, which may be described as organic design. Referring to his relationship with Goff, Joe Price wrote:

The relationship of the client to his architect should be one of faith and trust — for the architect should be able not only to follow the desires of his client, but also to actually think and become the image of his client. Bruce Goff gave to me a house that I would have designed for myself, if I myself had been a great architect.[16]

Goff's apparently rarefied world has the unsettling quality of being achieved by down-to-earth, but inspired means. Cast-off materials or cheap, mass-produced components are used out of context and to unlikely effect. Standard military hardware was used in a naval chapel; drilling booms framed an oil-field church;[17] and radiating ribs from Quonset huts formed the structure of the Ford house in Aurora, Illinois, in 1949.

Goff admired Wright's work and became his friend after receiving a gift of an original Wasmuth portfolio. Although Wright's advice may have influenced his planning, Goff never trained with Wright.[18] His Oklahoma houses of the mid-1950s have certain similarities with Usonian homes. Their geometry is strong and the family symbol of a fireplace occurs at their center. But the fireplace is supplemented in Goff's houses by a large television, whose external manifestation is a dominant aerial. The plans are also more open, with bedrooms integrated within the geometric form instead of forming an attendant wing. Carports are often the flourishes to a structure that is not just explicit, but celebrated. Main beams terminate in lighting lobes and suspend sheltering steel umbrellas in tension. Goff's work varies as much as his clients. Two house designs may be taken to demonstrate this. The Bavinger house of 1950 in Norman, Oklahoma, illustrates Goff's reaction to a virgin site with no constraints of nearby structures; and the Hyde house of 1965 in Kansas City, Kansas, shows his design strategy for a small site and suburban situation.

Gene Bavinger is an artist who teaches at the University of Oklahoma. His family disliked the restriction of boxlike houses and "wished a large open space in which all of their needs could be satisfied, and these included the usual functions of a house for a family of four plus the fact that it needed to also accommodate many interior plants, the growing of which is Gene's hobby."[19] The house was to be constructed by Bavinger himself, with help from students from the University of Oklahoma School of Architecture. Sandstone was to be used from the site, and the house's form was to grow organically out of the bed of the ravine from which it coils. Goff described his concept:

. . . the rock . . . was used in a continuous wall 96 feet long, which takes the form of a logarithmic spiral crawling up out of the ground near the entrance and coiling around a steel pole from which the entire roof, the interior stairs, and living area bowls and the bridge are hung.[20]

The house is one curving, ascending space. Its groundfloor level of native rock, with the kitchen at its center and sunken dining area, opens to the wooded ravine and contains a rock garden and pool with stepping stones. The roof is separated from the walls by continuous skylights and everywhere plants grow up toward these. Suspended stairs attached to the inner wall of the spiral lead to a series of bowls or nests, shaped like spoons and upholstered in gold carpet, which are also suspended in the space. Each bowl contains a separate activity, such as sitting or sleeping. Each can be secured by netting and screened by curtains, each incorporates a light beneath and is accompanied by a satellite closet, in the form of a copper-covered drum. This suspended system is analogous to the internal organs of some vast marine mollusk. As the rock-defined space narrows, the bowls and closets first nudge the encircling wall and then burst out into the sunlight. At the summit of the house the studio looks out from the ravine to the distant city as the structure flings itself into the air. Services are integral with the form: heating plant and the second floor bathroom are in the core, radial subfloor air ducts fan out to the perimeter, and an exhaust fan is located at the vortex.

The house has a tension, unknown in Wright's work, which is derived from the coexistence of two contrasting elements—the stone containing spiral and the suspension system, which includes an upper level bridge. The entire interior "is treated as a conservatory for plants and birds," Goff says. It is "a continuous flow of space wherein neither walls nor floor and ceiling are parallel."[21] The Bavingers built the house themselves over a 5-year period.[22]

162

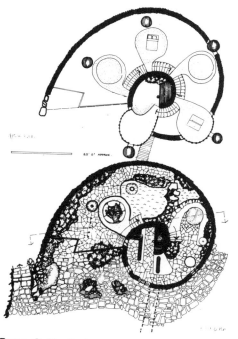

Bruce Goff's Bavinger house, plan, Norman, Oklahoma, 1950. The logarithmic sandstone spiral encircles a central steel mast.

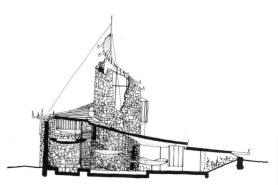

This section of the Bavinger house shows that the roofs, bridge, and bowls for sitting and sleeping are suspended from the mast.

The Bavinger house was built by its owners.

This interior view of the Bavinger house shows the exhaust fan at the apex.

Here, more completely than in any other house of this time, is an architectural expression of the way of life of the client, a sense of living in space three-dimensionally with furniture integral as part of the house itself, and close integration with nature indoors and out.[23]

The Hyde family had little furniture when they asked Goff to design their home. Mrs. Hyde provided the architect with a germinal idea since her favorite color was green and she loves quiet marine hues.[24] Their home presents a restrained appearance to the street, befitting the home of a surgeon, and is clad with standard asbestos siding, painted a dignified dark green. Two long beams, machicolated with ornament, emerge from the raised body of the house and link it by an entrance hall below to the garage. They terminate in bejewelled glass lights, emerald colored and quivering with antennae.[25] The house focuses on its toplit interior. The central area for entertaining is pyramid shaped. It is surrounded by the bedrooms, kitchen, and a lounging and dining area in flat-roofed bays. The whole space is carpeted. Under the rooflight at the center it is pale green, and the color ripples progressively from olive and emerald to deep sea green in the subsidiary bays. The great beams reappear inside, pointing toward the central rooflight from which a hooded flue is hung. The hearth beneath is of glazed mint-colored brick. The fireback of diagonally set gold mirror mosaic is placed against a low interior service pod containing bathrooms and laundry, which serves to break up the symmetry of the plan.

By day sunlight shimmers from diaphanous hangings and streams into the heart of the house, which resembles a wooded glade: sky and trees can be seen above. By night many small sparkling lights define the wigwam interior, which flickers with reflected firelight; the stars are visible through the apex. Because all bedrooms have sliding walls, every member of the family can lie in bed and share in the atmosphere of the house.

These two homes exemplify Goff's work and enlarge Wright's interpretation of organic architecture. They reveal tendencies that underlie Bruce Goff's design. Both houses are essentially great single rooms and both react closely with their sites. The Bavinger house typifies a theme of curvilinear planning, which continues into Goff's present work, whereas the Hyde house shows his fascination with crystalline form.[26]

His plans have a fugal quality, made up of slipping, interlacing, and superimposing figures, and they contain secondary systems, usually taking the form of satellite service or storage elements. Goff makes brilliant use of light and is uninhibited in his use of color. Like the Usonian houses, his designs engage the eye equally from 100 yards or 10 inches away. His concepts yield continued surprise and delight his clients. Goff's work still awaits a thorough evaluation.

Homemade Homes

Wright varied the concept of the house that his clients knew and wanted to the location and specific needs of the moment. Some late designs accepted the character of their owners as a starting point. Goff, on the other hand, invariably allows the life experience of his client to generate his approach. But what both architects have done is to put forward an *interpretation,* which is rooted in the client's personality, but which goes beyond it, sometimes spectacularly so. It is assumed that all mechanical and functional needs are met. The client may perhaps be gratified because the design projects a "super self-image," an image that may have been greater than his or her own imagination. The organic expression of personality in a dwelling could, however, be viewed as no less significant when achieved without an intermediary.

Since Wright's formulation of a method for the "poor man" to build his own home and a social milieu to promote this activity, many owner-built homes

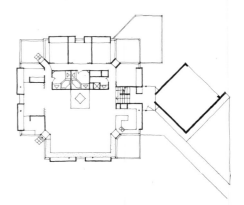

Bruce Goff's Hyde house, main floor plan, Kansas City, Kansas, 1965. All bedrooms can be opened to the central space.

164

The Hyde house is of varying hues of green. The carport is to the right.

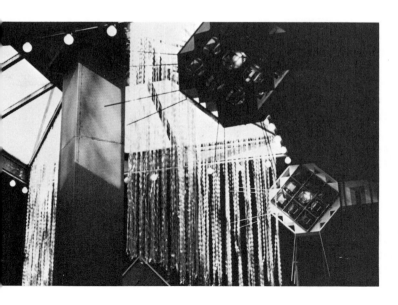

This detail of the Hyde interior shows that the beams linking the house with the garage terminate in the pyramidal interior with the lighting lobes. The chimney flue is at the center of the rooflight.

have appeared in the United States. This has occurred for a number of reasons that have little to do with Wright. They variously include a suitable economic climate; the existence of waste to provide building materials; a movement of population from cities to the country, which is statistically significant in the early 1970s,[27] and a lack of restrictive legislation in rural areas. Such homemade homes more than make up for the intellectual and functional content that good architects might have brought to them by their exuberance and inventiveness. They exemplify the character and variety that Wright sought to liberate.

Simon Rodia's "Watts Towers" in Los Angeles, built from 1921 to 1954, and Arnie Schmidt's "House of Windows" in Woodstock, New York, built during the 1950s, illustrate the pervasiveness of self-building. Such books as Boericke and Shapiro's *Handmade Houses: A Guide to the Woodbutcher's Art*[28] and such articles as Jan Wampler's "Imprint Architecture"[29] celebrate the extraordinary vitality and craftsmanship that people can bring to building their own homes. The interest that this has aroused has coincided with the rediscovery by architects of vernacular architecture[30] and a certain loss of faith in the effectiveness of the profession following spectacular failures in public housing and urban redevelopment.[31]

That self-building is not merely some form of therapy for rich nations has been shown by the work of John Turner and others.[32] It has been demonstrated that such methods are the only economic way for many people to obtain housing, certainly for those of low income in so-called Third World countries. Taliesin apprentices were already dropping out in the 1950s, and since then architectural students have become directly involved in many types of housing ventures. Self-expression in building can now be found down dirt roads anywhere, beyond the reach of building inspectors and code enforcers.

Building form may originate from a dedicated study of organic means to master a hostile environment. In exploiting the characteristics of light- and heavy-weight structures, Paolo Soleri's "Domehouse," completed near Phoenix, Arizona, in 1951 after he left Taliesin, typifies this attitude.[33] A lower cavelike room of concrete was placed in a hollow in the desert to entrain cooling winds, while above, a metal and glass dome incorporated a circular base-track, enabling segments to open or provide shade as it swiveled with the sun. A water spray was designed to cool the dome by condensation.

At Big Sur, California, in New Mexico, Colorado, the Ozarks, and New England, people are building the way their feelings, their climate, and their means suggest. Their homes are part of a search for a way of living that is more direct and natural than that of the cities many have left. Varying degrees of commitment to nonexploitive action have inspired their building, and this outlook may include a response to current global ecological and technical dilemmas. Organic architecture is making its appearance on a broad front.

The new self-builders work within two American traditions: that of the backyard inventor or "Yankee tinker," typified by Jefferson and Edison, and that derived from the ready availability of instructional books.[34] Wright looked to both traditions when he designed for clients who would carry out their own construction and when he popularized his skill and knowledge. He constantly strove for an architecture without pretense or sham, as he stated in 1951:

There is no secret of an "American Style" — in which any architect might find a "safe" grammar to carry from one job to the next. What most of the now world-wide followers of the organic . . . fail to understand is that there is no possible transfer of the same grammar from one genuine building to the other. The law of growth for the Johnson Helio-lab, for instance, is as different from that of Taliesin West, say, as the oak tree differs from the cactus. But both are alike in their inner concept and consistency of grammar. Each is true to itself.

What then can I tell contemporary architects except to seek an inner freedom — a sense of being — which will enable each to grasp for himself the freedom of his own idea? He will then find that the inner nature of his problem always carries right there, within itself, its own solution.[35]

Alternative Communities

Wright's cooperative communities were quickly engulfed by the advancing suburbs and became merely unconventionally communal groups of the middle class. Borsodi's work on self-sustaining homesteads was absorbed into the desperate search for remedies for the Depression. It was paralleled by the "subsistence farmsteads" of the New Deal and was continued by Milton Wend and others.[36] Such books as *How to Live in the Country without Farming* and *Five Acres and Independence* maintained the impetus generated at the School for Living near Suffern, New York, into the 1940s. Homesteading and communitarian experiments, however, offered no real alternative to postwar economic growth and technological optimism. Thus interest in them diminished until it was revived in the 1960s by two new factors: (1) dissatisfaction with the social aims of society; and (2) society's destructive and antiecological methods. It is not the purpose here to pursue the path heralded by Rachel Carson's *Silent Spring,* but only to point out the similarity between the critiques that have followed her work and those changes in attitude to which Wright looked for the establishment of organic culture.

Mass education is going to lose its hold on the people as organic culture comes to take the place of such sterilizing education. . . . If education would . . . forget its "to have and to hold" precepts and practices, allowing organic culture to come through with its great liberal sense of life, you would find that life can be trusted, perhaps that life is all that can really be trusted. And how

interesting you would find its variety of manifestation![37]

Those communities that have intentionally worked out communal and technical alternatives to the established way of life are important to the American present because they have investigated areas to which universities and research have only recently turned under the pressure of events. It has taken urban riots, a debilitating war, the energy crisis, and the brink of a second depression to affect a more general self-questioning. It is not fanciful to suggest that the germ of the little research stations of Broadacre City continues in the work of some alternative communities. It is work addressed not only to life in a developed country, but also to the relationship of that life to a hungry and undeveloped world.

The expertise being acquired in the energy sources of wind and sun in such communities as the Integrated Life-Support Systems Laboratories in New Mexico and in fish farming by such novel means as those of the New Alchemy Institute in Massachusetts[38] is freely available to those who will use it. This was to be precisely the role of Wright's "style centers" in informing the free Usonians of Broadacres. It is ironic that the Taliesin, which in Wright's lifetime raised its own food, generated its own hydropower, and built the Usonian houses, should be building a palace for a Persian princess 40 years later.

The Organic Community

The near half-century that has passed since Wright's first proposals for a reinvigorated, decentralized democracy to be achieved through Broadacre City has not made them less valid. As a scenario for the future, his ideas have been weakened by much that has since happened. Some of the changes would necessitate modification to prolong the utility of his scheme, just as any kind of model needs updating. Other developments reinforce

Broadacres' advantages. It is certainly more than just a lost opportunity.

The consensus of critical opinion to date is that Broadacre City was an unfortunate utopian error in the career of America's greatest architect. If these criticisms had been directed against the political and economic expectations that lay behind Broadacres, their authors might have commanded more attention, but they have not. They have arraigned Wright's plan for foreseeing the very events that have occurred. Decentralization has happened and its effects are everywhere apparent. In 1939 Wright told an audience of architects and planners in London:

And whether you believe what I have been saying or not, the great implements science has put into the hands of humanity are themselves carving out this new city that is to be everywhere and nowhere. They are going to build something like Broadacre City. Architects are not going to build it, I fear, because I see that as they are educated they are not competent even to see it. And so these natural agencies, these tremendous scientific forces, will build it without them.[39]

The interstate highways have been built, the people have ventured down them, followed by decentralized jobs and roadside businesses. But the poor have been left behind, a testimony to urban inhumanity, and the urban strips have desecrated the land with waste and advertising.

One example of city planning exists that contains some of the physical forms of Broadacre City. The new city of Milton Keynes in England has the all-important similarity of being conceived of as a network or an extendable grid of highways. Planning studies for this, the largest example of the British New Towns, began in 1960. Wright's concept was in the minds of the planning consultants, who studied Broadacre City at an early stage, but were able to discover little about it other than its general form and aims.[40] Milton Keynes is planned loosely about a 1-kilometer grid and is currently growing away from three existing towns, which will be merged under the direction of a new city corporation. It is intended to mix privately owned housing with that built and rented by the corporation and to supplement private cars with public transportation operating throughout the highway grid. A major highway and railway link the city to national lines of transport. Although the ubiquity of the concept is currently being eroded by such centralizing tendencies as a "new city shopping center," Milton Keynes appears to validate Wright's planning ideas.

It would seem that the energy crisis might deal a death blow to the automobile and, therefore, to decentralization. However, it is in the cities, which generate their own servicing complications and high energy demand, that the effects of the crisis will be most serious. Centralized urban transportation suffers from the universal problem of rush-hour peaking. It has been shown mathematically that public transportation works more efficiently with a population spaced linearly, rather than nodally.[41] Broadacre City offers such a possibility, where a comprehensive bus system on the 1-mile grid might be reached on foot or by bicycle.[42] Telecommunications, data processing, and electronic information networks — what Wright anticipated in his "electromagnetic communication" — all militate against the traditional reasons for centralization of the population. They make access to knowledge from remote locations and appraisal of decisions possible, and they require little energy to operate. Above all, they can be multidirectional and active.[43]

In Wright's lifetime, conventional servicing of dispersed communities was not economical. The supply of drinking water from remote reservoirs and piping of waste to distant sewage plants were, and are, impractical. Now, however, such technical means as solar stills, methane plant, composting of waste to fertilize soil, and the generation of energy by using sun, water, and

wind are available for local sources. Not only are these techniques possible, but they offer alternatives to the environmental dangers in the use of nonrenewable fossil fuels and nuclear power programs. What is becoming known as intermediate technology can, in fact, only operate in the context of a low-density population.[44]

The ecological critique of *Limits to Growth* and other findings of the early 1970s has, if nothing else, brought about an awareness of the shortage of resources in the face of a rising world population.[45] In this context, food production becomes a central issue and the Broadacre proposal of self-supportive land tenure acquires new relevance. It has been shown[46] that the energy utilization of Western industrialized farming is extremely high, and its output for a given acre of land can be less than that from the same acre devoted to fourteen houses with gardens.[47] Moreover, it is now known that industrialized farming can be destructive to soil structure and is polluting.[48] Its aim is to employ few workers to supply agriculturally passive urban concentrations.

In the world context, a labor-intensive rather than energy-intensive agriculture could achieve higher yields.[49] The indications are that Western advice and farming practices, of which the so-called Green Revolution is a part, when transferred to the Third World exacerbate social inequality and drive at least marginally self-supporting rural populations to dependence on cities.[50] A smaller basic unit than 1 acre might be required, but a land-use pattern along the lines of Broadacre City offers a way for developed nations to formulate an equitable, satisfying mode of life, and might be the only generally sustainable global model.

The major failing of Broadacres is its insistence on the primacy of individualism. The need for releasing the individual's potential is indisputable, but it is precisely a lack of understanding of those who may be different or

Milton Keynes New City, Buckinghamshire, England. The plan is a 1-km grid that takes account of existing features. It is growing away from three towns.

169

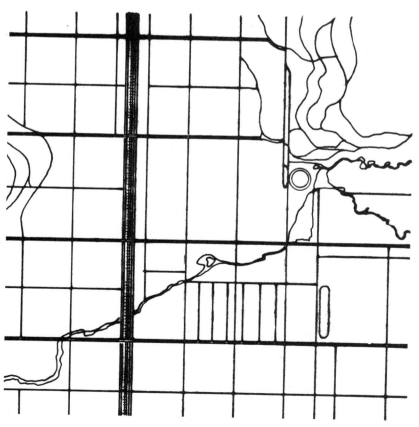

Broadacre City, Usonia. The plan is a 1-mile grid that takes account of existing features. Wright envisaged that it would grow away from existing cities and industrial concentrations.

poorer that can be encouraged by too great a stress on individual achievement. Much involvement in communal affairs would be necessary to redress the isolating tendencies of physical dispersal and potentially impersonal media and technology. If Broadacre City provided a sufficiently neutral context to sustain and allow self-expression, there would still remain the problem of social life, *res publica*.[51] There is in Broadacres the tendency toward Populism, which must be recognized in Wright's thinking. Historically, Populism is impatient with legality, which it regards as an abstraction, and favors the interests of privacy. It is ultimately the determination of society to agree to certain ethical and moral definitions that safeguard one individual's liberty from being invaded by that of another.

The present social situation has been summarized by Raymond Williams, in his wonderful book, *The Country and the City:*

The division and opposition of city and country, industry and agriculture, in their modern forms, are the critical culmination of the division and specialization of labor which, though it did not begin with capitalism, was developed under it to an extraordinary and transforming degree. Other forms of the same fundamental division are the separation between mental and manual labor, between administration and operation, between politics and social life. The symptoms of this division can be found at every point in what is now our common life: in the idea and practice of social classes; in conventional definitions of work and education: in the physical distribution of settlements; and in temporal organization of the day, the week, the year, the lifetime. Much of the creative thinking of our time is an attempt to re-examine each of these concepts and practices. It is based on the conviction that the system which generates and is composed by them is intolerable and will not survive.[52]

Broadacres was such an attempt at re-analysis. It takes its place among other planning concepts of this century — the Garden City, Linear Cities, and Ville Radieuse. But its strength lies in an acceptance of change and in its aim to create a balanced way of life for the individual, using hand and mind in voluntary association with others in natural surroundings.

Frank Lloyd Wright did not specify the means by which his reforms would be brought about. He regarded the development of society as an organic process, like the growth of a tree. The example of ecology shows that survival depends on the ability of species to adapt to change. At the present time, rapid technological change requires such adaptation of human society. Broadacre City and the houses that accompanied it offer a visual paradigm for social progress in Usonia that could be achieved by evolutionary, rather than revolutionary means.

Notes

Introduction

1 Buckminster Fuller's RIBA Discourse of 1962. Fuller's lecture was of such inordinate length that the *RIBA Journal* (Royal Institute of British Architects) asked him to summarize his argument for their publication. They also pointed out that this would save paper and trees. He refused to do so. Therefore the discourse was never published.
2 Reyner Banham, "The Home Is Not a House," *Arts in America*, April 1965, reproduced in *Architectural Design*, January 1969. Many architects' honeymoons with energy were taken further by the designs of the English *Archigram* group, whose initial demand was for disposable, short-life building.
3 John Dos Passos, *USA: The Big Money*, Houghton Mifflin, Boston, 1933, pp. 439, 440.
4 Frank Lloyd Wright, *The Future of Architecture*, Horizon, New York, 1953, p. 29.
5 Frank Lloyd Wright, *The Natural House*, Horizon, New York, 1954, p. 175.
6 Frank Lloyd Wright, *Taliesin*, Spring Green, Wis., 1940, p. 2.
7 Frank Lloyd Wright, *Two Lectures on Architecture*, The Art Institute, Chicago, 1931, p. 185.
8 Frank Lloyd Wright, *An Autobiography*, Faber & Faber, London, 1932, p. 142.
9 Alfred North Whitehead, *Process and Reality* (1929), Free Press, New York, 1969, p. 21.
10 Paul S. Henshaw, *This Side of Yesterday: Extinction or Utopia*, John Wiley & Sons, New York, 1971, p. 14.
11 Edward Frank, "Organic Philosophy, Organic Architecture and Frank Lloyd Wright," paper in the possession of the Avery Library, Columbia University, New York, 1963, p. 9.
12 Bruce Tegner, *Book of Kung Fu and Tai Chi*, Meditation 20, Bantam Books, New York, 1974. Lao-tse, or Laotze, has been variously translated from the Chinese. For example:

Many spokes unite to form the wheel
But it is the center that makes it useful.

When you shape clay into an urn
it is the space within that makes it useful.

Cut doors and windows in a room
the openings make them useful.

From the material comes profit
from the immaterial comes usefulness.

13 Wright, *The Future of Architecture*, p. 187.
14 Frank, op. cit., p. 16. Frank's paper is the clearest exposition on Wright's "organic" concept that I have found.
15 Wright, *The Future of Architecture*, p. 250.
16 Ibid., p. 230.

Chapter 1

1 Frank Lloyd Wright, *The Natural House*, Horizon Press, New York, 1954, p. 79.
2 Frank Lloyd Wright, *Architectural Forum*, vol. 68, January 1938.
3 George R. Collins, "Broadacre City: Wright's Utopia Reconsidered," paper read to the Four Great Masters of Modern Architecture Symposium, Columbia University, New York, 1961.
4 *Architectural Forum*, January 1938, pp. 77–80. Wright's detailed declaration was:

1 Visible roofs are expensive and unnecessary.
2 A garage is no longer necessary, as cars are made. A carport will do, with liberal overhead shelter and walls on two sides.
3 The old-fashioned basement, except for a fuel and heater space was always a plague spot. A steam-warmed concrete mat 4 inches thick laid directly on the ground over gravel filling, and the walls set upon that, is better.
4 Interior "trim" is no longer necessary.
5 We need no radiators and no light fixtures. We will heat the house the Roman way, that is to say, in or beneath the floors, and make the wiring system itself be the light fixtures, throwing light upon the ceiling. Light will thus be indirect, except for a few outlets for floor lamps.
6 Furniture, pictures, and bric-a-brac are unnecessary except as the walls can be made to include them or be them.
7 No painting at all, wood best preserves itself. Only the floor mat need be waxed.
8 No plastering in the building.
9 No gutters, no downspouts.
Now to assist in general planning what must or may we use, in our new construction? In this case, five materials: wood, brick, cement, paper, and glass. To simplify fabrication we must use the horizontal unit system in construction. (See lines crossing plans both ways making rectangles 2 feet by 4 feet.) We must also have a vertical unit system which will be the boards and batten-bands themselves, interlocking with the brick courses.

5 Ibid., pp. 78–79.

6 The very practical nature of Wright's proposals for the new home provides a revealing contrast with the polemical (and influential) "five points" of the new architecture of Le Corbusier. The columns, roof gardens, free plan, long window, and free facade of the French architect's archetype, or "object-type," were accepted by postwar architects as a powerful critique of traditional masonry architecture. This "object-type" was to be the inevitable visual form of mass production. Le Corbusier's concept resulted progressively in the *Villa Savoie* at Poissy, a "machine for living in," where the occupants were raised on stilts above the very countryside they had left Paris to enjoy; in "machines for hosteling-in," as at the *Pavilion Suisse* or *Cité de Refuge* in Paris, where brickwork crosswalls would have solved all the acoustic embarrassment the designs caused; in "machines for community-ing in" at Pessac, and the *Unité* at Marseilles, where inhabitants struggled to modify or humanize the archetype with which they were provided (*Unité* apartment blocks were sited north-south irrespective of locale); and the ultimate "machine for citying in," the ossified city plan: *Ville Radieuse*. Nothing could be more removed from Wright's view. The offspring of Le Corbusier's vision were such housing projects as Pruitt-Igoe, St. Louis, in the United States, now demolished, and much of the British public housing of the 1960s. Raising these buildings in the air has devalued the communal experience of the street, as shown by the urbanist Jane Jacobs, and brought about such problems as those identified in Oscar Newman's book, *Defensible Space*.

7 "A small house on the side street might have more charm if it didn't ape the large house on the avenue. . . ." Frank Lloyd Wright, *Architectural Forum*, January 1938, p. 78.
8 Norris Kelly Smith, *Frank Lloyd Wright: A Study in Architectural Content*, Prentice Hall, Englewood Cliffs, N.J., 1966. Robert C. Twombly, *Frank Lloyd Wright: An Interpretive Biography*, Harper and Row, New York, 1973.
9 Dining furniture had the qualities of De Stijl sculpture: Place settings were predetermined by built-in lights or flower vases and stately high-backed chairs.
10 Thorstein Veblen, *The Theory of the Leisure Class*, Chalto & Windus, London, 1925.
11 Wright, *Architectural Forum*, January 1938, p. 79.
12 Marjorie F. Leighey, "A Testimony to Beauty," in *The Pope-Leighey House*, Terry B. Morton, ed., National Trust for Historic Preservation, Washington, D.C., 1969, p. 60.
13 Herbert Jacobs, letter to the author, Nov. 4, 1973.
14 This can be seen, for example, in River Forest Tennis Club of 1906. Reyner Banham ("The Wilderness Years," *RIBA Journal*, December 1969) has ascribed this "striping" to Ocatillo Camp, 1928. He felt this to be a horizontal celebration of the Sahuaro cactus, whose form Wright enthuses over (*An Autobiography*, p. 273). However, the source of Wright's love of horizontality in the details of construction is older and meets the need for his "sense of shelter."
15 Richard MacCormac, "The Anatomy of Wright's Aesthetic," *Architectural Review*, vol. 143, no. 852, pp. 143–146, February 1968.
16 It is now common practice for architects to number grid lines. This enables an element to be accurately located by coordinates, and is fundamental to communications with the builder or others by telephone. The practice seems to have started with Wright on his blockwork houses of the 1920s, and by 1935, drawings of both the zoned house and Lusk house evidence it.
17 A contemporary analysis of this heating technique, printed in the *St. Louis Post-Dispatch* of May 26, 1940.
18 Wright, *The Natural House*, p. 167.
19 Wright was fond of inquiring if 5,000 people could negotiate the 2-ft corridor of a Pullman train, why could not five people in a home?
20 Herbert Jacobs, "A Client to the Rescue," *The New York Times*, Dec. 8, 1940; also Herbert Jacobs, *Frank Lloyd Wright: America's Greatest Architect*, Harcourt Brace, New York, 1965; Loren B. Pope, "Writer Finds Public Wants Homes of Modern Design, *The Evening Star*, Washington, D.C., Mar. 29, 1947; Loren B. Pope, "The Love Affair of a Man and His House," *House Beautiful*, vol. 90, pp. 32 – 34, 80, 90, August 1948; Lloyd Lewis, "Wright's Taylor-made Houses, " *Chicago Sun*, Jan. 25, 1943; Marjorie F. Leighey, loc. cit.
21 Frank Lloyd Wright, "Broadacre City," see caption "Collateral Detail Models," in *Architectural Record*, April 1935. John Howe, chief draftsman at Taliesin throughout the period, regards these houses as "the forerunners" of the Unsonians.
22 Frank Lloyd Wright, *Taliesin*, vol. 1, no. 1, 1934.
23 Wright, *The Natural House*, p. 69.

24 Bruce Brooks Pfeiffer is currently an historian at Taliesin and Director of Archives of the Frank Lloyd Wright Foundation, Taliesin Associated Architects.

25 John Howe, letter to the author, Dec. 31, 1973.

26 Wright, *Architectural Forum,* January 1938, p. 80.

27 Details of the Lusk house are contained in a letter sent by Jeanette C. Lusk to the author, dated Dec. 14, 1973.

28 Frank Lloyd Wright, letter to Robert D. Lusk, 1935, quoted by Frederick Gutheim, ed., *Frank Lloyd Wright on Architecture,* Duell, Sloane & Pearce, New York, 1941, p. 191.

29 Burton J. Goodrich, "At Taliesin," *Madison Capital Times,* Feb. 12, 1937. "The L-shaped plan and the wooden fence close in the rectangular corner lot. . . . The enclosed space is to be garden so intimate and natural as to become part of the living room, which comes out into it by means of the concrete floormat extending out in the form of a terrace. The garden may be said to come in through the large floor-to-ceiling glass doors. Several brick masses (so natural to the material) rise up out of the ground serving as walls, fireplaces, ventilation ducts, and chimneys. Binding these masses together are horizontal bands of wood (in the structural form known as board and batten), and glass with its delicate mullions webs itself between brick and wood now at eye level and then from floor to ceiling and again up against the sky to be opened for ventilation in the hot summer nights of this South Dakota region. . . . All spaces—living, study, dining, and sleeping have advantage of this scheme by breaking the otherwise flat roof up into a sawtooth to allow for the band of window ventilators over the rooms."

30 Jeanette C. Lusk, loc. cit. She recollects her experience with these agencies. "Government loans were about the only source of building funds in those days, and we couldn't build without one. The F.H.A. declared that because our house was 'different,' that it had been designed specifically for us and our personal requirements and way of life, that its re-sale value was nil. The Government had to figure in the re-sale value because many home-builders receiving loans defaulted on their payments."

31 "At Taliesin," *Capital Times,* Madison, Wis., Nov. 20, 1936; ibid., Jan. 23, 1938, Herbert Jacobs, "A Client to the Rescue," *The New York Times,* Dec. 8, 1940. *The Architectural Forum,* January 1938, pp. 77–79. Issue designed by Wright. "Usonian Architect," *Time,* Jan. 17, 1938. Includes cover and article.

32 See chronological list of Usonian houses, page 8.

33 The piece mentions an advertisement run in U.S. papers about low-cost housing and quotes from a number of letters received in response. Masselink is an invaluable source of information on Taliesin activities (in view of the lack of Wright's own papers). For example, he wrote a letter to George Beal on Dec. 5, 1936 (now in the Wright Collection at the Kenneth Spencer Research Library, University of Kansas, Lawrence, Kansas), which gives a vivid picture of Wright's work at that time. "Taliesin busy. It has a job, $¼ million, for an Administration Building for Johnson Wax. Foundations going in. . . . Kaufmann House nearing completion. Roberts House in Marquette almost finished with John as superintendent and a small $5,500 house in Madison this winter. Jim (Drought) and Benny (Dombar) supervisors. Then there is the Hanna House in Palo Alto to be started very soon. Mr. Wright will be going there soon to start work on it."

34 *The Pope-Leighey House,* Terry B. Morton, ed., Washington National Trust for Historic Preservation, 1969, p. 64. Pew house, Madison, Wisconsin, interview with author, October 1973.

35 The practice of having apprentices superintend construction was a normal part of Wright's architectural services (see Chapter 3) and was part of their architectural education in the Taliesin Fellowship. In this case, Drought and Dombar were supervisors. Letter of Eugene Masselink, see footnote 33.

36 Edgar Tafel, Charter Taliesin Fellow, in conversation with the author, Mar. 15, 1973.

37 Herbert Jacobs, letter to the author, Nov. 4, 1973.

38 Ibid.

39 Attested to by all nine resident owners interviewed by the author.

40 Frank Lloyd Wright, address to the Junior Chapter of the American Institute of Architects, New York, 1952. See also *Frank Lloyd Wright: Writings and Buildings,* Edgar Kaufmann and Ben Raeburn, eds., Meridian Books, New York, 1960, p. 285.

41 Wright, *The Natural House,* p. 220.

42 Ibid.

43 Kakuzo Okakura, *The Book of Tea,* Fox, Duffield & Co., New York, 1906; republished by Dover Publications, New York, 1964, p. 40.

44 Wright, *The Natural House,* pp. 80, 81. Wright's claim that his sandwich wall would be "termite proof" seems to be borne out. The only recorded damage was discovered in the Pope house when it was dismantled and moved to a new site by the National Trust for Historic Preservation.

45 Some fastidious housewives like Mrs. Leighey objected to the small ledges on the battens because they increased dust-gathering surfaces.

46 At the northern latitude of the lakeside location for the Schwartz house at Two Rivers, Wisconsin, both the client and his supervisor, Edgar Tafel, increased the insulation and wall thickness by incorporating studwork in certain walls.

47 Most builders and supervising apprentices tried to finish the floor in one progressive pour. The rough concrete was tamped level; then, after curing slightly, the Indian red-colored cement topping was steel troweled smooth and the module deeply marked with boards. Some builders preferred to allow for rolling progress, so that later, any crack marks that developed were on module lines. Great accuracy was required at this setting out.

48 In 1969 I found the Jacobs house had developed problems with its heating pipes. If serious, this problem will prove to be unremediable.

49 Account taken from the *St. Louis Post-Dispatch,* May 26, 1940, quoted in a letter by William Bernoudi, June 1940, to George and Helen Beal, now in the possession of the Kenneth Spencer Research Library, University of Kansas.

50 Frank Lloyd Wright, *An Autobiography,* Faber & Faber, London, 1932, p. 431.

51 During the summer of 1969, among the more than forty post-1937 Wright houses that I visited, none were air conditioned and all were a pleasure to be inside. Wright gave his own views on air conditioning in *The Natural House,* p. 175: "To me air conditioning is a dangerous circumstance. The extreme changes in temperature that tear down a building also tear down the human body. . . . If you carry contrasts too far too often, when you are cooled the heat becomes more unendurable. . . . The less the degree of temperature difference you live in, the better for your constitutional welfare."

52 *The Pope-Leighey House,* Morton, ed., p. 78.

53 Dorothy Johnson Field, *Taliesin* magazine, vol. 1, no. 1, 1934, Spring Green, Wis., pp. 13–16. Mrs. Field later expanded her ideas in *The Human House,* Houghton Mifflin Co., Boston, 1939.

54 Ibid.

55 The notion that Wright autocratically told his clients what they wanted is one of those legends not borne out by the facts. Those clients interviewed by me certainly felt their wishes had been noted and acted on. See, for example, Eugene R. Streich, "An Original Owner Interview Survey of Frank Lloyd Wright's Residential Architecture," *Environmental Design: Research and Practice,* 1, William J. Mitchell, ed., UCLA, January 1972, p. 13–10–1.

56 Wright, *The Natural House,* p. 165.

Chapter 2

1 Strictly speaking, the analogy is somewhat stretched, since what is known as the Carpentered-World Hypothesis merely demonstrates the extent to which people from Europeanized cultures utilize straight lines to see spatially. They are therefore susceptible to straight line illusions. The immunity of many Africans to these illusions might suggest that Westerners encounter similar difficulties with complex space (such as curved or faceted space, as in the Hanna house). The Guggenheim Museum provides some proof of this hypothesis. The totality of the warped space delights those visiting the building as much as it troubles the museum's directors in their search for a conventional interaction between painting and viewer. For more discussion on this see M. H. Segall, D. T. Campbell, and M. J. Herskovits, *The Influence of Culture on Visual Perception,* Bobbs-Merrill, Indianapolis, 1966.

2 The Hanna House is discussed in Appendix A: A Spatial Analysis of Usonian Houses.

3 Curtis Besinger, "To Appreciate the Pleasures of This House," and "How to Find the Art in Architecture," *House Beautiful,* vol. 105, no. 1, January 1963.

4 Ibid., p. 60.

5 "What Frank Lloyd Wright Said About This House," ibid., p. 71.

6 Whereas in the Hanna house the grid, side of hexagon, and vertical module were related to plywood sizes, in the Jester project the *circumference* was formed by multiples of 8-ft by 4-ft sheets. See Lionel March and Philip Steadman, *The Geometry of the Environment,* RIBA Publications, London, 1971.

7 Frank Lloyd Wright, *Architectural Forum,* vol. 88, p. 97, January 1948.

172

8 From the leaflet, "Personal Services of Frank Lloyd Wright," Taliesin, Spring Green, Wis., reprinted in Appendix B. "Dwelling houses upon urban lots will not be accepted. Acreage is indispensable." This is discussed in detail in Chapter 6.

9 Numbering taken from Pfeiffer's list, pp. 214–216 in *Frank Lloyd Wright: His Life, His Work, His Words,* by Olgivanna Lloyd Wright, Horizon Press, New York, 1967. This listing of projects appears to be incomplete. It omits published designs, such as the great Stanley Marcus house (1937) for Dallas, Texas, and the Muelberger house for Lansing, Michigan (1938), which were included in the 1938 and 1948 editions of *Forum.* It also omits such unpublished designs as the Notz house (1939) mentioned by Gordon Chadwick in the *Pope-Leighey House,* T. Morton, ed., National Trust for Historic Preservation, Washington, D.C., 1969, p. 30.

10 *The New York Times,* Apr. 19, 1959; Section 2, Mar. 18, 1962.

11 Now called the Pope-Leighey house following removal from the path of an interstate highway by the National Trust for Historic Preservation in 1964.

12 Russell Hitchcock illustrates this room in *In the Nature of Materials,* Duell, Sloan & Pearce, New York, 1942, Figure 394.

13 Turner's role is discussed in detail in Chapter 6.

14 For example, in concealed lighting through fretted plywood rather than the Jacobs' conduit-light, a rainwater-spout design that reduced splash-back on board and batten walls, etc.

15 See Chapter 6, Popularizing Organic Architecture.

16 Alvar Aalto visited this house in 1948. It is interesting to note that after this date he developed the "peeling" stepback as a theme of his planning. While observable in prewar work, it permeates such designs as the art gallery for Aalborg, Denmark, and his replanning of a section of Helsinki.

17 *The Pope-Leighey House,* op. cit.

18 The plan on p. 144 of *The Natural House* is not the one built, but an earlier version that was dropped for reasons of cost.

19 Loren Pope, "The Love Affair of a Man and His House," *House Beautiful,* August 1943. This is an unsolicited article that reads in part: "Where roof levels change, they are continuous inside as decks, or as an open trellis to accentuate this flow. This handling of changing levels or planes, and of proportions is so masterful that the interior space seems to come alive. After having experienced it, no one can ever go back to the painted box, which is all the ordinary house is, however elaborate. . . . The house gives you a sense of protection, but never of being closed in, and of leading you on beyond where your eyes can see."

20 Neither plan has been published. Russell Hitchcock's *In the Nature of Materials* contains some photographs of the Manson house.

21 Plan published in *Architectural Forum,* vol. 88, p. 69 (top right), January 1948.

22 Ibid., p. 79, top right.

23 Illustrated in *Architectural Forum,* January 1938.

24 Peter Blake, *Frank Lloyd Wright,* Master Builders Series, Gollancz, London, 1960, p. 106. ". . . a wood, brick, and glass version of the Barcelona Pavilion." The Winkler-Goetsch house is in fact more closely comparable with Mies' "Bachelor's House," exhibited at the 1930 Berlin Building Exposition. This demonstration building certainly exemplified all that was going on in contemporary European architecture. Its nonstructural glass and sculptural enclosing walls were contrasted with the regular column grid with a clarity that Le Corbusier only bettered in the *Villa Savoie* at Poissy. It was concerned with the polemics of the new architecture, its highly polished surfaces avoided any allusion to naturalism, and it was unspecific—there was no client, only the lifestyle was suggested.

Mies' work was included in the International Style Show in 1932 and the American Modern Architecture Show in 1934, both at New York's Museum of Modern Art. These exhibitions angered Wright because he felt that they implied that his own contribution was a thing of the past. It can certainly be said, however, that exposure to this material coincides with a simplified external appearance in Wright's buildings of the later thirties. The elaboration of detail of the blockwork houses of the twenties was left behind and contrast of materials was relied upon — using smooth rounded concrete with roughly coursed stonework at Falling Water, and cypress boarding with brickwork in the Usonians. It could be argued, however, that these simplifications were the result of the need to reduce costs and rationalize construction. They are, at any rate, only external manifestations of an architectural concept that is profoundly different from that of the Europeans, which makes any similarity in the plans of Wright's Winkler-Goetsch house and Mies' Bachelor's house superficial. For Wright, "the reality of the building is the space within," and the walls and other surfaces integrally shaped this; they were the structure. For the Internationalists, the essence of their buildings was an intellectual appreciation of the distinction between two systems, the regular structural steel frame and nonstructural walls often leading outside the grid or platte. This has been most clearly noted by Colin Rowe in his article, "Chicago Frame: Chicago's place in the modern movement," *Architectural Review,* vol. 120, pp. 285–289, November, 1956.

25 For the pre-fire photographs, see Henry Russell Hitchcock, *In the Nature of Materials,* Duell, Sloan & Pearce, New York, 1942, Figure 394.

26 Wright, *Architectural Forum,* January 1948, p. 199; see also Arthur Drexler, ed., *The Drawings of Frank Lloyd Wright,* Horizon Press, New York, 1962, pp. 170, 171.

27 Taliesin West typifies this. The axes of the plan are fixed by Camelback, Tabletop, and Superstition Mountains many miles away. The buildings form a smaller, more special place along the contours within this larger arena, and the many twists and turns in moving about the complex are intended to heighten an awareness of both and their interrelationship.

28 According to Donald Kalek, a member of the Taliesin Fellowship from 1965 to 1969, construction was so complex that daily classes were held on the site for the carpenters engaged in the work.

29 None of the former Taliesin apprentices with whom I spoke were able to divulge any more than the crumbling buildings themselves. Construction took place in wartime, which was in itself unusual. More accurate information must await publication of the archives.

30 The horizontal lapping of copper is similar to that on a well-known late house, the Clinton Walker house of 1952, on the beach at Carmel, California. The rolls of copper (at Carmel a ceramic material was used) are banded horizontally around the roof rather than run down its slope. This reveals one of Wright's important preoccupations — the treatment of plain surfaces. Linear elements are used to describe a sloping surface, as here in roof detailing, for the same reasons that fields at Taliesin were contour-ploughed long before this became a practice recommended by the Department of Agriculture. This was done in order to prevent runoff of topsoil. The treatment of the surface also revealed something of its nature. Internal wood trim was used in the Prairie houses and the living-room of Taliesin to delineate areas of plaster ceiling for similar reasons.

31 Interview with the author, October 1973. Mr. and Mrs. Carl Wall met at Olivette College, Michigan, and were married at the ages of 24 and 22 years, respectively.

32 As in the Hanna house, Wright recommended a Scott radio with remote speakers. This ready accommodation of technology within the fabric was already established by the concealed lighting of the Robie house of 1910 in Chicago, Illinois. In the Wall house, speakers were placed behind slots cut in the cypress, one each in the living area, dining area, bedroom, and workshop. Another portable speaker was placed in a footstool for use on the terrace.

33 This house was wrongly identified as the Roy Peterson residence in Racine, Wisconsin, in Wright's issue of *Architectural Forum,* January 1948, p. 71.

34 Ibid., p. 71.

35 The Richardson house was designed in 1941 for Livingston, New Jersey; World War II and the Richardsons' changed needs account for the house being built in 1951 in Glen Ridge, New Jersey.

36 Wright, *An Autobiography,* p. 430.

37 Of all Wright's clients interviewed by the author, Mrs. Lewis was the only one to refer to "Frank," rather than use the respectful, or reverential, "Mr. Wright."

38 All helped substantially, by the measures of the late 1920s, to bail Wright out of his financial troubles following the Miriam Noel affair and bank foreclosures. This resulted in the incorporation of his future earnings and redemption of Taliesin and its contents. For a full account see Wright, *An Autobiography,* pp. 259–264. See also, Robert Twombly, *Frank Lloyd Wright: An Interpretive Biography,* Harper & Row, New York, 1973, p. 154.

39 Wright, *An Autobiography,* p. 432, in which a letter from Woolcott to Wright is quoted: ". . . Lloyd [Lewis], whom I admire and enjoy, never did anything so wise in his life. Just to be in that house uplifts the heart and refreshes the spirit."

40 The Willey house (first project) of 1934 in Minneapolis, Minnesota, and the Kaufmann house of 1936 (Falling Water) in Bear Run, Pennsylvania, can be seen as prototypes for this. However, the blockwork Freeman house of 1922 in Los Angeles, or even the Hardy house of 1905 in Racine, Wisconsin, ultimately typify this approach. The Sturges and Oboler Usonians continue this strategy of site treatment, and later developments — such as the Grant house of 1945 in Cedar Rapids, Iowa, and the V. C. Morris house project of 1943 in San Francisco, California—terminate it.

41 In 1973 Twombly found that this laboratory monitored the costs and construction of the Jacobs house.

42 In a conversation with the author in November 1973, Mr. Pew said that this budget was not exceeded.

43 Ibid. In 1938 Wright was unwilling to accept the commission and tried to persuade the Pews to buy a 1-acre site elsewhere.

44 It is of interest that the house was first designed in brick. Although the Pews wanted stone, costs ruled this out until immediately before construction, when Wright found three stone masons and a source of materials at Spring Green.

45 See Appendix A, A Spatial Analysis of Usonians.

46 Mr. Pew took a professional interest in the maintenance of the house. He was not satisfied with the finish of the joinery, carried out by a Taliesin crew, and resanded and waxed all the cypress — to such an effect, that it is in better condition and color than the cypress in any other Usonian. He also cleaned down all the stonework.

47 The house has been mercifully saved from too much public exposure. Since the initial publicity following its completion, the Pews have never allowed photography of its interior.

48 Gregor Affleck, interview with the author, October 1973.

49 Turner's contribution is discussed in Chapter 3. The Affleck house was featured in *Progressive Architecture,* October 1946, and in *Architectural Forum,* January 1948.

50 Frank Lloyd Wright, *The Living City,* Horizon Press, New York, 1958, pp. 150, 151. A 4-acre subdivision with four free-standing houses, and a 2-acre total divided into four ½-acre lots with four "suntop-type" house plans. Wright's quadruple planning had considerable longevity. It first appeared in his 1902 quadruple block project, which linked four prairie houses into a 400-square-foot block and was developed an an entry entitled a "non-competitive plan," which he submitted in 1913 for the National Conference on City Planning competition. This was a four-house quarter-block proposal for the suburbs and was published in De Fries' *Frank Lloyd Wright: Ans dem Lebenswerke eines Architekten,* Ernst Pollok, Berlin, 1926.

51 Wright, *Architectural Forum,* January 1948, p. 80. ". . . and so this project is one of the best shots in our locker. In this scheme standardization is no barrier to the quality of infinite variety to be observed in Nature. No entrance to any dwelling in the group is beside any other entrance to another dwelling. So far as the individual can know, the entire group is his home. He is entirely unaware of the activities of his neighbors. There is no looking from front windows to backyards. . . . Playgrounds for the children, called sundecks, are here independent roof gardens placed where the mother . . . has direct supervision over hers. Family processes are conveniently centralized on the mezzanine next to the master bedroom and bath, where the mistress of the house can turn a pancake with one hand while chucking the baby into a bath with the other, father meantime sitting at his dinner, lord of it all, daughter meantime having the privacy of the front room below for the entertainment of her friends."

52 Curtis Besinger, a long-time member of the Taliesin Fellowship who was associated with many of the projects of this period, wrote this in a letter to George and Helen Beal on February 26, 1942. The letter is now in the possession of the Spencer Library, University of Kansas.

53 Wright, *Architectural Forum,* January 1948, p. 80.

54 Ibid., p. 48.

55 This problem occurred a number of times and caused several projects to be abandoned. Elsewhere clients had to be very active in Wright's behalf to overcome local opposition, as happened, for example, with Rebhuhn at Great Neck, Long Island. Wright would have nothing to do with state registration boards, nor would he deal with the American Institute of Architects. For an account of the government housing affair, see Talbot Wegg, "Frank Lloyd Wright versus the U.S.A.," *The American Institute of Architects Journal,* vol. 53, no. 2, pp. 48 – 52, February 1970.

56 No direct results came from the project. However, the berm concept was revived in the second Jacobs house of 1948 at Middleton, Wisconsin, and in the Keyes house of 1951 at Rochester, Minnesota.

57 Frank Lloyd Wright, *The Future of Architecture,* Horizon Press, New York, 1953, pp. 261, 262.

58 Some of the features that the FHA could not recommend to the funding banks included the cantilevers, board and batten walls, and lack of paint to woodwork. Applications were compared rigidly with a specified type of construction and rules concerning timber spans, etc.

59 Wright, *Architectural Forum,* January 1948, p. 79.

60 For these and other details I am indebted to Erling Brauner, an original coop member and chairman of the Art Department at Lansing, Michigan. In Brauner's opinion, Wright suffered very great personal disappointment at the cancellation of Usonia I.

61 See Chapter 5, Popularizing Organic Architecture. The Galesburg homes included the following designs, all of 1948 and all of textile block: Weisblatt, Pratt, and Eppstein. The Meyer house, also of 1948, is of conventional concrete block.

62 Textile block homes by Wright at Parkwyn included the Levin house of 1948, the McCartney and Brown houses of 1949, and the Winn house of 1950.

63 Illustrated in *Architectural Forum,* January 1948, p. 84.

64 See Chapter 4, Broadacre City.

65 These were the Friedman house of 1948, the Serlin house of 1949, and the Reisley house of 1950.

66 This, and other instances, shows that Wright was not always the dictatorial primadonna that some evidence suggests. However, there are some examples of his tyranical behavior. Louis Frank (the present owner of the Bazett house) describes Wright's arrival at dawn to inspect the planting on the lot, and Ben Raeburn of Horizon Press tells a story of Wright rearranging a client's furniture by night (the Carlsen house, 1950, Phoenix, Arizona). The most amazing event is described by Chadwick in *The Pope-Leighey House* (op. cit., p. 73). To emphasize that the execution of his designs should not deviate from his drawings, Wright had his apprentices physically destroy unsightly and badly built changes to the Oboler gatehouse.

67 Priscilla Henken, "Usonia Homes," *Journal of Housing,* October 1953, p. 319; see also, "A Broadacre Project," *Town and Country Planning,* June 1954, pp. 294–300. In addition, I am indebted to Priscilla Henken for an interview in 1969.

68 The communal areas of land are important for subjecting varying houses to a greater natural whole. They also maintain the site's indigenous character. Customary American practice is to fell and plant alien types of trees.

69 Henken, op. cit., pp. 294–300.

70 For example craftsmanship was necessary to achieve the accuracy required in modular work, corner construction in hexagonal designs, and later specifications for pointing. Vertical joints were flush and colored, usually like the brickwork, and horizontals were raked out (sometimes every third course, and sometimes painted gold).

71 Robert Twombly, op. cit., p. 254. "From 1946 through 1959 he received 270 house commissions, 38 in 1950 alone."

72 During this period Wright lived part of the time in New York and had a suite altered for his use at the Plaza Hotel. This was briefly known as Taliesin East. The museum design was constantly changed and improved. Besinger worked on three sets of working drawings.

73 The Usonian automatic and prefabs are discussed in Chapter 5.

74 Pfeiffer, archivist for Taliesin Associated Architects, lists the second Jacobs house as being designed in 1942; see Olgivanna Wright, *Frank Lloyd Wright: His Life, His Work, His Words,* Horizon Press, New York, 1966, p. 216. My own work suggests a date 1 year later. Although Pfeiffer's dates purport to be those for design, and therefore those for Wright's drawings, they occasionally differ from those given by clients. Many projects are also missing from Pfeiffer's list. But since he is, in effect, the only person allowed access to both drawings and archives, the matter must await definitive dating.

75 Herbert Jacob's letter to the author, Nov. 4, 1973.

76 When I visited the house in the summer of 1969, the solar gain inside was excessive. The large areas of glass might suggest a corresponding loss in winter. The performance of the south wall would be improved by incorporation of an external sunshade below the roof overhang, and by adding internal shutters. However, these were not, of course, intended by Wright. The external planting specified by him in the *Architectural Forum* article of January 1951, "A Portfolio of Wright Houses," included polychromatic planting to define the edge of the sunken garden and *dense evergreens.* Neither was carried out. This might have had the effect of providing summer shade while allowing solar penetration in winter because of the sun's lower altitude.

77 A perspective of this house, listed by Pfeiffer as being projected for Northampton, Ohio, appears in Arthur Drexler, *The Drawings of Frank Lloyd Wright,* Horizon Press, New York, 1962, p. 208.

78 Rosalie Tonkens, "How a Home Built by Frank Lloyd Wright Changed Couple's Life," *The New York Times,* Feb. 6, 1972.

79 Wright, *The Natural House,* pp. 161–164.

80 Desert concrete was made of large stones or boulders embedded in concrete. Although originated at Taliesin West, Scottsdale, Arizona, its use was not reserved for desert sites alone. A dry mix was used so that stones were not coated when placed in the mold or form work. Any stone was suitable and masonry skills were unnecessary.

81 *Northwest Architect,* vol. 33, no. 5, p. 46, July-August 1969. The Grants approached Wright because of their native building material: "He was understanding and truly interested in our desire to build a house of our own stone."

Chapter 3

1 "Begin with a Hoe: An Interview with Frank Lloyd Wright," *The Nation's Schools,* vol. 42, pp. 20–24, November 1948.

2 The greater part of Wright's *An Autobiography* deals with his emotional troubles. For the emotional and financial facts viewed more dispassionately, see Robert C. Twombly's *Frank Lloyd Wright: An Interpretive Biography,* Harper & Row, New York, 1973, chap. 6. For a general account of the period, see Reyner Banham's "The Wilderness Years," *RIBA Journal,* December 1969.

3 Frank Lloyd Wright, "The Hillside Home School of the Allied Arts: Why We Want This School," pamphlet, Spring Green, Wis., October 1931.

4 Ibid.

5 This seems to be the generally agreed upon account of how Wright came by Taliesin. However, what evidence there is suggests that Mrs. Wright was at this time supported by her three children, Jane, Maginel, and Frank. It does not seem then that she was in a position to buy the property.

6 Frank Lloyd Wright, *An Autobiography,* Faber & Faber, London, 1932, p. 150.

7 Norris Kelly Smith, *Frank Lloyd Wright: A Study in Architectural Content,* Prentice-Hall, Englewood Cliffs, N.J., 1966, p. 98.

8 Leonard K. Eaton, *Two Chicago Architects and Their Clients, Frank Lloyd Wright and Howard van Doren Shaw,* M.I.T. Press, Cambridge, Mass., 1969.

9 John Lloyd Wright, *My Father Who Is on Earth,* G. P. Putnam Sons, New York, 1946, p. 25.

10 Kelly Smith, op. cit., p. 96.

11 Good general accounts can be found in the following: John Humphrey Noyes, *History of American Socialisms,* 1870, now republished as *Strange Cults and Utopias of Nineteenth Century America,* Dover, New York, 1966; Arthur E. Bester, Jr., *Backwoods Utopias,* University of Pennsylvania Press, Philadelphia, Pa., 1950; Oswald and Liselotte Ungers, *Kommunen in der neuen Welt,* Kiepenheuer and Witsch, Germany, 1972.

12 Wright had two bouts of pneumonia in 1935 and 1936, so the change of climate was recommended by his doctor.

13 Kelly Smith, op. cit., chap. 2; see also pp. 103, 116, 157, 158.

14 Jean-Jacques Rousseau, *Emile,* J. M. Dent & Sons, London, 1911, p. 26.

15 Kelly Smith, op. cit., p. 118.

16 Grant Manson, "Wright in the Nursery," *Architectural Review,* vol. 113, June 1953, p. 349; Richard MacCormac, "Frank Lloyd Wright and the Kindergarten," *Environment and Planning B,* vol. 1, no. 1., Pion Ltd., London, 1974.

17 John Dewey, *The School and Society,* University of Chicago Press, Chicago, 1923.

18 Donald De Nevi, "The Educational Thoughts of Frank Lloyd Wright and Their Implications for the Education of Teachers," thesis for Department of Education at the University of California, Berkeley, 1969, p. 167. (University microfilms.)

19 Ibid.

20 Mildred Whitcomb, "An Interview with Frank Lloyd Wright," *Nation's Schools,* vol. 42, no. 5, November 1948.

21 De Nevi, op. cit., p. 168.

22 Mary Ellen Chase, *A Goodly Fellowship,* Macmillan, New York, 1939.

23 Weiss Turkel Fogh, "The Wizard's Cauldron," *The Cambridge Review,* May 9, 1969.

24 Ibid.

25 Wright also mentions in *An Autobiography* that "Taliesin was a Welsh poet, a druid-bard" (p. 150). Kelly Smith derives strength for his Camelot analysis from Wright's quote: "Taliesin, a druid, was a member of King Arthur's Roundtable." This reference appears to be from Wright's recollection made during an NBC telecast "A Conversation," of May 17, 1953, reproduced in *The Future of Architecture,* Horizon Press, New York, 1953, p. 17.

26 John Howe, "Reflections of Taliesin," *Northwest Architect,* vol. 33, no. 5, July-August 1969, p. 26.

27 Frank Lloyd Wright, "Charter Applicants for Fellowship," Spring Green, Wis., 1932.

28 Howe, loc. cit., p. 28.

29 Ibid., quoting Wright.

30 Ibid.

31 Wright, "Why We Want This School."

32 Twombly, *An Interpretive Biography,* pp. 147, 172, 173. "Neither relied on formal instruction; indeed some observers felt they gave no instruction at all. Both Masters (as they were called) emphasized the value of physical labor as a necessary prerequisite to self-knowledge and inner peace; both taught the importance of close contact with nature, and of music and dance as vehicles for achieving harmony of Being. The young people grew their own food, maintained the estates, and were expected to be completely loyal; they were isolated from, and considered themselves superior to, the outside world. Gathering en masse at least once a week at the Master's feet for an esoteric talk and a musicale, none of them could undertake any activity without specific permission or instruction." Twombly has developed his observations in an article "Organic Living: Frank Lloyd Wright's Taliesin Fellowship and Georgi Gurdjieff's Institute for the Harmonious Development of Man," *Wisconsin Magazine of History,* vol. 58, no. 2, State Historical Society of Wisconsin, Madison, Winter 1974–1975.

33 Jimmy Drought, letter to Helen Beal, Nov. 6, 1934, "As you have no doubt heard Gurdjieff has returned several times for various lengths of stay. . . ." See also Eugene Masselink's undated letter to George Beal, "Gurdjieff is here feeding us salad and soups that would knock the roof off Correll's Drug Store if ignited." Both letters are in the possession of the Kenneth Spencer Research Library, University of Kansas, Lawrence, Kansas.

34 Twombly points out the primacy of the circle in mystic thought and its occurrence in Wright's plans, as for example, in the Monoma Terrace project for Madison, Wisconsin, with its zodiacal and day-night symbols, as well as in the spiral (which is an endless circle) of the Guggenheim Museum. I feel that there may be some accuracy in Twombly's view. Wright's work on the Automobile Objective Project for Sugarloaf Mountain, Maryland, coincides with his meeting Olgivanna. However, it should be related to Wright's ongoing architectural concern with the exploration of "breaking the box," or attaining greater spatial freedom (see Chapter 2).

35 Helen Beal, letter to her parents from Spring Green, Wis., July 22, 1934 (Spencer).

36 Howe, op. cit., p. 27.

37 *Taliesin Eyes,* broadsheet, vol. 1, no. 1, Spring Green, Wis., Oct. 1, 1938, in the possession of the Kenneth Spencer Research Library, University of Kansas, Lawrence, Kansas. There are eight issues of the newsheet, the last is dated Nov. 24, 1938, and was written just before the impending caravan to Arizona.

38 Ibid., no. 2.

39 Ibid., no. 5.

40 Conversations between Edgar Tafel and the author in Liverpool, England, March 1973, and in New York City, October 1973.

41 Mabel Morgan, letter to Helen Beal, Aug. 17, 1938, in the possession of the Kenneth Spencer Research Library, University of Kansas.

42 Ibid., Aug. 31, 1938

43 Helen Beal, letter to her parents from Taliesin, June 6, 1934 (Spencer Library).

44 Ibid. Edger Tafel validates this description of the early organization in a letter to the author, Sept. 18, 1973. In a letter of June 26, 1934, Helen Beal brings a charming practicality to bear in her criticism of the management of Taliesin: "The whole thing is being run on a very small budget but by people who have no conception of how to get the most out of a dollar. I find it most interesting because there is the foundation here for a very interesting experiment and plan but no system for carrying it out. To me it is tragic that a good thing seemingly is not being allowed to develop to full bloom because of lack of management."

45 Curtis Besinger, letter to the author, Dec. 26, 1973. Other details were derived from conversations between Besinger and myself at Lawrence, Kansas, in November 1973. For other descriptions of Taliesin see: Howe, "Reflections of Taliesin," *Northwest Architect;* Robin Boyd, "Taliesin Weekend," memorandum for Elizabeth Gordon, 1958, in the Wright Collection, University of Kansas. Elements of this were later reproduced in several issues of *House Beautiful.*

46 Besinger, ibid.

47 A good account of American farming practice during the 1930s, written from the organic point of view, it to be found in Louis Bromfield's

Malabar Farm, Ballantine Books, London, 1971.

48 Peter Blake, *Frank Lloyd Wright,* Master Builders Series, Gollancz, 1960; also George Collins, "Broadacre City: Wright's Utopia Reconsidered," paper to symposium at Columbia Unversity, 1961; also Twombly, *An Interpretive Biography,* p. 175.

49 Wright, *An Autobiography,* p. 24.

50 "At Taliesin," was the title of a column that ran in the Madison *Capital Times* for some 15 years. Occasionally it was by Wright, occasionally by named apprentices, but was usually anonymous.

51 Wright, *An Autobiography,* p. 359.

52 Jimmy Drought, letter to George and Helen Beal, Mar. 8, 1938, in possession of the Spencer Library, University of Kansas.

53 Howe, op. cit., p. 27.

54 Wright, *An Autobiography,* pp. 271 – 276. The chief sources for Ocatillo are Russell Hitchcock's *In the Nature of Materials,* plates 276 – 280; also Wright, *Architectural Forum,* vol. 68, January 1938.

55 Mabel Morgan, letter to George and Helen Beal, Jan. 20, 1938, in possession of the Spencer Library, University of Kansas.

56 Edward Frank, "Organic Philosophy, Organic Architecture, and Frank Lloyd Wright," paper in the possession of the Avery Library, Columbia University, New York. The design process for the Kaufmann house was attested to by Gregor Affleck in an interview with the author in October 1973.

57 Besinger, loc. cit.

58 Jack Howe, letter to the author, Jan. 5, 1975. For example, referring to the "All Steel" houses (1937) for a Los Angeles client in the steel business, Howe wrote, ". . . floors, walls (including window units), and roofs were all constructed of the same U-shape, 16-gauge steel units. I made the drawings for this developing some plans from the Two-Zone house, some from Usonian houses." These drawings are reproduced in *The Drawings of Frank Lloyd Wright,* Arthur Drexler, ed., Horizon Press, New York, 1962, pp. 141 – 144.

59 Curtis Besinger, letter to the author, Sept. 23, 1974.

60 Ibid.

61 Ibid.

62 Ibid.

63 Besinger thought that this indicated an awareness of history, in that rag papers had a better life expectancy than those made from wood pulp.

64 Besinger, loc. cit.

65 Ibid.

66 Ibid.

67 This is borne out by all the clients I have interviewed.

68 The only case I have discovered of clients being unprepared or ignorant of what they were embarking on was that of the Euchtmans in Baltimore, Maryland, 1940. "They were untypical clients. They only approached Wright because Usonians offered a way out of the problem of their site: they had bought a lot, then found the sewer was too high to allow a 'normal' house to be built, i.e., a basement was out. Wright never met them . . . they didn't really understand what they'd got into. They had no kids and were cleanliness fanatics. They fitted extra carpeting and plastic covers to the furniture." Conversation with Gordon Chadwick, New York, November 1973. The Bazetts, in Hillsborough, California, 1940, sold their house shortly after it was completed, but the problem seems to have been a marital one.

69 Howe, "Reflections of Taliesin," p. 29. "All were treated equally, whether theirs was a modest house or a mansion. The wealthy, however, were encouraged to give 'Fellowships' (an Oxbridge idea) and some responded magnificently. Four, including Francis W. Little of Minneapolis, were lifelong patrons of Mr. Wright."

70 Ibid.

71 Bernard Schwartz, interview with the author, November 1973.

72 Ibid.

73 See Appendix B, "The Personal Architectural Services of Frank Lloyd Wright."

74 Eugene R. Streich, "An Original Owner Interview Survey of Frank Lloyd Wright's Residential Architecture," *Environmental Design: Research and Practice,* William J. Mitchell, ed., University of California at Los Angeles, January 1972, p. 13-10-4. "In some cases where cost was a factor, Wright's staff dimensionally scaled down the design, while keeping the original concept intact."

75 Howe, loc. cit.

76 Streich, op. cit., p. 13-10-3.

77 Frank Lloyd Wright, letter to Francis Little, Nov. 3, 1913, in possession of the Metropolitan Museum of Art, New York.

78 Howe, loc. cit.

79 Gordon Chadwick, "The Challenge of Being a Taliesin Fellow," *The Pope-Leighey House,* Terry B. Morton, ed., National Trust for Historic Preservation, Washington, D.C., 1969, p. 64.

80 Ibid., p. 66.

81 Ibid.

82 Ibid., p. 69.

83 Edgar Tafel, interviews with the author, 1972 and 1973.

84 Jimmy De Reuss, "What We Learned from Frank Lloyd Wright," *House and Home,* February 1959.

85 Chadwick, op. cit., p. 67.

86 Ibid., p. 72.

87 Stanley and Gertrude Rosenbaum, interview with the author, November 1973.

88 Wright, *The Natural House,* p. 178.

89 Wright did not include this Usonian church in the lists of his work. His plan to site the building partly above a carpark, using the fall of the site, was rejected by city officials. The radical lightweight construction of steel grillage sprayed with gunnite cement, with walls only 4 inches thick, also met stiff resistance. After continued obstruction by the authorities, Wright eventually withdrew, design changes were made, and construction completed without his approval.

90 John Howe, letter to the author, Jan. 5, 1975.

91 Harold Turner, interview with the author, November 1973.

92 Professor Beal, interview with the author, November 1973.

93 Copy of a Wright letter made by George Beal in the Spencer Library. The letter is undated, but my research on the collection and my discussions with George Beal, Professor of Architecture at Kansas University throughout the period, all suggest a date around the late 1930s.

Chapter 4

1 Alexander Meiklejohn, *Education between Two Worlds,* Harper & Row, New York, 1942, p. 190.

2 Lucia and Morton White, *The Intellectual versus the City,* New American Library, New York, 1942. The Whites find parallels between Wright's ideas and Marxism, while Meyer Schapiro, himself a Marxist, denounced Wright as a fascist in his article "Architect's Utopia," *Partisan Review,* vol. 4, March 1938.

3 I have in mind here Howard's concept of unified land ownership in particular. Within his garden cities, the whole built-up area and its accompanying agricultural belt was to be under quasipublic or trust ownership. Planning control through leasehold covenants and the ability to incorporate social need with land value were the results. The need to ensure that the development of land took into account community interest, inspired many attempts to legislate in England. These began with Lloyd George's "People's Budget" and the attempted Liberal reforms of 1909, and continue to the present *Community Land Bill* of 1975, under which local government will eventually be required to purchase all development land at existing use value. The Conservative party has already announced that it will repeal this act. Wright's economic aims were never generally achieved in the United States. They are discussed further in this chapter.

4 Schapiro, loc. cit.; *Fabian News,* December 1898, quoted by F. J. Osborn in his preface to Ebenezer Howard, *Garden Cities of Tomorrow,* Faber & Faber, London, 1946. The latter suggested that the garden city would only have ben of use to the Romans who laid out Britian's cities:

Now Mr. Howard proposes to pull them all down and substitute garden cities, each duly built according to pretty coloured plans, nicely designed with a ruler and compass. The author has read many learned and interesting writers and the extracts he makes from their books are like plums in the unpalatable dough of his utopian scheming. We have got to make the best of our existing cities, and proposals for building new ones are about as useful as would be arrangements for protection against visits from Mr. Wells' Martians.

The assumption that building the new must necessitate demolishing the old is one that Wright's most trenchant critic, Kelly Smith, also makes.

5 H. G. Wells, *Anticipation,* Chapman and Hall, London, 1901. I am indebted at this point to Colin Ward for his article, "Say It Again, Ben!" in the *Bulletin of Environmental Education,"* vol. 43, no. 72, p. 19, Town & Country Planning Association, November 1974. Wells continues:

It is not too much to say that the London citizen of the year AD 2000 may have a choice of nearly all England and Wales . . . as his suburb, and that the vast stretch of country from Washington to Albany may be all of it "available" to the active citizen of New York and Philadelphia before that date.

It will certainly be a curious and varied region, far less monotonous than our present English world, still in its thinner regions, at any rate, wooded, perhaps rather more abundantly wooded, breaking continuously into park and garden, with everywhere a scattering of houses. . . . Each district, I am inclined to think, will develop its own differences of type and style.

6 Projects that had advanced to fullscale mockups or models and working drawings included the San Marcos in the desert resort near Chandler, Arizona, and the St. Marks-in-the-Bowery apartments in New York, in my opinion one of his finest large-scale projects. This became the "city dwellers' tower" for Broadacre City.

7 Frank Lloyd Wright, "Being the Kahn Lectures for 1930," *Modern Architecture*, Princeton University Press, Princeton, N.J., 1931.

8 Frank Lloyd Wright, *The Disappearing City*, William Farquar Payson, New York, 1932.

9 Broadacre City was also presented in Chicago in 1932. "Wright drew the biggest crowd to attend the City Club forum since the war. . . . He told of his Broadacre City idea." *Capital Times*, Madison, Wis., Feb. 18, 1932. Other secondary sources to those in the text are: *American Architect*, March 1935; *Watson Lectures*, London, 1939, published in the May 19, 1939 *Builder* and included in Wright's *The Future of Architecture*, Horizon Press, New York, 1953.

10 Frank Lloyd Wright, *Architecture and Modern Life*, Harper & Brothers, New York, 1938; *When Democracy Builds*, University of Chicago Press, Chicago, 1945; *The Living City*, Horizon Press, New York, 1958.

11 Frank Lloyd Wright, "A Conversation with Mies van der Rohe," *Taliesin*, Spring Green, Wis., 1935; this is a monologue of many pages with never an utterance from Mies.

12 Work on the model started a year before, in 1934, and continued by day and night. "We don't know the date here anymore . . . this model has started us all on the way to insanity, and the fear of April 1 is almost dreadful." Edgar Tafel, letter, Monday ? (sic), 1935, to the Beals, from Taliesin West, in the Spencer Library, University of Kansas.

13 Exhibitions were frequently financed or arranged by old Wright clients. For example, the one in Washington, D.C. was organized by Mrs. Avery Coonley, and the one in Marquette, Michigan, by Mrs. Abby Roberts.

14 The 1970 U.S. Census reported 74.9 million suburbanites, an increase of 25 percent over 1960, and outnumbering those in cities and rural areas. *Time* magazine ran a surveyed and computerized feature on this phenomenon entitled, "Suburbia: A Myth Challenged," on Mar. 15, 1971.

15 *Architectural Record*, April 1935, p. 248. Other unfootnoted quotes are also from this source.

16 This was literally a building to visit for leisure, containing a planetarium, restaurant and shops, surrounded by a continuous spiral coil of ramped carparking. Wright placed his 1925 project for Sugar Loaf Mountain, Maryland, in the Broadacre Model.

17 *Architectural Record*, loc. cit.

18 Wright, *The Living City*, p. 174.

19 *Architectural Record*, loc. cit.

20 Ibid.

21 Wright, *The Living City*, p. 137.

22 Frank Lloyd Wright, radio address at the opening of the Industrial Arts Exposition in New York, reported in the *Weekly Home News*, Spring Green, Wis., May 9, 1935.

23 Wright, *Taliesin*, Spring Green, Wis., vol. 1,

no. 1, 1934, pp. 6–7; reprinted in *Architectural Record*, loc. cit.

24 *Architectural Record*, loc. cit.

25 "Nature mocks our man-made efforts, throws the man aside at least, and taking a little here and there goes on with her work. To work with her is wisdom. To go against her is failure or worse." Wright, radio address, loc. cit.

26 Curtis Besinger, letter to the Beals, Mar. 8, 1943. ". . . Mr. Wright has spent most of his time this winter in writing. The first part in completing his 'Autobiography,' which will be coming out in April. Since then on Broadacre City. The Broadacres material was originally in the last book of the Autobiography but he decided to leave it out and try to make a separate book of it." Letter in the possession of the Kenneth Spencer Library, University of Kansas, Lawrence, Kansas.

27 Frank Lloyd Wright, Book Six, "Broadacre City," *An Autobiography*, The Taliesin Press, Spring Green, Wis., 1944, p. 29.

28 Ibid., p. 28.

29 Kelly Smith, *Frank Lloyd Wright: A Study in Architectural Content*, Prentice Hall, New York, 1966, p. 155.

30 Lionel March, *Frank Lloyd Wright: An Architect in Search of Democracy*, three broadcasts on the BBC, with the Third Program in January 1970: (1) "The Chicago Years to the New Deal, 1890–1935"; (2) "The Society and its City"; (3) "The Individual and his Home." The second broadcast was published in *The Listener*, vol. 83, no. 2144, Apr. 30, 1970, as "Imperial City of the Boundless West: Chicago's Impact on Frank Lloyd Wright." I quote here the first broadcast, p. 3.

31 Stephen Alexander, "Frank Lloyd Wright's Utopia," *New Masses*, vol. 15, June 18, 1935, p. 28. His comment that Wright ". . . is virtually alone among the architects of this country in his approach to the fundamental problems of presentday architecture as primarily socio-economic . . ." is more accurate and less prejudiced than many later comments; Meyer Schapiro, op. cit., pp. 42–47; George R. Collins, "Wright's Utopia Re-considered," paper in symposium, *Four Great Makers of Modern Architecture*, Columbia University, New York, 1961. It is notable that the most trenchant criticism of Broadacres has come from New York. This has disregarded the reality of the "drive-in" environment of millions of Americans and is written from the standpoint at once most far removed from the Midwest, South, and Far West way of life, and the one place in the United States where possession of a car can be a disadvantage.

32 Kelly Smith, op. cit., pp. 153, 154.

33 March, op. cit., first broadcast, p. 4.

34 Ibid., second broadcast, p. 2.

35 Ibid., third broadcast, p. 2.

36 Even Venetian gondolas were brought in to authenticate the canals of the Classical vision. Celebratory postcards and memento picture albums of the Exposition can still be found in antique shops all over the Midwest.

37 I am thinking of the cynical attempt by Burnham to buy Wright for the service of Classicism by a paid-up study at the Beaux Arts in Paris, described in Wright's *An Autobiography*, pp. 123–124. This must be counted one of the factors decisively contributing to his conviction about the necessity for an honest, *organic* architecture.

38 March, op. cit., second broadcast, p. 3.

39 Ibid., third broadcast, p. 4.

40 Ibid., second broadcast, p. 4.

41 Alvin Boyarsky, "Chicago à la carte: The City as an Energy System," *Architectural Design*, December 1970.

42 March, op. cit., first broadcast, p. 6.

43 I am thinking of the control of railroad and lumber interests, the proscription of corruption of the political machine, and numerous laws in the interest of working men and public health. For example, see Robert Maxwell, ed., *La Follette*, Prentice Hall, Englewood Cliffs, N.J., 1969.

44 The speech was given at the opening of the Arts and Crafts Society at Hull House. See Kaufman and Raeburn, eds., *Buildings & Writings*, pp. 56–73. Wright founded his aesthetic outlook on industrial elements (a use of the machine that pre-dates the Italian Futurists). Where Broadacre City eventually "tamed" industry into a nonpolluting, liberating, and integrative role, the Futurists enthused over the very noise, flames, and smoke that Le Corbusier (and CIAM, and therefore European planning orthodoxy) felt had to be quarantined in Ville Radieuse into Zones Industrielles. Lionel March developed this parallel in his second broadcast, p. 5, noting that whereas Wright's formative years were spent in an emergent twentieth-century city, Le Corbusier was confronted by the "Grand Design" of the established nineteenth century in Paris.

45 March, op. cit., first broadcast, p. 7.

46 Wright, *An Autobiography*, Book Six, p. 5.

47 Henry George, *Progress and Poverty*, Appleton & Co., New York, 1882, p. 104.

48 March, loc. cit.

49 Emma Goldman, *Living My Life*, vol. 1, Alfred Knopf Inc., New York, 1931, p. 462.

In my travels through the United States I had always found university towns the most indifferent to the social struggle. American student bodies were ignorant of the great issues of their native land and lacked sympathy with the masses. I was therefore not enthusiastic when Ben (her manager at the time — J.S.) suggested our invading Madison, Wisconsin. Great was my surprise when I discovered an entirely new note in the University of Wisconsin. I found the professors and pupils vitally interested in social ideas, and a library containing the best selection of books, papers, and magazines. Professors Ross, Commons and Jastrow and several others proved to be exceptions to the average American educator. They were progressive, alive to the problems of the world, and modern in the interpretation of their subjects.

Earlier Goldman had registered some doubts as to the commitment of Jane Addams (pp. 375–376). Visiting Hull House some time after Kropotkin, she found Addams and her colleagues affecting Russian dress and referring to their late guest as "Prince," a title he had long eschewed. However, by the standards of the *Attentat*, or political assassination favored by Berkmann and Emma Goldman's associates, Hull House would no doubt have a certain redolence of half-hearted liberalism.

50 Farmers' wealth, unlike that of holders of stock, was represented by their buildings and property, which were taxed. Faced with high taxes, tariffs, and the cost of rail shipping — the one practical mode of transportation for their produce — they staked future crops on bank

loans and found falling prices. The railroads also controlled the political machine.

51 March, op. cit., first broadcast, p. 11. March demonstrated that this connection had a personal basis; the younger son, "Phil" La Follette, resigned as secretary to Frank Lloyd Wright Incorporated (the legal body for which Wright worked) in order to become governor. March wrote:

The progressives' platform contained planks which are to be found in Wright's discussion of society, *The Living City*. This comes as no surprise since both Wright and the La Follettes shared intimately a common background in Wisconsin and the "Wisconsin Idea." The progressives were: *for* the right of men and women to own their own homes, their farms and their places of employment but *against* corporate and absentee ownership; *for* the public ownership of all utilities of common necessity including the media of communication — radio, telephone, post — the media of mass and bulk transportation, and the medium of exchange (the progressives stood for the national control of the country's banking business); they were *for* full employment, full social security, free education and health services; *for* co-operative marketing of food and the abolition of speculation and profiteering in its distribution; *for* the right of workers to organise as they choose; *for* free speech and thought, and *for* untrammeled investigation into all social injustices. The programme was designed to recover the essential ideals of the American constitution for a broadbased democracy in a world dominated by vast corporate interests and industrial enterprises.

52 Reyner Banham, *Los Angeles: The Architecture of Four Ecologies*, Penguin Press, London, 1971, pp. 78–83.
53 John L. Wright, *My Father Who Is on Earth*, G. P. Putnam Sons, New York, 1946, p. 31.
54 March, op. cit., third broadcast, p. 2; Frank Lloyd Wright, *Modern Architecture*, the Princeton Lectures, 1930, lecture six, "The City"; see also Wright's *The Living City*, pp. 81–83.
55 Frank Lloyd Wright, "Broadacre City," *Architectural Record*, April 1935, p. 244.
56 *Taliesin*, op. cit., a conversation with Mies Van der Rohe.
57 March, op. cit., first broadcast, p. 10. March points out that Gesell's works in English were distributed from San Antonio, Texas. "Owen D. Young was a notable representative for the United States at international monetary meetings during this period and, according to Irving Fisher, he was there actively promoting Gesellian ideas: in particular criticizing the gold standard and pressing for some international means of stabilizing exchange." The case is one of strong supposition and must await the opening of the Taliesin archives to scholars for confirmation.
58 Ibid., p. 9. "Irving Fisher, the outstanding American economist, writing on booms and depressions in 1933, thought that Gesell's proposal offered the speediest way out of the great Depression, and that in the long run it would be the best regulator of monetary velocity."
59 Ibid.
60 Silvio Gesell, *The Natural Economic Order*, Philip Pye, trans., Frohnan: Neo Verlag, Berlin, 1929; also London, P. Owen, 1958, p. 11.
61 March, op. cit., p. 15.
62 Byron Keeler Mosher, letter to the author, Nov. 16, 1974. But he stressed that the importance of technocracy to Taliesin was minimal.

63 Veblen lent strength to Wright's views on evolutionary social progress. He was skeptical of industrial change because: (1) The industrial system still had a margin of safety before collapse; (2) The technicians, who could play a revolutionary role, were unaware and imbued with the ideology of absentee ownership; (3) The working class, essential for revolution, was, through its unions, only interested on improving its lot within the existing system; and (4) The general population showed no sign of questioning the status quo.
64 Henry Elsner, Jr., *The Technocrats: Prophets of Automation*, Syracuse University Press, Syracuse, N.Y., 1967, p. 30.
65 C. H. Douglas, *Social Credit*, C. Palmer, London, 1924, p. 49.
66 *Architectural Record*, April 1935, p. 245.
67 Ruskin here footnotes ". . . and if not land; still less the water."
68 John Ruskin, "Letters to Working Men," *Fors Clavigera*, letter 89, vol. 8, September 1880. "Whose Fault Is It? To the Trade Unions of England." He goes on: "You must get your land by the law of labour . . . buying never to let go . . . and this, therefore, is practically the first thing you have to bring in by your new Parliaments (following enfranchisement) a system of land tenure, namely, by which organised classes of labouring men may possess their land as corporate bodies, and add to it — as the monks once did, and as every single landlord can, now."
69 March, op. cit., third broadcast, p. 8.
70 Ibid.
71 Ibid.
72 Ibid. This monograph was also a report to the President's Committee.
73 Ibid., third broadcast, p. 7.
74 *Kahn Lectures*, Lecture six, "The City," Princeton University, 1930; also in more detail in the lecture to the National Terracotta Society, Chicago, 1930.
75 Paul and Percival Goodman, *Communitas*, Random House, New York, 1947, p. 87.
76 "A Graphic Guide to Decentralization and Some Simple Facts on Reconversion," 78th Cong., 2d Sess., S. Res. 190, Oct. 7, 1944.
77 Ralph Borsodi, *Flight from the City*, Harper & Row, New York, 1933.
78 Rita Davidson and William Smull, "Bryn Gweled: A Co-operative Homestead Development in Pennsylvania," *Pencil Points*, March 1946, pp. 65–88. The community was a Rochdale cooperative, and homes were planned along Usonian lines, taking advantage of untouched, natural materials and optimal orientation. One architect, Paul Beidler, described them as "solar houses."
79 Wright, *London Lectures*, second lecture, 1939.
80 Ibid., third lecture.
81 The cemeteries were also in the woods. Tree cropping was to be integrated with the local economy in a hard-headed way. Lionel March notes in his second broadcast that the report on agriculture and forestry by O. E. Baker of the Department of Agriculture to President Hoover's Committee on Social Trends is mentioned frequently in *Architecture and Modern Life*, by Wright and Baker Brownell.
82 March, op. cit., third broadcast, p. 2.
83 Frank Lloyd Wright, "In the Cause of Ar-

chitecture II," *Architectural Record*, vol. 34, pp. 405–413, May 1914.
84 Frank Lloyd Wright, "Broadacre City: A New Community Plan," *Architectural Record*, April 1935, p. 247.
85 Wright, *An Autobiography*, Book six, pp. 3, 4.
86 Wright, "In the Cause of Architecture," *Architectural Record*, vol. 23, pp. 155–222, March 1908.
87 Wright, *The Living City*, pp. 193, 194.
88 Wright, *An Autobiography*, Book six, p. 14.
89 From Wright's radio address in New York City, op. cit., reproduced in *Weekly Home News*, May 9, 1935.
90 The full list is given in Appendix F. In his letter to the Beals, written at Taliesin West, Mar. 8, 1943, Curtis Besinger states that the petition had been sent "in the hope that it might be considered as a part of Post-War Planning." Letter in the Spencer Library, University of Kansas.
91 From the third lecture, *London Lectures*, May 1939. These are reproduced in Wright's *The Future of Architecture*, Horizon Press, New York, 1953, pp. 261, 262.

Chapter 5

1 Frank Lloyd Wright, *The London Lectures*, second lecture, 1939; also reprinted in *The Future of Architecture*, Horizon Press, New York, 1953, p. 250.
2 All nine of the resident Usonian owners whom I interviewed, and two of the pre-war owners who have moved, consistently voted for Roosevelt and the New Deal. Stanley Rosenbaum, for example, was familiar with Meiklejohn's concept of education and was deeply interested in the TVA and "alternative communities." Many owners still regretted Roosevelt's failure to nationalize the banks 35 years later.
3 Lionel March, *Frank Lloyd Wright: An Architect in Search of Democracy*, third BBC broadcast, January 1970, p. 8.
4 Ibid, pp. 6, 7, 8.
5 Talcott Parsons, discourse to the Social Theory Section of the 42nd meeting of the American Society of Sociologists, December 28, 1947.
6 Joseph K. Folsom, "Changing Values in Sex and Family Relations," *American Sociological Review II*, October 1937, pp. 717–726. "Decline in obedience of children as a value in parent-child relations as the family assumed egalitarian patterns" was reported. "The diminishing differential of adult-child privileges implied increasing provision for the specific requirements of children."
7 Irving Rosow, "Modern Architecture and Social Change," M.A. thesis, Wayne State University, Detroit, Michigan, 1948, pp. 50–52.
8 Ibid., p. 86.
9 Ibid., pp. 108–109.
10 Ibid., p. 108.
11 William Lescaze, *On Being an Architect*, G.P. Putnam Sons, New York, 1942. This quote by the dean of a prominent school of architecture is repeated by Rosow, ibid., p. 90.
12 Rosow, op. cit.
13 "A Little Private Club," *Life*, vol. 5; this article was reprinted in *Architectural Forum*, vol. 69, November 1938, pp. 331–340.

14 George Nelson and Henry Wright, *Tomorrow's House,* Architectural Press, New York, 1945.

15 Ayn Rand, *The Fountainhead,* Bobbs Merrill, New York, 1943.

16 See Chapter 3, p. 27.

17 Eugene Streich, "An Original Owner Interview Survey of Frank Lloyd Wright's Residential Architecture, *Environmental Design: Research and Practice,* William J. Mitchell, ed., University of California at Los Angeles, January 1972.

18 See Chapter 3, also transcripts of conversations with Wright's clients in Minnesota, 1969; John Howe, "Reflections of Taliesin," *Northwest Architect,* July-August 1969, pp. 35–47, 63, 65–77.

19 Dudley Spencer, interview with the author, August 1969.

20 *Northwest Architect,* op. cit., p. 45ff.

21 Ibid., p. 76; quoted by Mrs. Grant from the book *Taliesin Drawings,* by Edgar Kaufmann, Jr.

22 Scott and Helen Nearing, *Living the Good Life,* chap. 3, Schocken Books, New York, 1954.

23 *Northwest Architect,* op. cit., p. 76.

24 See Chapter 2. Wright's method of casting rocks into concrete in the mold appears to have originated at Taliesin West during the late 1930s.

25 Wright's six years in Japan enabled him to write as perceptively of its architecture as anyone in the English language:

The Japanese have never outraged wood in their art or in their craft. Japan's primitive religion, "Shinto," with its "be clean" ideal, found in wood ideal material and gave it ideal use in that masterpiece of architecture, the Japanese dwelling. . . .
In Japanese architecture may be seen what sensitive material let alone for its own sake can do for human sensibilities, as beauty, for the human spirit.
Whether pole, beam, plank, slat, or rod, the Japanese architect got to the forms and treatments of his architecture out of tree nature, wood wise, and heightened the natural beauty of the material by cunning peculiar to himself.
The possibilities of the properties of wood came out richly as he rubbed into it the natural oil of the palm of his hand, ground out the soft parts of the grain to leave the hard fiber standing, an "erosion" like that of the plain where flowing water washes away the sand from the ribs of the stone. . . .
And when we see the bamboo rod in their hands seeing a whole industrial world interpreting it into articles of use and art that ask only to be *bamboo,* we reverence the scientific art that makes wood *theirs.*
The simple Japanese dwelling with its fences and utensils is the *revelation of wood.*

Quoted from Frederick Gutheim, "Wood," *In the Cause of Architecture,* 1928, p. 117.

26 Bob Berger, interview with the author, August 1969; also Gloria Berger, letter to the author, Jan. 14, 1974.

27 Wright, op. cit., pp. 204–207.

28 Rosalie Tonkens, "Having a Home Built by Frank Lloyd Wright Changed Couple's Life," *The New York Times,* Feb. 6, 1972.

29 Wright, address at Masonic Temple, Detroit, Mich., typescript in possession of the Kenneth Spencer Research Library, University of Kansas, Lawrence, Kansas.

30 Frank Lloyd Wright, *The Natural House,* Horizon Press, New York, 1954, pp. 161–164. This design is of considerable interest to British architects because it pre-dates the panel and frame construction developed by Walter Segal during the 1960s. Segal's 4-ft, 4-in. module is the same as Wright's, however, his structural frame is irregular, made of 6 by 2 in. posts, and his composite sandwich panels are held by regular cover plates bolted back to back at 4-ft, 4-in. centers. Wright was able to use regular 4 by 4 in. structural posts, and his "Cemesto" panels, with an insulation core, faced each side with cement/asbestos, were held in place by quarter-round wood moldings. The Usonian houses themselves are a different way of achieving the low-cost assembly that Segal set himself.

31 Henry Russell Hitchcock, *In the Nature of Materials: the Buildings of Frank Lloyd Wright, 1887–1941,* Duell, Sloan & Pearce, New York, 1942, pp. 67, 121–122. Ready-cut, duplex apartments were built in 1915 in Milwaukee and elsewhere without supervision.

32 "Here Is Pre-fabrication's Biggest News for 1957," *House and Home,* vol. 10, pp. 117–121, December 1956.

33 Wright, *The Living City,* pp. 70–71.

34 Twombly, *An Interpretive Biography,* p. 255.

35 Wright, AIA address, Detroit, Michigan, May 27, 1954 (see footnote 29).

36 Frank Lloyd Wright, *The Living City,* Horizon Press, New York, 1958, pp. 148–149.

37 Ibid.

38 Interview with its owner, November 1973, who took the prototype off the company's hands, after the design failed to go into production.

39 Frank Lloyd Wright, "The House of the Future," address to the Cincinnati Convention, *The National Real Estate Journal,* vol. 33, July 1932.

40 Kathryn Morgan-Ryan, "On the Rolling Prairie . . . Oskaloosa, Iowa," *House and Home,* March 1958, pp. 90–104.

41 Ibid., p. 94.

42 Ibid., p. 93.

43 Jimmy de Reuss, *House and Home,* February 1959, p. 126.

44 Ibid.

45 Ibid., p. 128.

46 Ibid.

47 For example, "Seven Lessons from Frank Lloyd Wright," *House and Home,* vol. 6, November 1954; "Three New Houses by Frank Lloyd Wright," *House and Home,* vol. 14, August 1958.

48 *House and Home,* vol. 10, pp. 136–141, September 1956.

49 Ibid., p. 136.

50 Ibid., p. 137–141.

51 Wright stood absolutely for self-expression in the individual or culture. The image he usually employed to represent slick, imported superficiality was that of "Marybud" on the farm dolled up in her Hollywood finery. He saw himself expressing an indigenous Usonian culture in the teeth of foreign importation—first the Columbian Exposition, then the International Style. In 1914 he wrote in *In the Cause of Architecture II:* "The ideal of an organic architecture is no mere license for doing the thing that you please to do it in order to hold up the strange thing when done with the 'see what I have made' of childish pride."

Chapter 6

1 Frank Lloyd Wright, *The Future of Architecture,* Horizon Press, New York, 1953, p. 265.

2 Ibid., p. 277.

3 Frank Lloyd Wright, "Broadacre City: A New Community Plan," *Architectural Record,* April 1935, p. 247.

4 "To say upon an occasion like this that I love America and her early ideal of democracy is to write myself down as a mere politician or the usual sentimental fool. Nevertheless I say it. It is my first line, and I believe, will be my last sentiment." Radio address by Frank Lloyd Wright at the opening of the Industrial Arts Exposition in New York, reported in the *Weekly Home News,* Spring Green, Wis., May 9, 1935.

5 Frank Lloyd Wright, *The Living City,* Horizon Press, New York, 1958, p. 166.

6 The design for this project (1930) was modified to form the largest of the houses presented in the collateral models accompanying the Broadacres exhibit. These ran from a minimal house up to the five-car home.

7 This was discussed in 1939 in the third and fourth Watson lectures dealing with what should happen to the cultural inheritance of London; Wright, *The Future of Architecture,* p. 260.

8 Wright, *Architectural Record,* p. 247.

9 Wright, *The Living City,* pp. 193, 194.

10 Ibid., p. 193.

11 He has, however, projected designs for larger elements of the existing environment, such as his Circle Center Development for Bartlesville, Oklahoma, in 1956.

12 Herb Greene, Introduction to *Portfolio of the Work of Bruce Goff,* The Architectural League of New York and the American Federation of Arts, 1970. Goff himself has said: "The term Architect implies that a building is structurally sound, but implies also in a building an imaginative character expressive of its use, with integrity to economic requirements, to site, climate, materials, through which a building becomes inherently of its own style, both timely and timeless. Every building from the smallest to the largest, for any purpose, any place, anyone or any time deserves to become Architecture." Takenobu Mohri, *Bruce Goff in Architecture,* Kenchiku Planning Center Co. Ltd., Tokyo, 1970, p. 67.

13 Mohri, ibid., p. 210.

14 I am referring to the Dewlen Aperture project, Amarillo, Texas, of 1957, the Bass house project, Tulsa, Oklahoma, of 1956, and the Duncan house, Cobden, Illinois, of 1965.

15 Bartlesville, Oklahoma, of 1957. This house is best reviewed in "Fantastic Architecture," *L'Architecture d'Aujourd hui,* June-July 1962; and *The Kenchiku,* 1969.

16 Mohri, op. cit., p. 210. Price continued by describing Goff's design process:

"To enable guests to relax, to prevent any feeling of formality, I wanted everyone to sit on the floor. This was, and still is, almost unheard of in America, but because of this even strangers would appear as friends, and freedom from conformity would automatically commence. But there are serious problems with Americans sitting on the floor, for one, it gets hard—so soften it with four inches of carpet and foam pad. Without support, the back gets tired, therefore the walls are sloped, running the soft carpet up them, and even continuing it onto the ceiling where it can in turn soften the indirect light, making the source almost invisible. How then can people converse when they are lined up reclining on a wall? Sink a hexagonal pit in the center of the room for conversations, the carpet flowing throughout, surrounding a medallion in the center of the pit; this in turn can then be made to rise from the floor so it can contain a bar and stereo system—and, since music must be a basic principle of this house, give the main room a triangular shape so that by placing the speakers in one corner the house itself takes the form of a speaker horn, the deep rug along the walls acting as a baffle. By insisting that people leave their shoes at the door (another shock for Americans), no dirt will be carried in, and now the rug can be snow white and envelope each person as a cloud. As is here apparent, one simple thought can and did evolve into many different aspects, some directly connected, others indirectly, but all because of the simple directive that people should sit relaxed upon the floor.

17 U. S. Navy Seebee Chapel, Camp Parks, California (1944), Hopewell Baptist Church, Oilfield near Edmono, Oklahoma (1949).

18 Peter Gommon, "Bruce Goff and the Architecture of America," graduate dissertation at the Liverpool School of Architecture; interview of Goff by Gommon, summer 1969; in 1964, Lionel March and Philip Steadman were told by Goff in his Kansas City office that it was on Wright's specific advice that he "hardened up" the geometry of the Price house; the earlier first project of 1954 (Greene, *Portfolio,* p. 10) was comparatively willful and unstructured.

19 Mohri, op. cit., p. 205.

20 Ibid.

21 Ibid.

22 I visited the house and interviewed the Bavingers in November 1973. Bavinger worked on it fulltime one summer, and at other times on weekends. It consumed two bank loans and all his earnings. Like Wright's first Usonian, it attracted visitors, and like the Jacobs, the Bavingers charged $1 a tour. When the number of visitors reached 600 in one weekend, Gene Bavinger put up a studio dome alongside the house. This he obtained free, like he did the steel mast — wheedling the latter from an oil company. It is made of two links of drill stempipe and supports a live load of 78,000 pounds. Such key details as the detailing of the skylight framing and junction with the rough stonework he evolved himself. A neighboring architect told him that he, Gene, could "figure them out in less time than he could." The house's apparent unsuitability as an environment for raising children is belied by the Bavinger baby's uneventful pleasure in crawling everywhere. His parents cite the example of Indians on a reservation near Oklahoma City who live and raise children on a cliff.

23 Mohri, op. cit., p. 205.

24 My information was gained in a visit and interview with Mrs. Hyde in November 1973. I am also indebted to David Henderson for his subsequent interview with the Hydes.

25 The faceted lenses on these beams, as well as the diagonal "stained glass" on all the doors, turn out to be dime store ashtrays.

26 This shows clearly in the inside–outside ambiguities and spatial overlays of the Wilson house of 1950 in Pensacola Bay, Florida, and in the Pollock house of 1958 in Oklahoma City. The geometric planning discipline is at its most se-

vere and restricted in the plans for the Bass house project of 1956 for Tulsa, Oklahoma, and the Gutman house of 1958 in Gulfport, Mississippi. This last has an aerodynamic "flying saucer" form and has ridden out many destructive hurricanes. The theme continues in more recent homes like the Nicol house of 1966 in Kansas City, Kansas.

27 "America's Third Century: A Survey," *The Economist,* vol. 39, Oct. 25, 1975. "Immigration out of the rural, or non-metro, areas was 500,000 a year in the 1950s, just under 300,000 in the 1960s. Between 1970 and 1973, the latest years for which there is data, there was a population rise in America's non-metro, i.e., rural, areas of just over 350,000 a year. The next crisis of lifestyles will be re-ruralization."

28 Art Boericke and Barry Schapiro, *Handmade Houses,* Scrimshaw Press, San Francisco, 1973.

29 Jan Wampler, "Imprint Architecture," *Architecture Plus,* vol. 2, no. 4, pp. 88–99, July-August 1974.

30 This was perhaps signalled by Bernard Rudofsky's exhibition "Architecture without Architects," at the Museum of Modern Art in 1964, and his subsequent book of the same name published by Doubleday, Garden City, N.Y., 1964. A revival of visual romance followed, which organized new building functions within the accretive forms of such vernacular paradigms as traditional hill villages. This has become known as the "crumble aesthetic," and is probably best known in the work of Moishe Sadfi, such as the Habitat apartment building in Montreal.

31 The best known example is the demolition, by the U. S. army, of Yamasaki's prize-winning apartments in St. Louis, Missouri. Aspects of this tendency are chronicled in Robert Goodman's *After the Planners,* Penguin Books, London, 1972, and Oscar Newman's *Defensible Space,* Macmillan, New York, 1972.

32 John Turner, *Freedom to Build: Dweller Control of the Housing Process,* Collier-Macmillan, London, 1972.

33 "Desert House Is Roofed with a Movable Dome to Shade It in Summer, Open It in Winter," *Architectural Forum,* vol. 95, pp. 150–152, June 1951.

34 Recent examples of this lively tradition are the *Whole Earth Catalog,* The Portola Institute, Random House, New York, 1968–1971; and Ken Kearn's *Owner-Built Home,* Ken Kearn Drafting, Oakhurst, Calif., 1971. The *Catalog* ended its final edition with a section for its successors on "How to do a Whole Earth Catalog." Such journals as *Popular Mechanics Illustrated* have continued a "how-to-do-it consciousness," which is as old as the Republic. Daniel Beard's *Shelters, Shacks and Shanties,* Charles Scribner's Sons, 1914, summarized techniques of shelter learned from Western scouts' need to survive, which were in turn often learned from the Indians. Pioneers learned to operate covered wagons with the *Emigrant's Guide to California* (published circa 1850) by their side.

35 Frank Lloyd Wright, "Portfolio of Wright Houses," *Architectural Forum,* vol. 94, p. 93, January 1951.

36 Kearn, op. cit., epilog.

37 Wright, *The Future of Architecture,* pp. 277, 248.

38 The New Alchemy Institute publishes the

New Alchemy Newsletter from Box 342, Woods Hole, Mass. 02543. The work of the Integrated Life-Support Systems Laboratories has been reported in *Lifestyle, Mother Earth News,* and *Undercurrents* magazines, and to a wider audience in the *Los Angeles Times,* Jan. 1, 1973 in an article by J. Dreyfuss, "Unique Dome Home Harnesses Sun and Wind: New Mexico House Is First Totally Heated, Powered by Elements." The Institute operates reconditioned Jacobs' windplants. Marcellus Jacobs manufactured and sold $50 million worth of wind-generator units from the 1930s to 1956.

39 Wright, *The Future of Architecture,* p. 277.

40 Lord Llewelyn-Davies, letter to the author, Oct. 31, 1975. "While we were interested in Broadacre City we did not find it possible to get very much material on the ideas behind it and I do not think we went into any depth in studying it." The planning consultants were Llewelyn-Davies and Weeks, London.

41 Lionel March, "Spatial Organization of Hyperurban Societies," *RIBA Journal,* Mar. 21, 1968; see also, "Homes Beyond the Fringe," RIBA *Journal,* August 1967, and working papers of the Cambridge University Centre for Land Use and Built Form Studies.

42 This would be a compromise of Ivan Illich's proposals in **Energy and Equity** (1973), for the use of the bicycle as the sustainable standard of transportation to which the Third World would develop, and developed countries would develop. It is notable that research in the use of flywheels now substantiates those advantages of efficiency and reduction of fuel consumption for which Wright looked; flywheel-buses operate in Germany. There are also two models of pedal-driven cars now on the market: the PPV by Environmental Vehicles, Inc., of Sterling Heights, Michigan, and the Pedicar by Environmental Tran-Sport Corporation of Windsor, Connecticut.

43 I have in mind the potential of telecommunications to support informational and professional activities in the home, as Wright anticipated. The development of linguistic software and such interface characteristics as voice recognition can make the telephone a terminal comparable with sophisticated service bureaus for a data network. It might be acoustically coupled with the domestic television and a video-cassette storage unit. Research on lasers may yield greater possiblities, but co-axial cable allows up to 108 separate television channels. The means are clearly available to originate, rather than passively consume, media information. Although political problems are involved, feedback allows instantaneous polling—and has already been so used in television debates. The joint committee on communications of the National Academy of Engineering, along with the Connecticut Research Council, sponsored by Housing and Urban Development stated in June 1971:

It is the goal of the NAE-CRC joint committee to demonstrate that imaginative applications of communications technology to business, education, government, health, and cultural pursuits can stimulate the development of a new living pattern that fully utilizes the nation's land resources. Specifically, it is the NAE-CRC thesis that all the inventions have already been made to permit the design of special broadband (high capacity data carriers) communications sytems

which will allow these activities to be conducted more effectively in small communities, scattered throughout the nation. In the small communities of a new rural society, the problems now plaguing large cities would remain manageable.
It is important to stress that the intent is not to deurbanize the United States, but to give the 100 million Americans the option to live and work in either the existing urban or a new rural community.

A rural repopulation policy, such as this implied, was one of the strategic conclusions of the New Rural Society Program study carried out for HUD by Fairfield University with the Goldmark Communications Corporation, Contract No. H-1694, May 1973. The effect of (briefly) supplying sophisticated hardware to a rural region and two banks in Connecticut was tested. The Joint Unit for Planning Research at University College, London, which was one of the subcontracting consultants for this report, has continued work on the effects of telecommunications on physical planning, including the degree of psychological acceptance of substitution for intercourse, and is currently dubious about a great degree of change. The situation seems best summarized by John Goddard, geographer at the London School of Economics:

In terms of locational trends, few planners have yet come to grips with the likely impact of rapid developments in communications technology that are now taking place. Interdisciplinary research in such fields as Communications Engineering, Industrial Psychology, Business Administration, Architecture, and Geography is urgently required to assess the implications of communications developments in Organizational structure and Location in particular, and City Structure in general.

John Goddard, and J. Andersen, *Current Approaches to Human Geography in Sweden,* London School of Economics Discussion Paper no. 33, 1968.

44 Solar collectors will not operate if they are shaded by neighboring buildings. There is little purpose to composting organic waste without a garden on which to spread it. Windmill blades becoming detached in a storm can travel through the air at speeds of 700 mph and could be a hazard in high-density housing.
45 D. L. Meadows et al., *The Limits to Growth: A Global Challenge,* Universe Books, New York, 1972. The other principal statements on the environmental case are in: Paul R. and Anne H. Ehrlich, *Population, Resources, Environment,* W. H. Freeman and Company, San Francisco, 1970 and 1972; and "Blueprint for Survival," *The Ecologist* magazine, January 1972. These views have been opposed, among others, by W. Beckerman, *In Defence of Economic Growth,* Jonathan Cape, London, 1974.
46 Gerald Leach, "The Energy Costs of Food Production," paper presented to the Man/Food Equation Symposium at the Royal Institution, London, Sept. 20–21, 1973. An illuminating correspondence in *The Times* followed the publication of an article, "Pointing the Way to More Rational Use of Energy," by Lord Rothschild (technical advisor to the British Government), on Jan. 9, 1974. Rothschild quoted the energy accounting figures of D. Pimental et al. (*Science,* 1973, pp. 182, 443) for American maize production. Dr. Blaxter of the Rowett Research Institute of Aberdeen found his conclusions too optimistic:

Even if we ignore inputs of energy to make herbicides, insecticides, fungicides, and pharmaceuticals and do not consider the energy required to make and replace tractors and implements which farmers use, and which of course depreciate, the energy input as fossil fuels into farming amounts to 47.1×10^9 Mcal each year, that is considerably more than the 35.4 that we obtain as food. The output to input ratio is not, as for maize, as favourable as the 2.8 Lord Rothschild quotes but is only 0.75. For individual farm products the ratio varies appreciably, from values of well over 2.0 for grains, through values of 1.1 for main crop potatoes to 0.3 for milk and 0.16 for eggs.
In *The Times,* Jan. 14, 1974, Leach pointed out on January 11 that: Overall, United Kingdom farming consumes about 6% of the total energy supplies of the nation, while food manufacturing, distribution and sales consume a further 8 per cent — giving a total energy output/input ratio a good deal lower than 0.2. In contrast, the most "primitive" agricultural societies, farming with no more than muscle power and an odd steel-tipped tool, achieve energy ratios in the region of 15 to 20, though their yields per acre are one quarter to one half of ours.

47 Best and Ward, *The Garden Controversy,* Department of Agricultural Economics, Wye College, Kent, England, 1956. This summarized a previous unpublished study by the Agricultural Land Service Research Group of the Ministry of Agriculture and Fisheries. Patricia Pringle calculated output per house-plot acre at 14 houses/acre in 1970 to be £94.70. Gross yield per acre of tillage for 1969/70 was £71, plus 25 percent for better than average land, was £88. See Pringle, "All Hands to the Spade," *Undercurrents,* London, 9, pp. 35–40, 1975. "Back gardens and allotments are still recognized as having the highest productive yield of all land due to crop rotation and personal involvement rather than monoculture and mechanization." One might add composting as a factor.
48 The effects of monocultural practices are now well known. The nitrogen-fixing qualities of rotation, with leys and natural manuring, are replaced by artificial fertilizers. These progressively destroy soil humus and reduce the population of microorganisms that give it friability. The results are poor drainage and falling yields, after initial gains. Greater applications of fertilizers and more powerful machinery to work the intractable soil become necessary. These cause soil compaction and tighten a vicious spiral.
49 The greater the use made of labor, the greater is the likelihood for good husbandry and smaller allotments of land; and the greater the use made of machinery, the greater is the need for capital and larger units of land. The Third World problem that most exacerbates the growth of population is unemployment. Dr. Abbas Ammar, Deputy Director-General of the International Labor office placed "overt" urban unemployment in poor nations in 1972 at 15 to 20 percent. According to him, "the total under-utilization of labor in both rural and urban employment was estimated at 30 to 40 percent; labor-intensive forms of production were required." The success of the "Dig for Victory" campaign in Britain in 1944, when gardens produced 10 percent of all home-grown food while the adult population was involved in the war effort, is well known. The National Farmers Union farm accounts scheme of 1965 indicated that output from British farms of 0 to 50 acres was £60 per acre, 51 to 150 acres was £40, 151 to 300 acres was £35, and over 300 acres was £32.
50 Dr. Norman Borlaug, who won a Nobel prize for developing the new strains of rice upon which the Green Revolution is partly dependent, agrees that the gains are only short-term. Their effects may prove counterproductive. The new plant strains only perform well when farmed by industrialized methods. Consequently, large landowners grow and benefit from them, since only they can afford the necessary capital. Smaller landowners are eliminated and tenants dispossessed. This process is endemic in poor nations as Brazil has shown:

The land in the South, especially in the state of Parana and earlier also in São Paulo itself, which was divided into relatively small homestead properties, came to be concentrated into large holdings precisely when it was invaded by the capitalist expansion of coffee and other cash crops. In consequence, the standard of living of a large part of the landed population fell in the train of this capitalist development. It was during the capitalist expansion of the 1920s and 1940s and the lesser expansion of the 1950s that the concentration of land ownership increased, tenant farmers were transformed into agricultural wageworkers, and the level of living of the majority declined. During the 1930s, on the contrary, and in some places in the 1950s, these trends were in the reverse direction: de-concentration of landholding, increased smallholders and tenants, higher standards of living for the rural population. But when the United States withdrew its sugar quota from Cuba and parcelled it out among its "friendly" nations, Brazil among them, and in consequence the demand for northeastern sugar briefly rose again, sugar was planted right into the peasants houses, in the words of the now imprisoned Governor of Pernambuco; and their living standards suffered accordingly.

Andre Frank, *Capitalism and Underdevelopment in Latin America,* Part III C: "The Development of Underdevelopment in Brazil," Pelican Books, London, 1969 and 1971, p. 227. As the experience of India has shown, with crop failure and famine in such states as Behar, impoverished peasants leave for the cities.
51 Taliesin certainly offered no model for communal democracy. I find this one of the most valuable points made by Professor Kelly Smith on Wright's make-up. He accounts for the vacillation and polarity in his thinking by the Rousseauistic difficulty of resolving the demands of the individual and society. He found Wright's "conception of a society of responsible but absolutely free individualists . . . an impossible notion" and suggested that this lay behind his personal difficulties and attitude to the city. Smith quoted Rousseau's *Emile:* "He who would preserve the supremacy of feelings in natural life knows not what he asks. Ever at war with himself, hesitating between his wishes and his duties, he will be neither a man nor citizen." In *Frank Lloyd Wright: A Study in Architectural Content,* Prentice-Hall Inc., Englewood Cliffs, N.J., 1966.
52 Raymond Williams, *The Country and the City,* Chatto and Windus, London, 1973, pp. 304, 305. Williams' book uses English literature and social thought to trace the effect of the rise of

capitalism on the English city and country. It offers an important paradigm for current Third World developments. He also points out that there is an undeveloped formulation of decentralization in revolutionary thought, and quotes:

Engels' writings on socialism as "abolishing the contrast between town and country, which has been brought to its extreme point by present-day capitalist society." Williams comments, "Marx and Engels wrote that the housing question could never be solved while 'modern big cities' were maintained, and that only with socialism could we restore 'the intimate connection between industrial and agricultural production" (p. 304).

Williams analyzes the ambiguity in the socialist argument, containing as it does Marx and Engels' view of "the idiocy of rural life." Yet it is from this rural quarter that the revolutionary forces of the last 40 years have come. China is now the most successful country in combating the primacy of the cities and building up a self-reliant decentralized social structure. More recently, Cambodia appears to offer a modern example of instant, and imposed, decentralization.

182

Appendix A
A Spatial Analysis of Usonian Houses

Any experience of Wright's domestic designs of the 1937–1950 period shows a remarkable sense of naturalness and ease, yet simultaneous conceptual rigor. Wright was able to conjure extraordinary spatial variety from minimal materials and dimensions. This ability was achieved through a structural vocabulary that was developed throughout his life. It consists of a three-dimensional field of grid lines through which the solid elements of the building are slid and located, and enables the voids, covered spaces, windows, other openings, and no-form forms such as terraces and car courts to be both integral to the whole and equally meaningful. Indeed the use of the grid allows what is implied by the perceived form of the building to be as important as what is explicit. It is this quality that gives the houses their perceptual richness and meaning, that endears them so much to their owners.

The Usonian houses develop and simplify the methods of grid planning that were first used in the Prairie houses. Geometric systems had an obvious fascination for Wright as can be seen in his earlier Sullivanian ornament and sketch plans. He himself suggests in the first book of *An Autobiography* that the origins for this were his close childhood observation of plants, crystals, and rock formations. His perception was already conditioned however by his kindergarten experience. Grant Manson, who first pointed out the formative nature of Froebel's precepts in Wright's early life, observed that "the child was encouraged to see that geometric forms underlie all natural objects."[1] Nevertheless an anomaly exists. The configuration of geometric grids is inorganic, and their use to create an "organic" architecture therefore presents a problem.

Early Grid Planning

It is impossible to underrate the importance of geometrical organization in Wright's work. The origins of this design tool have been shown by MacCormac to lie in the "gifts" of Froebel.[2] As an educational pioneer, he may be compared with Maria Montessori, and his toy-patterns were calculated to inculcate an appreciation of structure and expectation of unity into the world of the child. MacCormac showed that Wright derived a philosophy as well as a design discipline from the kindergarten. He had absorbed experiences with his hands and eye,[3] which were intended by Froebel to be an instrument in a system of education. This he based upon a "pantheistic conception of nature." Its aim was to bring about an understanding of "Natural Law" that would

simultaneously develop the powers of reason and convey a sense of the harmony and order of God: "God's works reflect the logic of his spirit and human education cannot do anything better than imitate the logic of nature."[4]

The basis of the patterns in the kindergarten handbooks was the geometry of crystallography, which Froebel had studied and which he took to be representative of the structure of all matter.

183

The Evans house, Chicago, Illinois, 1908. Richard MacCormac's analysis of typical Prairie house geometry shows the tartan grid planning condensed to its starkest point.

Wright's inclination to look for unity in nature was confirmed for him by the writings of Herbert Spencer, which Sullivan gave him to read. The 19th-century confusion between organic and inorganic growth was articulated by Spencer, who as late as 1898 "could still assert that the growth of crystals and organisms was 'an essentially similar process.'"[5] MacCormac suggested that it was from the manuals of Froebel and the biological terms of Sullivan that Wright derived the characteristic meanings of some of his personal design vocabulary: he cited nature, organic, crystallization, integration, efflorescence, and structure. Wright's view of the need for integral ornament that is a celebration of structure is a neglected subject. It is nicely contained in the word "efflorescence"; however, this lies outside the present discussion.

When a child played with Froebel's blocks, he did so in a disciplined 19th-century manner upon gridded boards and under rules which anticipated certain relationships. Similarly the mat-making or plaiting "gifts" were carried out within an obvious operational discipline. MacCormac showed that Wright set out to build an architecture woven into a *three-dimensional* grid. He demonstrated that the Prairie houses were a literal projection of their complex and often irregular planning grids. These took a "tartan" form, A-B-A, A-B-A-C-A-D, or A-B-A-C-A-D-A-C-A-B-A. Wright was not concerned that the grid pattern should be symmetrical. This provided a means by which every element of the building could be coordinated into a whole. It also solved an endemic architectural problem, the potential divorce between the intellectual organization of the plan and the physical experience of an observer; with Wright they became one and the same, concept and experience. A vocabulary of forms was used to translate or express the grid at all points — the solid rather than pierced balconies, planters, bases of flower urns, clustered piers, even built-in seats were evocations of a house's underlying structure. This process reached its most complex point in the rhythmic overlays and punctuating piers of the Martin house in Buffalo, New York, of 1904 and its most taut expression in the Evans house in Chicago, Illinois of 1908, where the cruciform core of the plan (with the usual suppressed domestic quarter) was held as if magnetically between terminal piers.

Sites and Movement Patterns

The early work, named after its region, the Prairies, is for the most part placed upon flat ground, within the enveloping grid of the city subdivisions.[6] In organizing his clients' lots, which were themselves a subdivision of the block, into a matte of tartan grid lines, Wright was grounding an architecture of definition. The property boundary formed an enforced limit to a framing of activities and forms that spiraled in to inglenook seats at the symbolic core of family hearth. It was an architecture that was organic in the sense of "the parts being integrate with the harmonious whole," but esentially inorganic, in the sense that it did not need to take account of nature's accidents. Almost the only exception is the Glasner house in Glencoe, Illinois, of 1905, with its bridge across a ravine to a tea house,

which may be seen as a point of departure for later developments. The grid planning of Usonians was to become looser by allowing nature to carry out a dialog with the geometry of the house.

MacCormac gave a crucial insight into the grammar of Wright's design. However, one further element of the early work has not attracted attention: the use of movement and careful organizing of its pattern. This was to be an important element by which Wright sought to tie the geometry of the later designs into their sites.

The plan of the Cheyney house in Oak Park, Illinois, of 1904 is an instructive example of the use of the early tartan grid. This encompasses the whole site and controls the way in which the house makes contact with the streets around it. Their grid, in turn, is a part of the grid over the whole state of Illinois, of which Chicago is the climax, as well as a part of the 1-mile grid of the 19th-century Continental Survey, which extends throughout the Western United States. However, the house also displays a curiously wandering and shifting manner of approach. To reach the interior, a visitor is required to make many turns along paths, which are deflected by such manifestations of the grid as steps and planters. At each turn the house and its site are observed in a new relationship. The same process continues into the interior. This way of moving and seeing have nothing to do with the axial, simplistic approach of the classical tradition, but much in common with Eastern architecture. It was common practice in Japanese urban housing to enter the small lot by bridging a street water channel and traversing a minute forecourt or garden to the entrance. The first symbolized a transfer from public to private domain, and the second, involving careful planting and paving, meant experiencing an indirect approach through many kinds of texture and transparency. The dimensions for all this rarely exceeded 20 ft. In Versailles and the classical tradition everything is subject to instant bombast. In traditional Japanese architecture, house and garden progressively reveal more of their nature as they are traversed.

Wright made his first contact with a culture that was to fascinate him for the rest of his life in the Japanese pavilion at the Columbian World's Fair in 1893. The Winslow house in River Forest, Illinois, of that year was his first mature design. It displays a simple axial, symmetrical approach, sustained within by a similarly balanced room plan. However, interior movement is circular around the central fireplace core, and the symmetry is eroded by a rear porch and the kitchen and porte-cochere. The Heller house of 1897 and the Husser house of 1899, both in Chicago, were narrow, deep, plans projected very clearly from tartan grids. However, the movement pattern of both designs was one of traversing strips in the grid between the offset symmetries of the main rooms. In the Waller project of 1898 in River Forest, Illinois, this movement pattern was used to combat a strongly axial plan that incorporated diagonals and an octagonal room — one of Wright's favorite devices of the time.

In 1905 Wright made his first visit to Japan. It is very likely that the insistent modular organization of traditional Japanese architecture, based on the tatami floormat, reinforced his conviction of the need for grid planning. But his work after this date increasingly substituted a wandering, devious route pattern across and about the grid for the more simple progression up and down tartan strips of earlier designs. The six turns and spiral approach to the livingroom seat of the Gale house of 1909 is matched in the Robie house and other work. It is most clearly in evidence in the Emil Bach house of 1915, in Chicago, Illinois. This square plan design shudders under the effect of the grid upon it, indented, pier punctuated, and layered outside with trellises.[7] The site is treated, albeit very quietly, as an obstacle course for the visitor to traverse. He is required to mount steps and negotiate garden elements that are all subterranean eruptions of the grid before ricocheting through the overlapping spaces of the interior. By the time the spiral pull of the spaces have deposited him safely by the chimney core in the dining area, he has executed eleven turns.

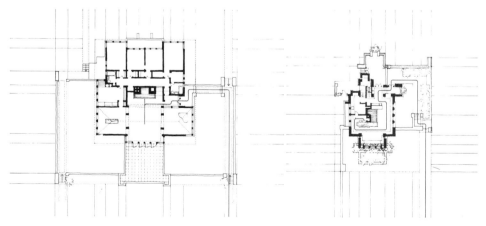

The Cheyney house, Oak Park, Illinois, 1904. The tartan grid plan is combined with a meandering movement pattern.

The Bach house, Chicago, Illinois, 1915. The intricate movement pattern is established at the sidewalk and continues into the interior. The plan is basically that of the one-zone house of 1934.

By the time he left Chicago, Wright possessed a vocabulary of a crystalline organization that contained a shifting manner of movement about it. He summarized his design process;

In the logic of the plan what we call standardization is seen to be fundamental groundwork in architecture. All things in nature exhibit this tendency to crystallize; to form mathematically and then to conform, as we may see. There is the fluid, elastic period of becoming, as in the plan, when possibilities are infinite. New effects may then originate from the idea or principle that conceives. Once form is achieved, however, that possiblity is dead so far as it is a positive creative flux.[8]

Later Developments

In Los Angeles Wright was confronted by sites that were almost never flat. The Millard house of 1921 in Pasadena was embedded into the side of a ravine. The Storer house of 1922 lay on the acute bend of one of the contour roads of the Hollywood Hills. The Freeman house of 1922, perched on the side of these hills, was entered from above with bedrooms below. The Ennis house of 1923 crowned a ridge in the Griffith Park area. Wright was obliged to extend his grid downwards from the floor level of his designs (metaphorically speaking) to encounter local topography, and by this means contrived to use terraces and retaining walls to tie his concept into the site. The vocabulary of these houses of the 1920s, of concrete block and paving, is therefore found all over the site, both above and up to 50 ft below them. At a functional level this gives easy access to the house up the contours or from the house to the terraces. At the conceptual level it allows nature in the form of the demands of the site to penetrate Wright's geometric grid or "field,"[9] and co-exist there with the solid elements of the house.

The Freeman house, Los Angeles, California, 1922. The three-dimensional grid of the "textile block" forms a cage within which solid and pierced blocks and windows are interwoven.

The grid in these houses became a regular one determined by the module of blocklength horizontally and blockcourse vertically. This construction system, named "textile block" by Wright, incorporated two-way steel reinforcement and could be given a patterned surface according to the mold used. It became a crucial stage in his struggle to unite inside space with outside space—to "break the box" as he termed it. It marked the transition from the mature and complex geometrical organization of the Prairie houses to the freer, yet more rational ordering of space in the Usonian houses. It was at this point that the reinforced blockwork dictated a vertical module corresponding regularly with the courses and enabled Wright to open up the corner, most dramatically in the Freeman house. Here the plate glass-to-glass corner windows run through two stories. They are framed up with horizontal muntins, continuing the line of mortar joints course by course, and result in an extraordinary ambiguity where apparently weightless blocks intersect with the glass. In the Storer and Millard houses Wright was able to dissolve the solids of his walls in a pierced, shimmering screen of textured, partially glazed blocks. They become a diaphonous membrane that sifts space flowing into and out of the interior. The contrast with Wright's early description of his aspirations with this problem could not be greater. In 1908 he wrote:

I used to gloat over the beautiful buildings I could build if only it were unnecessary to cut holes in them.[10]

In 1932 he declared with a sense of achievement:

Now came clear an entirely new sense of architecture, a higher conception of architecture . . . space enclosed . . . this interior conception took architecture entirely away from sculpture, away from painting and entirely away from architecture as it had been known in the antique. The building now became a creation of interior space in light. And as this sense of the interior space as the reality of the building began to work, walls as walls fell away.[11]

The advance in his grasp of spatial organization shown in the concrete block houses was clearest in the last building of this type, the Lloyd Jones house of 1929 in Tulsa, Oklahoma. Its walls are made up equally of alternating vertical strips of glass and blockwork, the one divided by horizontal glazing bars and the other by cement courses. Faceted glass bays or prows plough through these walls as a literal crystallization of the planning grid. The artificial lighting and ventilation is integrated within pierced textile blocks.

The Kaufmann weekend house, "Falling Water," of 1935 built near Ohiopyle, Pennsylvania, is also important in the development of Wright's pre-Usonian designs. It is of course the most celebrated example in his work of the relationship between a house and its site. The spectacular form of the building, poised over its waterfall, has tended to obscure the nature of the strong contrast between the two and to substitute an image of conjunction of house and site. The house, although it is cantilevered from highly organic masses of stonework, is essentially composed of concrete horizontals with steel-framed glazing, both of which are inimical to the

forms of the woods around it. Its grid planning, however, represents a turning point. It is a particularly lyrical example of the penetration of nature into the field of the house. Native rock is allowed to come through the floor, and this acts both as the base for the fire and as the psychological foundation for the design.

Usonian Grid Planning

The three-dimensional grid of the Usonian houses was regular and an inherent part of the locational process of their building.[12] Horizontal dimensions were 2 by 4 ft, or occasionally other subdivisions of the 8 by 4 ft plywood sheet and other board materials. The vertical module was 1 ft 1 in., or the distance between batten centers in the board and batten walls. Brick courses were laid to coincide with this dimension and were also a secondary vertical dimensioning system.[13] The planning grid was therefore a "cage" made up of locational "fixes," which were in turn determined by practical considerations of building materials and process.

Both planes of the Usonian grid-field were used to locate each element in space. They determined the broad enclosure of internal and external areas and every detail of interpenetration between the two. Wright's skill lay in the perfect coordination of horizontal and vertical systems to manipulate the character of every part of this "family" of houses. If a part of the structure rose above ceiling height, such as the chimney masses and raised clerestory roofs, it encountered the vertical grid. If a part of the concrete floormat or brick base dropped to a lower level or to deal with a falling site, it again was gripped by the module and conditioned by it. This organization of the vertical dimension is a real advance on that of the Prairie houses. In homes which are small it gives a broad unfussy appearance and unifies disparate elements. The 1 ft 1 in. band forms a "layering" system of stripes. These control and regulate the heights of every visual element — the main structural features such as eaves and clerestory lines, planters and retaining walls, tops of doors and internal decks, and fittings such as built-in furniture, bookshelves, tables, and worktops. As a result these all unite into an unobtrusive combination of calm horizontality, slipping past and apparently through brickwork and windows.

Usually there are three plans for each Usonian house. There is the floor plan. There is a "deck" plan at door-top height. And there is a high-level ceiling plan, which applies either to sloping ceilings or raised clerestory areas depending on whether there is a pitched or a flat roof. These plans do not necessarily coincide. The experience of Wright's interiors is one of immediate enclosure by means of walls, although these walls are more liberating than enveloping and always slip out of view toward some unseen point. The space that a person moves through is accompanied by a contrasting system that operates above his head. This is formed by Wright's characteristic "decks." These, like many of the elements of his architecture, originated in the Prairie houses. They are flat ledges of wood construction normally about 2 ft in width and always some 6 ft 6 in. above the floor. They are an important component of Wrightian interiors since they stream throughout the chief spaces at door-top height and

1   Visually unify areas whose boundaries may be complex.
2   Carry the lighting system; concealed lights above to give indirect light reflected from the ceiling and recessed downlights to wash the drapes and illuminate the perimeter of rooms.[14]
3   Incorporate track for drapes.
4   Provide a surface for bowls or decoration; this was where Wright placed his beloved pine boughs.
5   Integrate inside with outside: the soffit of the deck continues above all windows to become the exterior roof overhang.

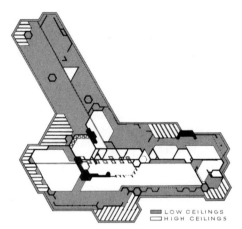

LOW CEILINGS
HIGH CEILINGS

The configuration of the Hanna house decks contrasts with the floor plan below and the sloping ceiling above. In most flat-roofed Usonians the raised ceilings are in the clerestory lanterns.

The upper-level ceilings have the property of dramatizing the main spaces of the Usonians. In post-1945 houses these are often sloping and give a restful, containing "cap" to the interior. This is similar to what is popularly known in America as a "cathedral ceiling." With Wright the inner space always conforms to the exterior form; there is no such spatial "cheat" as a loft space. However, the majority of Usonian houses have flat upper roofs, surrounded by clerestory windows. These give an open character to the space, akin to partially removing the roof, as the sky and nearby trees become visible inside. Moreover, the clerestory daylight is modified by the fretted plywood through which it filters. The interior is also animated by raking sunbeams that can be especially beautiful at the end of the day when the lower part of the house may be in shadow.

The combined effect of architectural treatment at these three plan levels is to give Wright's space an extraordinary richness, which is simultaneously lucid, deceivingly artless, and geometrically controlled. The lower part of his spaces is both containing and beckoning, leading the eye to a point beyond view. The decks give the interiors a sense of breadth and repose that corresponds with the overpowering horizontality of the exteriors. And twin scales of door and ceiling

height provide contrast, which exaggerates the low character of intimate spaces and height of living areas and persuades the eye that the house is larger than it actually is.

Wright demonstrated a final subtlety in the Usonian houses that had cypress-boarded rather than plywood ceilings. He used the boards' linear nature to emphasize the direction of movement through his spaces. The direction of the boarding corresponds with the flow of the space below so that the characteristic spiral movement pattern is dramatized by interlocking boards exercising a slow turn above. The result is analogous to sand ridges formed by the tide or current in water. The boards stream along above circulation areas, swirl around corners, and curl into backwaters over spaces of repose. In the living areas of the extended Sondern house and the Schwartz house, the safe, terminal nature of reaching the fireplace is emphasized, and in the Lloyd Lewis and Pew houses the center of the room is delineated. The latter was an early feature of Prairie house rooms, which required a point of emphasis where the upper floor prevented any deep modulation of the ceiling. Dining rooms, such as that of the Evans house of 1908, contained leaded, stained-glass panels above the table.[15] The Pew house has a similar effect, where beautifully miter-cut cypress forms a recessed vortex that holds down and occupies the center of a room with meandering boundaries. The only hexagonal Usonians having boarded ceilings are the Wall and Richardson houses of 1941. In the former the boarding curls about sections of the main space like flower petals, and in the latter it laps down and underlines the triangular form of the living area.

The grid plan became a conditioning and unifying structure. Wright increasingly exploited the potential ambiguity of overlapping different bands of the grid. This took architectural form in both the detailing and the interpenetration of the masses of the houses. In the fenestration of the Hanna house of 1936, the hexagonal grid was mirrored in the glazing rhythm of the west facade. The existence of an external "boundary zone" is suggested by the universal overhanging eaves and trellises, and by such features as the corner

"eyelids" of the Pew house of 1940, where each second floor bedroom has a corner window shaded by an individual overhang. The same combination of a manifestation of the grid-field with an environmental advantage occurs in an element common to all the Usonian designs. The ranges of casement windows are designed to open within and under the eaves overhang. In doing this they reinforce the separate entity of the boundary zone and create a space that is both inside and out; in the case of the glazed doors this can be readily appreciated. They also change from being elements that lie along one plane of the grid, the facade, into those at right angles to it, modifying the relationship between interior and exterior. The practical result is windows in shade, which can be opened during the rain.

Gardens were conceived as an integral part of the grid format or as a continuation of the level system conditioned by it. This may be seen in the original Usonian models displayed at Hillside in Spring Green, Wisconsin, although not many of the designed schemes were realized. The Lloyd Lewis house of 1940, however, displays the intended "layering" of the garden, where the vertical rhythm of the brick piers of the loggia is continued in walks and parallel strips of flower planting. In the Hanna house the grid successfully united the building with its surroundings. Then as the owners' lifestyle required larger gatherings, it naturally ordered terraces and carparking levels, built some 25 years later.

In the broad massing of Usonian houses Wright used the grid to unify and intersect the wings of his pollywog plans. The brick base, capped by its rowlock course of brick headers, underlay everything and tied together the 30, 60, and 90° angles of such plans as the Armstrong house of 1939. A falling plan like that of the Pope house of 1940 resulted in the entrance from the higher level being upon the brick. Then to enter the lower living area, steps were cut down through the brick to reach the concrete floormat of the main floor. Lower bedroom wings normally line through with the lower walls of living areas, while the latter are capped by higher ceilings upon the clerestory strip windows. The houses can be read as low, wandering, boarded forms

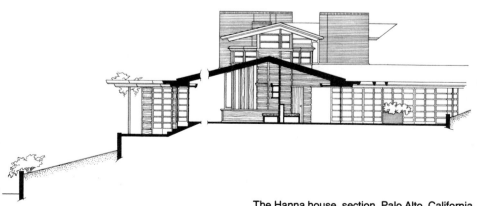

The Hanna house, section, Palo Alto, California, 1936. The position of the interior decks is clearly shown. It lines through with the heads of all doors, contains concealed lighting, and continues outside into the overhanging eaves.

186

topped by clerestorys or as a high, glazed living area into which lower wings were slid.

All these many elements were most eloquently combined in the 1941 project for the Sundt house, designed for Madison, Wisconsin. The site, by the shore of one of the two Madison lakes, entered the grid-field of the house by means of a triangular boat dock. The plan was broadly of V form, with the living area in the apex. It consisted of a superimposition of many triangles, some displaced and others interlocking in the manner of an after-image. These allowed spaces to overlap in an unprecedented way. The carport was to be a part of the entry loggia, but also a corner of the major triangle of the house. The design could be read as this basic format, with a lantern projected vertically from it over the living area and a bedroom wing projected horizontally. Or it could be read as a dominant living-room triangle with subservient outer triangles, some only partially stated, for sitting by the fire, writing, and eating. The south terrace by the dining table can be viewed as part of an underlying base or symmetrical adjunct to the living area (emphasized by the raised, boarded ceiling), as a part of the driveway area, or as a central element of a half-stated triangular pond. The pond itself, as well as the driveway, suggest a system of greater triangles, forever moving out from the house. As the model at Hillside shows, the Sundt house would have matched these geometrical abstractions with all the resources of Wright's Usonian vocabulary and would have been a spatial tour de force. Some idea of his intentions can be gained from the Richardson house, also planned in 1941, in Glen Ridge, New Jersey, which is similar but does not have such a strong geometric relationship with its site.

Grid Plan and Movement Pattern

There is an evident "fit" between the sites for Wright's Usonian houses and the geometry he selected for them. The way in which movement patterns were integrated with this enabled him to relate the user to features of the site that were often at a great distance. The sensations were manipulated in the manner of stage handling, giving glimpses of selected points such as a rock, a tree, or a mountain, and reserving the crowning view as a surprise, held back until the last. As previously noted, this occured very clearly in the desert designs for the Pauson house of 1940 and Wright's own home, Taliesin West.

The rectilinear designs are for the most part a concession to the surroundings of urban sites and grid street plans. At times Wright used a rectangular grid in this context, but set his house at a 45° angle to the street. This had the effect of improving orientation or view, as in the Pew and Schwartz houses, and of highlighting the individuality of the home. In all cases the geometry that was chosen — even in the circular cluster and one and two radii organization of such later developments as the second Jacobs house of 1942 and the Sol Friedman house of 1949 — achieves an inevitability that becomes truly marvelous in homes with dramatic sites.

The Palmer house of 1950, in Ann Arbor, Michigan, can stand for many others. The design

is fused with a tiny hillock in thick woods, now somewhat suburban, and is of a V form. It has a twin core plan based on the 60° triangle, or one-sixth of the hexagon. The living area at its prow leads out to a gently falling slope, while the two wings, garage and bedrooms, slide along the edge of increasingly steep drops. The V is itself wrapped around the top of the hillock and also contains a car court. From the road below a triangular pier (of the workshop) indicates the house above, and the driveway slopes up into the receiving arms of the car court and into the "field" of the grid. This grid has become an indissoluble part of the site, and even some distance from the house itself it can be encountered quite informally as a small triangle of brickwork or a light. Outside the livingroom a long step, made of the red-colored concrete of the floormat, slips out of the grass and is revealed as a manifestation of the grid. The geometry of the design extends outward, not stopping at the walls of the building. Wright himself referred to this as "watching out for the ends" of a design.[16] His treatment of house and site suggests that it would be possible to dig trenches anywhere in the site and discover the bones of the grid below grade. His act of design grasps "force-lines" or vectors, which, although unrecognized, always existed in the site. He perceives them as natural features, draws them quietly together, and knots them inexorably with the grid.

The achievement of Wright's Usonian houses in the grammar of his architecture was to develop a quite abstract geometric planning grid that ordered all the spaces and parts to the whole. The discrepancies and opportunities of nature, in the form of the features of each site, were allowed to "invade" this grid and to carry out a dialog with it. The houses were the result of both. Looking back at what he had done at the end of his life, Wright summarized his design process;

Kindergarten training, as I have shown, proved an unforseen asset: for one thing, because all my planning was devised on a properly proportional unit system. I found this would keep all to scale, ensure consistent proportion throughout the edifice, large or small, which thus became — like tapestry — a consistent fabric woven of interdependent, related units, however various.
So from the very first this system of "fabrication" was applied to planning even in minor buildings. Later I found technological advantages when this system was applied to heights. In elevation, therefore, soon came the vertical module as experience might dictate. All this was very much like laying warp on the loom. The woof (substance) was practically the same as if stretched upon this predetermined warp. This basic practice has proved indispensable and good machine technique must yield its advantages. Invariably it appears in organic architecture as visible features in the fabric of the design — insuring unity of proportion. The harmony of texture is thus, with the scale of all parts, within the complete ensemble."[17]

Notes

1   Grant Manson, "Wright in the Nursery," *Architectural Review*, June 1953.
2   Richard MacCormac, "The Anatomy of Wright's Aesthetic," *Architectural Review*, February 1968; and "Froebel's Kindergarten Gifts

and the Early Work of Frank Lloyd Wright," *Environmental and Planning Bulletin*, vol. 1, pp. 29–50, 1974.
3   See Frank Lloyd Wright, *An Autobiography*, Faber & Faber, London, 1932, p. 17.
4   MacCormac, *Architectural Review*, op. cit., p. 1.
5   MacCormac, *Environment and Planning Bulletin*, op. cit., p. 36.
6   The Hardy house of 1905, in Racine, Wisconsin, is the most obvious exception to the general rule.
7   Henry Russell Hitchcock illustrated this design in *In the Nature of Materials*, Duell, Sloane & Pearce, New York, 1947.
8   *Architectural Record*, January-February, 1928. Quoted in *Frank Lloyd Wright: Writings and Buildings*, op. cit., pp. 221, 222.
9   I use the word in the sense of "magnetic field."
10 Frederick Gutheim, ed., *Frank Lloyd Wright On Architecture*, op. cit., p. 38. From "In the Cause of Architecture I," *Architectural Record*, March 1908.
11 Kaufmann, Edward, ed., *An American Architecture: Frank Lloyd Wright*, Horizon Press, New York, 1955, p. 217. I must confess that I reached this comparison only to find that it had been already made by Edward Franks in his paper, "Organic Philosophy, Organic Architecture, and Frank Lloyd Wright," op. cit., p. 21.
12 See Chapters 1 and 3.
13 Vertical measurements from datum are frequently given both as increments of board and batten and numbered brick courses.
14 The downlights were not purchased components; they were made on site as an integral part of the joinery of the decks. The cut-out varied with the planning grid used, as did the glare-baffle. Aluminum foil was often stuck above as a reflector.
15 Hitchcock, op. cit., p. 145.
16 This was the subject of Alden Dow's contribution to the symposium "Four Great Masters of Modern Architecture," held at Columbia University, New York, 1961, in the possession of the Avery Library.
17 Frank Lloyd Wright, *A Testament*, Horizon Press, New York, 1957. Quoted by Kaufmann, op. cit., pp. 306–307.

Appendix B
The Personal Architectural Services of Frank Lloyd Wright

The personal architectural services of Frank Lloyd Wright are available for ten percent of the cost of the completed building which invariably includes the planting of the grounds and major furnishings considered as part of the building scheme. The fee is the same for a million dollar building or for a five thousand dollar dwelling: divided in three parts as follows:

1 3 percent of proposed cost of the building when preliminary studies are accepted. These however may be modified without additional charge until entirely satisfactory to client and architect.

2 5 percent additional for the working drawings and specifications payable when in the architect's estimation they are complete and ready for bids but with the understanding that should the building cost more than the client has stipulated or is willing to pay, the architect will modify the drawings to bring the costs within reason. Adjustment of this second portion of the fee is to be made when plans are approved by the owner or when contracts are let.

3 2 percent to complete the fee of ten percent for the architect's supervision during construction. Payable from time to time during construction and when the building is completed to the client's satisfaction. A final adjustment of the fee according to the total cost of the completed building to bring the total fee of ten percent of completed cost exclusive of ground is to be made when requested by the architect.

Superintendence satisfactory to architect and client is to be arranged at the client's expense. Traveling expenses necessary and incurred by the architect in direct connection with his work are to be paid from time to time on architect's certificate.

The architect undertakes to itemize mill work and material for the building, lets contracts for piece work and eliminates the general contractor where possible by sending a qualified apprentice of the Taliesin Fellowship at the proper time to take charge, do the necessary shopping and hold the whole building operation together, checking cost layouts, etc., and endeavor to bring the work to successful completion. This apprentice is to be lodged and fed by the owner, his necessary traveling expenses paid for by the owner who also pays the apprentice $25.00 per week for his services so long as he is required on the work. This not only saves most of a general-contractor's fee but both client and architect are better assured of the results of such simplifications and extensions of space as are characteristic of the new methods of building which are inevitably involved.

Before the architect proceeds with the design of any building an accurate topographical survey of the property showing all natural slopes and features such as rock outcroppings, trees, etc., roads, neighboring buildings and service lines for water, sewer, gas and light together with a complete list of the client's requirements should be on record. Dwelling-houses upon urban lots will not be accepted. Acreage is indispensable.

The services of Frank Lloyd Wright are exclusively owned by The Frank Lloyd Wright Foundation.

Appendix C
Agreement between Contractor and Owner for Construction of Usonian Buildings

THIS AGREEMENT made the _____ day of _____ in the year Nineteen Hundred and _____ by and between _____ _____ Contractor and _____ Owner, WITNESSETH that the Contractor and the Owner for the considerations hereinafter named agree as follows:

ARTICLE 1. SCOPE OF THE WORK. The Contractor shall furnish all materials and perform all of the work on the Drawings and described in the Specifications entitled

prepared by FRANK LLOYD WRIGHT acting as and in these Contract Documents entitled Architect; and the Contractor shall do everything required by this Agreement, the General Conditions, the Specifications and the drawings to the complete satisfaction of the Architect.

ARTICLE 2. TIME OF COMPLETION. The work to be performed under this Contract shall be commenced _____ _____ and shall be substantially completed _____

ARTICLE 3. THE CONTRACT SUM. The Owner shall pay the Contractor for the performance of the Contract, subject to additions and deductions provided therein, in current funds as follows _____
Where the quantities originally contemplated are so changed that application of the agreed unit price to the quantity of work performed is shown to create a hardship to the Owner or the Contractor, there shall be a equitable adjustment of the Contract to prevent such hardship.

ARTICLE 4. PROGRESS PAYMENTS. The Owner shall make payments on account of the Contract as provided therein, as follows:

On or about the tenth day of each month seventy-five percent of the value based on the Contract prices, of labor and materials incorporated in the work and of materials suitably stored at the site thereof up to the first day of that month, as estimated by the Architect, less the aggregate of previous payments, and upon substantial completion of

the entire work, a sum sufficient to increase the total payments to eighty-five per cent of the Contract price _____
Payments to be made only upon certificate from the Architect.

ARTICLE 5. ACCEPTANCE AND FINAL PAYMENT. Final payments shall be due thirty days after substantial completion of the work provided the work be then fully completed and the Contract fully performed.

Upon receipt of written notice that the work is ready for final inspection and acceptance, the Architect shall make such inspection, and when he finds the work acceptable under the Contract and the Contract fully performed he shall issue a final certificate, over his own signature, stating that the work provided for in this Contract has been completed and is accepted by him under the terms and conditions thereof, and that the entire balance found to be due the Contractor, and noted in said final certificate, is due and payable.

Before issuance of final certificate the Contractor shall submit evidence satisfactory to the Architect that all payrolls, material bills, and other indebtedness connected with the work have been paid.

If after the work has been substantially completed, full completion thereof is materially delayed through no fault of the Contractor, and the Architect so certifies, the Owner shall, and only upon certificate of the Architect and without terminating the Contract, make payment of the balance due for that portion of the work fully completed and accepted. Such payment, shall be made under the terms and conditions governing full payment, except that it shall not constitute a waiver of claims.

ARTICLE 6. THE CONTRACT DOCUMENTS. The General Condtions of the Contract, the Specifications and the Drawings, together with this Agreement, form the Contract, and they are as fully a part of the Contract as if hereto attached or herein repeated. The following is an enumeration of the Specifications and Drawings:

IN WITNESS WHEREOF the parties hereto have executed this Agreement, the day and year first above written.

Witness _____

Witness _____

THE GENERAL CONDITIONS OF THE CONTRACT FOR THE CONSTRUCTION OF USONIAN BUILDINGS

ARTICLE 1. EXECUTION, CORRELATION AND INTENT OF DOCUMENTS—The Contract Documents shall be signed in duplicate by the Owner and the Contractor. In case the Owner and the Contractor fail to sign the General Conditions, Drawings or Specifications, the Architect shall identify them.

The Contract Documents are complementary, and what is called for by any one shall be as binding as if called for by all. The intention of the documents is to include all labor and materials, equipment and transportation necessary for the proper execution of the work.

ARTICLE 2. DETAIL DRAWINGS AND INSTRUCTIONS—The Architect shall furnish with reasonable promptness, additional instructions, by means of drawings or otherwise, necessary for the proper execution of the work. All such drawings and instructions shall be consistent with the Contract Documents, true developments thereof, and reasonably inferable therefrom.

The work shall be executed in conformity therewith and the Contractor shall do no work without proper drawings and instructions.

ARTICLE 3. COPIES FURNISHED—Unless otherwise provided in the Contract Documents the Architect will furnish to the Contractor, free of charge, all copies of drawings and specifications reasonably necessary for the execution of the work.

ARTICLE 4. SHOP DRAWINGS—The Contractor shall submit with such promptness as to cause no delay in his own work or in that of any other Contractor, two copies of all shop or setting drawings and schedules required for the work of the various trades, and the Architect shall pass upon them with reasonable promptness, making desired corrections, including all necessary corrections. The Contractor shall make any corrections required by the Architect, file with him two corrected copies and furnish such other copies as may be needed. The Architect's approval of such drawings or schedules shall not relieve the Contractor from responsibility for deviations from drawings or specifications, unless he has in writing called the Architect's attention to such deviations at the time of submission, nor shall it relieve him from responsibility for errors of any sort in shop drawings or schedules.

ARTICLE 5. DRAWINGS AND SPECIFICATIONS ON THE WORK—The Contractor shall keep one copy of all drawings and specifications on the work, in good order, available to the Architect and to his representatives.

ARTICLE 6. OWNERSHIP OF DRAWINGS AND MODELS—All drawings, specifications and copies thereof furnished by the Architect are his property. They are not to be used on other work and, are to be returned to him on request, at the completion of the work. All models and approved shop drawings are the property of the Owner.

ARTICLE 7. SAMPLES—The Contractor shall furnish for approval all samples as directed. The work shall be in accordance with approved samples.

ARTICLE 8. MATERIALS, APPLIANCES, EMPLOYEES — Unless otherwise stipulated, the Contractor shall provide and pay for all materials, labor, water, tools, equipment, light power, transportation and other facilities necessary for the execution and completion of the work.

Unless otherwise specified, all materials shall be new and both workmanship and materials shall be of good quality. The Contractor shall, if required, furnish satisfactory evidence as to the kind and quality of materials.

The Contractor shall at all times enforce strict discipline and good order among his employees, and shall not employ on the work any unfit person or in the judgment of the Architect any one not skilled in the work assigned to him.

ARTICLE 9. SURVEYS, PERMITS AND REGULATIONS—The Owner shall furnish all surveys unless otherwise specified. Permits and licenses of a temporary nature necessary for the prosecution of the work shall be secured and paid for by the Contractor. Permits, licenses and easements for permanent structures or permanent changes in existing facilities shall be secured and paid for by the Owner, unless otherwise specified.

The Contractor shall give all notices and comply with all laws, ordinances, rules and regulations bearing on the conduct of the work as drawn and specified. If the Contractor observes that the drawings and specifications are at variance therewith, he shall promptly notify the Architect in writing, and any necessary changes shall be adjusted as provided in the Contract for changes in the work. If the Contractor performs any work knowing it to be contrary to such laws, ordinances, rules and regulations, and without such notice to the Architect, he shall bear all costs arising therefrom.

192

ARTICLE 10. PROTECTION OF WORK AND PROPERTY—The Contractor shall continuously maintain adequate protection of all his work from damage and shall protect the Owner's property from injury or loss arising in connection with this Contract. He shall make good any such damage, injury or loss, except such as may be directly due to errors in the Contract Documents or caused by agents or employees of the Owner. He shall adequately protect adjacent property as provided by law and the Contract Documents.

The Contractor shall take all necessary precautions for the safety of employees on the work, and shall comply with all applicable provisions of Federal, State and Municipal safety laws and building codes to prevent accidents or injury to persons on, about or adjacent to the premises where the work is being performed. He shall erect and properly maintain at all times, as required by the conditions and progress of the work, all necessary safeguards for the protection of workmen and the public and shall post danger signs warning against the hazards created by such features of construction as protruding nails, hod hoists, well holes, elevator hatchways, scaffolding, window openings, stairways and falling materials; and he shall designate a responsible member of his organization on the work, whose duty shall be the prevention of accidents. The name and position of the person so designated shall be reported to the Architect by the Contractor.

Any compensation, claimed by the Contractor on account of emergency work, shall be determined by agreement or Arbitration.

ARTICLE 11. INSPECTION OF WORK—The Architect and his representatives shall at all times have access to the work wherever it is in preparation or progress and the Contractor shall provide proper facilities for such access and for inspection.

If the specifications, the Architect's instructions, laws, ordinances or any public authority require any work to be specially tested or approved the Contractor shall give the Architect timely notice of its readiness for inspection, and if the inspection is by another authority than the Architect, of the date fixed for such inspection. Inspections by the Architect shall be promptly made, and where practicable at the source of supply. If any work should be covered up without approval or consent of the Architect, it must, if required by the Architect, be uncovered for examination at the Contractor's expense.

Re-examination of questioned work may be ordered by the Architect and if so ordered the work must be uncovered by the Contractor. If such work be found in accordance with the Contract Documents the Owner shall pay the cost of re-examination and replacement. If such work be found not in accordance with the Contract Documents the Contractor shall pay such cost, unless he shall show that the defect in the work was caused by another Contractor, and in that event the Owner shall pay such cost.

ARTICLE 12. SUPERVISION—The Contractor shall keep on his work, during its progress, a competent superintendent and any necessary assistants, all satisfactory to the Architect. The superintendent shall not be changed except with the consent of the Architect, unless the superintendent proves to be unsatisfactory to the Contractor and ceases to be in his employ. The superintendent shall represent the Contractor in his absence and all directions given to him shall be as binding as if given to the Contractor. Important directions shall be confirmed in writing to the Contractor. Other directions shall be so confirmed on written request in each case.

The Contractor shall give efficient supervision to the work, using his best skill and attention. He shall carefully study and compare all drawings, specifications and other instructions and shall at once report to the Architect any error, inconsistency or omission which he may discover, but he shall not be held responsible for their existence or discovery.

ARTICLE 13. CHANGES IN THE WORK—The Owner with the Architect's approval without invalidating the Contract, may order extra work or make changes by altering, adding to or deducting from the work, the Contract Sum being adjusted accordingly. All such work shall be executed under the conditions of the original contract except that any claim for extension time caused thereby shall be adjusted at the time of ordering such change.

In giving instructions, the Architect shall have authority to make minor changes in the work, not involving extra cost, and not inconsistent with the purposes, of the building, but otherwise, except in an emergency endangering life or property, no extra work or change shall be made unless in pursuance of a written order from the Owner signed or countersigned by the Architect, or a written order from the Architect stating that the Owner has authorized the extra work or change, and no claim for an addition to the contract sum shall be valid unless so ordered.

The value of any such extra work or change shall be determined in one or more of the following ways:

    (a) By estimate and acceptance in a lump sum.
    (b) By unit prices named in the contract or subsequently agreed upon.
    (c) By cost and percentage or by cost and a fixed fee.

If none of the above methods is agreed upon, the Contractor, provided he receives an order as above, shall proceed with the work. In such case and also under case (c), he shall keep and present in such form as the Architect may direct, a correct account of the cost, together with vouchers. In any case, the Architect shall certify to the amount, including reasonable allowance for overhead and profit, due to the Contractor. Pending final determination of value, payments on account of changes shall be made on the Architect's certificate.

Should conditions encountered below the surface of the ground be at variance with the conditions indicated by the drawings and specifications the contract sum shall be equitably adjusted upon claim by either party made within a reasonable time after the first observance of the conditions.

ARTICLE 14. CLAIMS FOR EXTRA COST—If the Contractor claims that any instructions by drawings or otherwise involve extra cost under this contract, he shall give the Architect written notice thereof within a reasonable time after the receipt of such instructions, and in any event before proceeding to execute the work, except in emergency endangering life or property, and the procedure shall then be as provided for changes in the work. No such claim shall be valid unless so made.

ARTICLE 15. DEDUCTIONS FOR UNCORRECTED WORK—If the Architect and Owner deem it inexpedient to correct work injured or done not in accordance with the Contract, an equitable deduction from the contract price shall be made therefor.

ARTICLE 16. DELAYS AND EXTENSION OF TIME — If the Contractor be delayed at any time in the progress of the work by any act or neglect of the Owner or the Architect, or of any employee of either, or by any separate Contractor employed by the Owner or by changes ordered in the work, or by strikes, lockouts, fire, unusual delay in transportation, unavoiadable casualties or any causes beyond the Contractor's control, or by delay authorized by the Architect pending arbitration, or by any cause which the Architect shall decide to justify the delay, then the time of completion shall be extended for such reasonable time as the Architect may decide.

No such extension shall be made for delay occurring more than seven days before claim therefor is made in writing to the Architect. In the case of a continuing cause of delay, only one claim is necessary.

If no schedule or agreement stating the dates upon which drawings shall be furnished is made, then no claim for delay shall be allowed on account of failure to furnish drawings until two weeks after demand for such drawings and not then unless such claim be reasonable.

This article does not exclude the recovery of damages for delay by either party under other provisions in the contract documents.

ARTICLE 17. CORRECTION OF WORK BEFORE FINAL PAYMENT — The Contractor shall promptly remove from the premises all materials condemned by the Architect as failing to conform to the Contract, whether incorporated in the work or not, and the Contractor shall promptly replace and re-execute his own work in accordance with the Contract and without expense to the Owner and shall bear the expense of making good all work of other contractors destroyed or damaged by such removal or replacement.

ARTICLE 18. CORRECTION OF WORK AFTER FINAL PAYMENT – Neither the final certificate nor payment nor any provision in the Contract Documents shall relieve the Contractor of responsibility for faulty materials or workmanship and, unless otherwise specified, he shall remedy any defects due thereto and pay for any damage to other work resulting therefrom, which shall appear within a period of one year from the date of substantial completion. The Owner shall give notice of observed defects with reasonable promptness. All questions arising under this article shall be decided by the Architect subject to arbitration.

ARTICLE 19. THE OWNER'S RIGHT TO DO WORK – If the Contractor should neglect to prosecute the work properly or fail to perform any provision of this contract, the Owner after three days' written notice to the Contractor may, without prejudice to any other remedy he may have, make good such deficiencies and may deduct the cost thereof from the payment then or thereafter due the Contractor, provided, however, that the Architect shall approve both such action and the amount charged to the Contractor.

ARTICLE 20. OWNER'S RIGHT TO TERMINATE CONTRACT – If the Contractor should be adjudged a bankrupt, or if he should make a general assignment for the benefit of his creditors, or if a receiver should be appointed on account of his insolvency, or if he should persistently or repeatedly refuse or should fail, except in cases for which extension of time is provided, to supply enough properly skilled workmen or proper materials, or if he should fail to make prompt payment to subcontractors or for material or labor, or persistently disregard laws, ordinances or the instructions of the Architect, or otherwise be guilty of a substantial violation of any provision of the contract, then the Owner, upon the certificate of the Architect that sufficient cause exists to justify such action, may, without prejudice to any other right or remedy and after giving the Contractor seven days' written notice terminate the employment of the Contractor and take possession of the premises and of all materials, tools and appliances thereon and finish the work by whatever method he may deem expedient. In such case the Contractor shall not be entitled to receive any further payment until the work is finished. If the unpaid balance of the contract price shall exceed the expense of finishing the work including compensation for additional managerial and administrative services, such excess shall be paid to the Contractor. If such expense shall exceed such unpaid balance, the Contractor shall pay the difference to the Owner. The expense incurred by the Owner as herein provided, and the damage incurred through the Contractor's default, shall be certified by the Architect.

ARTICLE 21. CONTRACTOR'S RIGHT TO STOP WORK OR TERMINATE CONTRACT – If the work should be stopped under an order of any court, or other public authority, for a period of three months, through no act or fault of the Contractor or of anyone employed by him, or if the Architect should fail to issue any certificate for payment within seven days after it is due, or if the Owner should fail to pay to the Contractor within seven days of its maturity and presentation, any sum certified by the Architect or awarded by arbitrators, then the Contractor may, upon seven days' written notice to the Owner and the Architect, stop work or terminate this contract and recover from the Owner payment for all work executed and any loss sustained upon any plant or materials and reasonable profit and damages.

ARTICLE 22. APPLICATIONS FOR PAYMENTS – The Contractor shall submit to the Architect an application for each payment, and, if required, receipts or other vouchers, showing his payments for materials and labor, including payments to subcontractors as required by Art. 31.

In applying for payments, the Contractor shall submit a statement and, if required, itemized in such form and supported by such evidence as the Architect may direct, showing his right to the payment claimed.

If payments are made on account of materials delivered and suitably stored at the site but not incorporated in the work, they shall, if required by the Architect, be conditional upon submission by the Contractor of bills of sale or such other procedure as will establish the Owner's title to such material or otherwise adequately protect the Owner's interest.

ARTICLE 23. CERTIFICATES OF PAYMENTS – If the Contractor has made application as above, the Architect shall, not later than the date when each payment falls due, issue to the Contractor a certificate for such amount as he decides to be properly due.

No certificate issued nor payment made to the Contractor, nor partial or entire use or occupancy of the work by the Owner, shall be in acceptance of any work or materials not in accordance with this contract. The making and acceptance of the final payment shall constitute a waiver of claims by the Owner, other than those arising from unsettled liens, from faulty work appearing after final payment or from requirement of the specifications, and of all claims by the Contractor, except those previously made and still unsettled.

ARTICLE 24. PAYMENTS WITHHELD–The Architect may withhold or, on account of subsequently discovered evidence, nullify the whole or a part of any certificate to such extent as may be necessary to protect the Owner from loss on account of:
    (a) Defective work not remedied.
    (b) Claims filed or reasonable evidence indicating probable filing of claims.
    (c) Failure of the Contractor to make payments properly to subcontractors or for material or labor.
    (d) A reasonable doubt that the contract can be completed for the balance then unpaid.
    (e) Damage to another Contractor.
    When the above grounds are removed payment shall be made for amounts withheld because of them.

ARTICLE 25. CONTRACTOR'S LIABILITY INSURANCE – The Contractor shall maintain such insurance as will protect him from claims under workmen's compensation acts and from any other claims for damages for personal injury, including death, which may arise from operations under this Contract, whether such operations be by himself or by any subcontractor or anyone directly or indirectly employed by either of them. Certificates of such insurance shall be filed with the Owner, if he so require, and shall be subject to his approval for adequacy of protection.

ARTICLE 26. FIRE INSURANCE – The Owner shall effect and maintain fire insurance upon the entire structure on which the work of this contract is to be done to one hundred per cent of the insurable value thereof, including items of labor and materials connected therewith whether in or adjacent to the structure insured, materials in place or to be used as part of the permanent construction including surplus materials, shanties, protective fences, bridges, or temporary structures, miscellaneous materials and supplies incident to the work, and such scaffoldings, stagings, towers, forms, and equipment as are not owned or rented by the contractor, the cost of which is included in the cost of the work. EXCLUSIONS: This insurance does not cover any tools owned by mechanics, any tools, equipment, scaffoldings, stagings, towers, and forms owned or rented by the Contractor, the capital value of which is not included in the cost of the work, or any cook shanties, bunk houses or other structures erected for housing the workmen.

ARTICLE 27. DAMAGES – If either party to this Contract should suffer damage in any manner because of any wrongful act or neglect of the other party or of anyone employed by him, then he shall be reimbursed by the other party for such damage.

Claims under this clause shall be made in writing to the party liable within a reasonable time at the first observance of such damage and not later than the time of final payment, except as expressly stipulated otherwise in the case of faulty work or materials, and shall be adjusted by agreement or arbitration.

ARTICLE 28. LIENS – Neither the final payment nor any part of the retained percentage shall become due until the Contractor, if required, shall deliver to the Owner a complete release of all liens arising out of this Contract, or receipts in full in lieu thereof and, if required in either case, an affidavit that so far as he has knowledge or information the releases and receipts include all the labor and material for which a lien could be filed; but the Contractor may, if any subcontractor refuses to furnish a release or receipt in full, furnish a bond satisfactory to the Owner, to indemnify him against any lien. If any lien remain unsatisfied after all payments are made, the Contractor shall refund to the Owner all moneys that the latter may be compelled to pay in discharging such a lien, including all costs and a reasonable attorney's fee.

ARTICLE 29. SEPARATE CONTRACTS – The Owner reserves the right to let other contracts in connection with this work. The Contractor shall afford other contractors reasonable opportunity for the introduction and storage of their materials and the execution of their work, and shall properly connect and coordinate his work with theirs.

If any part of the Contractor's work depends for proper execution or results upon the work of any other contractor, the Contractor shall inspect and promptly report to the Architect any defects in such work that render it unsuitable for such proper execution and results. His failure so to inspect and report shall constitute an acceptance of the other contractor's work as fit and proper for the reception of his work, except as to defects which may develop in the other contractor's work after the execution of his work.

To insure the proper execution of his subsequent work the Contractor shall measure work already in place and shall at once report to the Architect any discrepancy between the executed work and the drawings.

194

ARTICLE 30. SUBCONTRACT – The Contractor shall, as soon as practicable after the execution of the contract, notify the Architect in writing of the names of subcontractors proposed for the principal parts of the work and for such others as the Architect may direct and shall not employ any that the Architect may within a reasonable time object to as incompetent or unfit.

The Contractor agress that he is as fully responsible to the Owner for the acts and omissions of his subcontractors and of persons either directly or indirectly employed by them, as he is for the acts and omissions of persons directly employed by him.

Nothing contained in the contract documents shall create any contractual relation between any subcontractor and the Owner.

ARTICLE 31. RELATIONS OF CONTRACTOR AND SUBCONTRACTOR – The Contractor agrees to bind every Subcontractor and every Subcontractor agrees to be bound by the terms of the Agreement, the General Conditions, the Drawings and Specifications as far as applicable to his work, including the following provisions of this article, unless specifically noted to the contrary in a subcontract approved in writing as adequate by the Owner or Architect.

This does not apply to minor subcontracts.

The Subcontractor agrees—

(a) To be bound to the Contractor by the terms of the Agreement, General Conditions, Drawings and Specifications, and to assume toward him all the obligations and responsibilities that he, by those documents, assumes toward the Owner.

(b) To submit to the Contractor applications for payment in such reasonable time as to enable the Contractor to apply for payment under Article 22 of the General Conditions.

(c) To make all claims for extras, for extensions of time and for damages for delays or otherwise, to the Contractor in the manner provided in the General Conditions for like claims by the Contractor upon the Owner, except that the time for making claims for extra cost is one week.

The Contractor agrees—

(d) To be bound to the Subcontractor by all the obligations that the Owner assumes to the Contractor under the Agreement, General Conditions, Drawings and Specifications, and by all the provisions thereof affording remedies and redress to the Contractor from the Owner.

(e) To pay the Subcontractor, upon the payment of certificates, if issued under the schedule of values described in Article 22 of the General Conditions, the amount allowed to the Contractor on account of the Subcontractor's work to the extent of the Subcontractor's interest therein.

(f) To pay the Subcontractor, upon the payment of certificates, if issued otherwise than as in (e), so that at all times his total payments shall be as large in proportion to the value of the work done by him as the total amount certified to the Contractor is to the value of the work done by him.

(g) To pay the Subcontractor to such extent as may be provided by the Contract Documents or the subcontract, if either of these provides for earlier or larger payments than the above.

(h) To pay the Subcontractor on demand for his work or materials as far as executed and fixed in place, less the retained percentage, at the time the certificate should issue, even though the Architect fails to issue it for any cause not the fault of the Subcontractor.

(j) To pay the Subcontractor a just share of any fire insurance money received by him, the Contractor, under Article 26 of the General Conditions.

(k) To make no demand for liquidated damages or penalty for delay in any sum in excess of such amount as may be specifically named in the subcontract.

Nothing in this article shall create any obligation on the part of the Owner to pay to or to see to the payment of any sums to any Subcontractor.

ARTICLE 32. ARCHITECT'S STATUS – The Architect shall have general supervision and direction of the work. He is the agent of the Owner only to the extent provided in the Contract Documents. He has authority to stop the work whenever such stoppage may be necessary to insure the proper execution of the Contract.

As the Architect is, in the first instance, the interpreter of the conditions of the Contract and the judge of its performance, he shall side neither with the Owner nor with the Contractor, but shall use his powers under the contract to enforce its faithful performance by both.

ARTICLE 33. ARCHITECT'S DECISIONS – The Architect shall, with in a reasonable time, make decisions on all claims of the Owner or Contractor and on all other matters relating to the execution and progress of the work or the interpretation of the Contract Documents.

The Architect's decisions shall be final.

ARTICLE 34. ARBITRATION – All disputes, claims or questions subject to arbitration, under this contract shall be submitted to arbitration in accordance with the provisions, then obtaining, of the Standard Form of Arbitration Procedure of The American Institute of Architects.

The Contractor shall not cause a delay of the work during any arbitration proceeding, except by agreement with the Owner.

ARTICLE 35. USE OF PREMISES–The Contractor shall confine his apparatus, the storage of materials and the operations of his workmen to limits indicated by law, ordinances, permits or directions of the Architect and shall not unreasonably encumber the premises.

The Contractor shall not load or permit any part of the structure to be loaded with a weight that will endanger its safety.

The Contractor shall enforce the Architect's instructions regarding signs, advertisements, fires and smoking.

ARTICLE 36. CUTTING, PATCHING AND DIGGING–The Contractor shall do all cutting, fitting or patching of his work that may be required to make its several parts come together properly and fit it to receive or be received by work of other contractors shown upon, or reasonably implied by, the Drawings and Specifications for the completed structure, and he shall make good after them as the Architect may direct.

Any cost caused by defective or ill-timed work shall be borne by the Contractor.

The Contractor shall not endanger the work of any other contractor save with the consent of the Architect.

ARTICLE 37. CLEANING UP – The Contractor shall at all times keep the premises free from accumulations of waste material or rubbish caused by his employees or work, and at the completion of the work shall remove all his rubbish from and about the building and all his tools, scaffolding and surplus materials and shall leave his work "broom clean" or its equivalent, unless more exactly specified. In case of dispute the Owner may remove the rubbish and charge the cost to the several contractors as the Architect shall determine to be just.

ADDENDA

Appendix D

Organic Architecture Meets the International Style

The following is a dialog that took place during the question and answer period at the London Lectures in May 1939. For the Third Lecture, see *The Builder,* May 12, 1939, and *The Future of Architecture*, Horizon Press, New York, 1953, pp. 268–272.

These lectures were the only give-and-take clash between Wright's organic architecture and Le Corbusier and the International style, as expressed by an audience of young architects. Le Corbusier went to Madison, Wisconsin, in 1935, and some members of the fellowship attended his lecture at the University of Wisconsin. He was obviously hoping for an invitation to visit Taliesin, but none came.

I include this exchange not so much for the way it reveals the upper-class sentiments mouthed by a pre-war British architect, but because the attitudes of being "like sailors on a ship" exactly reflects the basis of Le Corbusier's *Ville Radieuse*. This was the *cellule,* the minimal apartment of the *Loi Loucheur* from which he built up his continuous 13-story apartment blocks and later *Unites d'Habitation.* It was this thinking that was built into post-war high-rise housing in Britain, much of which is now uninhabitable.

Question from member of audience: Mr. Frank Lloyd Wright has said that houses should be built in order that people might live happily in them and that those houses should be suited to the needs of the family. A working-class family with several children who have to live in three or four rooms can still be very happy, and, since they live in such a small space, they become like sailors on board ship; they learn to respect each other's requirements, and when they go out into the world they are good-natured and have very many qualities which stand them in good stead. I doubt very much whether it would be any advantage to them to have an acre or two, because they could not keep it in order. If the population of England was spread out at the rate of an acre per head, England itself would be ruined as a playground for those who live in the towns and take their holidays enjoying the country; there would be semi-suburban conditions all over the kingdom. It is different in America, with its large areas.

Another point is that there is no better man than the Cockney soldier and no one who can bear hardship with greater fortitude and cheerfulness. I think that is due to the fact that he has lived what I may call a battleship existence through living in crowded quarters; his wife can lean out of the window and talk comfortably to her neighbor. There is much to be said for such a life. People who may be perfectly happy in such conditions may be led into desiring to have a motorcar and into feeling that they must spend something every time they want to have some pleasure, and I do not think that that is at all necessary. . . .

Reply by Wright: Is that drudge-a-day life the beau ideal, then, of modern civilization—the battleship existence of which you speak? If it is then I think the speaker perfectly right, and suggest that the more we can compress our people the better; the less space we give them the more effective the result will be. And in that case I really do not see why they should need as much space as they have got now; why not put the pressure on still stronger and deprive them of still more, so that they may fight even better? Because they have not known a better life, probably will not know it in this generation or the next, I suppose where ignorance is bliss, 'tis folly to be wise!

The existence the speaker describes is, however, to me a negation of life rather than any affirmation of it. I deplore the circumstances in which such lives must be spent. It is just that kind of thing that the modern movement and life itself go up against. It is true that human life may be satisfied or habituated under pressures to adapt itself to whatever circumstances, even the bombing of women and children as modern warfare. But is life to end there? Why did Englishmen go to the new country we call ours now? Why have we this great new nation and this new country? It is because, long ago, Englishmen said No to that idea of yours, sir. Some of them would not accept it. Were they worse men than the Cockney soldier? Even the slums, on your assumption, may be very fruitful. Maintaining them might produce excellent results of which we are not yet aware. Perhaps were we to abolish "the battleship-life" of the slums it would do a great deal to abolish war, which would be a great disaster to the human race, would it not? Perhaps the admirable Cockney is a soldier just because of his "battleship existence." Perhaps humanity itself now labors under fearful threat of war because of this ideal disciplinary character of the "battleship-life" lived by citizens in tight quarters and in slums.

I feel, however, that to be humane we must stand for the philosophy of freedom rather than for any philosophy of battleship sacrifice whatever, because what has the fighting Cockney soldier achieved in life, so far, by his fighting except *the need for more Cockney soldiers?*

What worth having has civilization to show gained from these human sacrifices? What? Unless more and more airplanes flying overhead destroying women and children in masses, now legitimate as modern warfare? I can think of nothing more degrading in this world.

Appendix E

Taliesin Memorabilia

Charter applicants for Fellowship accepted and at work in temporary quarters at Taliesin October 25th, 1932. All are taking part in the construction of the Fellowship buildings under the direct leadership of Frank Lloyd Wright.

Meantime the studio for architecture and private studios for the men, the studios for sculpture and painting, the little theatre, living rooms and conference rooms, private studios for women, water and sewer system; barns and servants building, the directors house and farmers cottage are either completed or well under way. The foundations are in for the kitchen and dining rooms. The buildings for shopwork will be begun next spring, also the several cottages for associates. Garages and filling station will be built.

Meantime the following apprentices are sharing in the making of the Fellowship plant and working on plans and models for the buildings for the Broadacre City.

Stephen Arneson, A.I.T. Chicago	Architecture	Michael Kostanecki, †‡ T.H. Danzig	Architecture
Elizabeth Bauer, Vassar (B.A.)	Architecture	Fred. L. Langhorst, Cornell (B.A.)	Architecture
William A. Bernoudy, Washington U.	Architecture	Yen Liang, Pekin, U. of Penn. (B.A.)	Architecture
Robert Bishop, Swarthmore (B.A.)	Architecture	Rudolph Mock, † Basel, E.T.H. Zurich	Architecture
Visscher Boyd, U. of Penn.	Architecture	Chandler Montgomery, Ohio State U. (B.A.)	Sculpture
Christel Tessa Brey, Vassar	Architecture	Charles L. Morgan, U. of Illinois	Architecture
Willets Burnham, Winnetka H.S.	Architecture	Robert K. Mosher, U. of Mich. (B.S.)	Architecture
William Deknatel, Paris Beaux Arts	Architecture	Isamu Noguchi, *†§ Guggenheim Fellowship	Sculpture
Geraldine Deknatel, Paris Beaux Arts	Architecture	Takehiko Okami, Tokyo, Imperial U.	Architecture
Abe Dombar, U. of Cincinnati	Architecture	William Wesley Peters, M.I.T.	Architecture
James Drought, U. of Wisconsin	Landscape	Louise Dees-Porch, Wellesley, Antioch	Architecture
Robert B. Ebert, U. of Wisconsin	Architecture	Samuel Ratensky, † U. of Penn.	Architecture
Chas. Edman, Jr., Northwestern U.	Architecture	Manuel Sandoval, * Nicaragua	Crafts
William Beye Fyfe, Yale	Architecture	Irving Shaw, U. of Minn., U. of Chicago	Architecture
Mendel Glickman,* Tri State U.	Civil Engineering	Lewis E. Stevens, U. of Michigan	Architecture
Robert Goodall, † U. of Illinois	Architecture	Edgar A. Tafel, New York U.	Architecture
Phillip Holliday, U. of Wisconsin (B.S.)	Painting	Elizabeth Weber, Chicago Art. Ins.	Architecture
John H. Howe, Evanston H.S.	Architecture	Svetlana Wright, Hillcrest H.S.	Painting
Karl E. Jensen, † Copenhagen, Denmark	Architecture		
Heinrich Klumb, † Cologne, S.H.B.	Architecture	*Honor Fellowships.	
Else Klumb, Cologne. T.L.S. Bonn	Crafts	†Taliesin men.	
Yuan Hsi Kuo, Shanghai, U. of Penn.	Architecture	‡Returned to Poland.	
		§Returned to Tokyo.	

Friends of the Fellowship

Jane Addams, Chicago
Cyrus Adler, Chicago
Prof. and Mrs. Walter Agard, Madison, Wis.
Mr. and Mrs. Henry Allen, Wichita, Kan.
Thomas Amlie, Elkhorn, Wis.
Sherwood Anderson, Marion, Va.
Barrett Andrews, New York City
C.R. Ashbee, London, England
Franz Aust, Madison, Wis.

Jean Badovici, Paris
George Banta, Menasha
Aline Barnsdall, Los Angeles
Mrs. Maginel Wright Barney, New York City
Dr. Walter Curt, Behrendt, Germany
Robert Benchley, New York City
Mr. and Mrs. E.A. Bernhard, Buenos Aires
Ernest Bloch, Switzerland
Sophie Braslau, New York City
Joseph Brewer, Grand Rapids, Mich.
Baker Brownell, Evanston
George Bye, New York

Dr. Alexander Chandler, Chandler, Arizona
Sheldon Cheney, Berkeley
Stuart Chase, Redding, Conn.
Jan Chiapuso, Chicago
P.M. Cochius, Leerdam, Holland
Mrs. Avery Coonley, Washington, D.C.
Senor and Senora Jose Cortez, Rio de Janeiro
Cecil Corwin, New York City
Dr. Lucio Costa, Rio de Janeiro
Jean Cranmer, Denver
George Cranmer, Denver
Thomas Craven, New York

Walter Davidson, New York City
Senor and Senora Nestor DeFigueredo, Rio de Janeiro
H. De Fries, Dusseldorf
John Dewey, New York
Muriel Draper, New York City

Albert Einstein, Princeton
Frau Elsa Einstein, Princeton
Arato Endo, Tokyo

Mrs. Maud Fangl, New York City
Arthur Farwell, Lansing, Michigan
M. Framjii, Bombay, India
Paul Frankl, New York
Buckminster Fuller, Bridgeport, Conn.

Mrs. John W. Garrett, Baltimore, Md.
Mr. and Mrs. Samuel Glassenberg, Wilmette, Ill.
Bruce Goff, Tulsa
Walter Gropius, Germany
Angel Guido, Buenos Aires
Dr. and Mrs. William Norman Guthrie, New York City

Mme. Hani, School of the Free Spirit — Tokyo
Douglas Haskell, New York
H. De Cronin Hastings, London
Josef Hoffman, Vienna
Knud Lonberg Holm, New York City
George Howe, Philadelphia, Pa.

Alfonso Iannelli, Chicago

Jens Jensen, Chicago
Ralph Jester, New York City
Dr. Alvin Johnson, New York City
Chester Lloyd Jones, Madison

Georgia Jones, Tulsa
Richard Lloyd Jones, Tulsa

Albert Kahn, Detroit
Ely Kahn, New York
Fiske Kimball, Philadelphia, Pa.
William Kittredge, Chicago
Rockwell Kent, Ausable Forks, N.Y.
A. Lawrence Kocher, New York
Walter Kohler, Kohler, Wisconsin
Michael Kostanecki, Warsaw, Poland

Horacio Acosta Y Lara, Montevideo, Paraguay
Dean Ellis F. Lawrence, Eugene, Oregon
Suzan Lawrence, Springfield, Ill.
Vladimir Lazovich, Zagreb, Yugoslavia
Lloyd Lewis, Chicago
Dr. Max Lieberman, Berlin
Count and Countess Lubiensky, Tokyo

Albert MacArthur, Phoenix, Arizona
Alfred MacArthur, Chicago
Charles MacArthur, Hollywood
Stanley Marcus, Dallas, Texas
Mr. and Mrs. Darwin D. Martin, Buffalo, N.Y.
Madame Warren McArthur, Los Angeles
Harold McCormick, Chicago
Alexander Meikeljohn, Madison
Eric Mendelsohn, Berlin
Dr. M. Mikkelsen, New York
Mrs. Alice Millard, Pasadena
Edna St. Vincent Millay, New York
Dr. Ku Hung Ming, Peking, China
Edwin Morgan, Rio de Janeiro
Professor Karl Moser, Zürich
Dr. Herbert Moses, Rio de Janeiro
Paul Mueller, Chicago
Lewis Mumford, Amenia, N.Y.
Bishop Mardary, Belgrade, Jugoslavia

Aisaku Nayashi, Tokyo

Bishop Francis O'Connell, Chicago
Georgia O'Keeffe, New York
Baron Okura, Tokyo
José Clemente Orozco, New York
José Ortega, Madison
J.P. Oud, Rotterdam, Holland

Stamo Papadaki, Athens, Greece
Dorothy Parker, New York
George Parker, Janesville, Wis.
Harry F. Pebbles, Oak Park, Ill.
Mrs. Andrew Porter, Swarthmore, Pa.

Antonin Raymond, Tokyo
Noemi Raymond, Tokyo
Diego Rivera, New York
Boardman Robinson, Colorado Springs
Dr. Charles H. Ross, Madison

Eliel Saarinen, Bloomfield Hills, Michigan
Carl Sandburg, Chicago
Dr. Ferdinand Schevill, Chicago
Cyril K. Scott, Denver
Julie Siberiakov, Batoum, Russia
Mm. Maria de Silva, Rio de Janeiro
Lee Simonson, New York City
Edward Steichen, New York
Eugene Steinhof, Vienna
Mallet Stevens, Paris
Ashton Stevens, Chicago
Alfred Stieglitz, New York
Frederick Stock, Chicago
P.J. Stokvis, Arnhem, Holland
Leopold Stokowski, Philadelphia

Takehiko Okami, Tokyo
Norman Thomas, New York
Kameki Tsuchiura, Tokyo

Señor Uriburi, Madrid
Dr. J.S. Uriburi, Madrid

Madame Maria Valazzi, Milan, Italy
Mies Van Der Rohe, Germany

200

Richard Waldo, New York City
Mrs. Sarah Adler Weil, Chicago
William Allen White, Wichita, Kansas
H.T.H. Wijdeveld, Amsterdam, Holland
Dr. Walter Willcox, Eugene, Oregon
Alexander Woollcott, New York
John Wright, Michigan City
Lloyd Wright, Los Angeles

Fellows*

Stephen Arneson, St. Paul, Minn.
Margaret Asire, Westerville, Ohio
Yvonne Bannelier Wood, Paris, France
Betty Barnsdall, Hollywood, Cal.
Elizabeth Bauer, Princeton, N.J.
Paul Beidler, Lehighton, Pa.
Christel Tessa Brey, Chicago
William Bernoudy, St. Louis, Mo.
Robert Bishop, Swarthmore, Pa.
Ernest Brooks, Tulsa, Oklahoma
Vissher Boyd, Philadelphia, Pa.
Willets Burnham, Winnetka, Ill.
Alfred Bush, New York City
William Deknatel, Paris, France
Geraldine Deknatel, Paris, France
Abe Dombar, Cincinnati, Ohio
Alden B. Dow, Midland, Michigan
Vada Dow, Midland, Mich.
James Drought, Milwaukee, Wis.
George Dutton, San Francisco
Ruth Dutton, San Francisco
Charles Edman, Jr., Monte Vista, Colorado
A.C. Van Elston, Muscoda, Wis.
Stanhope B. Ficke, Davenport, Iowa
Sally S. Ficke, Cambridge, Mass.
William Beye Fyfe, Oak Park, Ill.
Mendel Glickman, Milwaukee, Wis.
Phillip Holliday, Fairmount, Ind.
John H. Howe, Evanston, Ill.
Karl E. Jensen, Copenhagen
Else Klumb, Cologne
Heinrich Klumb, Cologne
Michael Kostanecki, Krakow, Poland
Frederick Langhorst, Elgin, Ill.
John Lautner, Marquette, Mich.
Yen Liang, Peiping, China
Charles Grey Martin, Bedford, Ia.
Eugene Masselink, Grand Rapids
Rudolph Mock, Zurich, Switzerland
Chandler Montgomery, Chicago
Robert Mosher, Bay City, Michigan
Takehiko Okami, Tokyo
Wm. Wesley Peters, Evansville, Ind.
Louise Dees Porch, Reading, Mass.
Samuel Ratensky, Brooklyn, N.Y.
Nicholas Ray, La Crosse, Wis.
Manuel Sandoval, Nicaragua
Irving Shaw, Minneapolis
Mary Roberts, Marquette, Mich.
Henry Schubart, New York City
Lewis Stevens, Milwaukee
Edgar Tafel, New York City
Elizabeth Weber, Wilmette
Svetlana Wright, Taliesin
Thomas Wigle, Detroit
Harry Yardley, Philadelphia

*Attendance and graduation from these institutions:
U. of Michigan; Institute Fetan, Switzerland; Vassar; U. of Pennsylvania; Washington U.; Swarthmore; Beaux Arts, Paris; U. of Cincinnati; Columbia; Kalamazoo College; Princeton; Northwestern; U. of Wisconsin; Harvard; Emma Willard; Yale; U. of Illinois; Cornell; Marquette U.; M.I.T.; Ohio State; Imperial U., Tokyo; Wellesley; U. of Minnesota; Smith; New York U.; Chicago Art Institute; T.L.S. Bonn; E.T.H. Zurich; A.I.T. Chicago; Sorbonne.

Appendix F

Broadacre City Petition, 1943

We, the undersigned, respectfully ask that the Administration of our Government authorize Frank Lloyd Wright to continue the search for Democratic FORM as the basis for a true capitalistic society now known as Broadacre City. We believe that work should immediately be declared a worthy national objective and the necessary ways and means freely granted him to make such plans, models and drawings as will enable our citizens and other peoples to comprehend the basic ideas the plans, models and drawings represent and which, without political bias or influences will be invaluable to our people when peace is being considered.

A NON-POLITICAL LIST OF AMERICAN CITIZENS

ARCHITECTS	DIRECTORS OF INSTITUTIONS	LANDSCAPE ARCHITECTS
ARTISTS	EDITORS	PREACHERS
CAPITALISTS	EDUCATORS	WRITERS
CIVIL AUTHORITIES	LAWYERS	

NOTE: I have desired to present a characteristic non-political group of Americans but have asked only for the names of some of the well-known men and women who have known me and my work. If desired the list should be extended to include thousands of our best citizens engaged in the occupations listed above.

Frank Lloyd Wright

Henry J. Allen, Editor and Public Servant, Wichita
Thurman Arnold, Department of Justice, Washington, D.C.
Franz Aust, Landscape Architect, University of Wisconsin

Alfred Barr, Jr., Director, Museum of Modern Art, New York, N.Y.
Charles A. Beard,* Author and Historian, New Milford, Conn.
Thomas Benton, Mural Painter, Kansas City, Mo.
Joseph Brewer, President, Olivet College, Olivet, Michigan
John Stewart Bryan, President, William and Mary College

Leslie Cheek, Director, Baltimore Art Institute
Chris L. Christenson, Dean, Agricultural College, Madison
Marc Connelly, Writer, Hollywood
Thomas Craven, Writer, New York, N.Y.
Paul Philippe Gret, Architect, Philadelphia
John Stewart Curry, Artist, Madison

John Dewey, Philosopher, New York, N.Y. (in hospital)

Albert Einstein, Scientist, Princeton, N.J.
William T. Evjue, Editor and Publisher, The Capital Times, Madison

Marshall Field,* Publisher and Editor, Chicago and New York
Clark Forsman, Housing Administrator (in England)
Buckminster Fuller, Mead Mechanical Engineer, Washington, D.C.

Norman Bel Geddes, Industrial Designer, New York, N.Y.
Walter Gropius, Architect and Educator, Cambridge, Massachusetts
Harold M. Groves, Economist, University of Wisconsin
William Norman Guthrie, Preacher, Stamford, Connecticut

Paul R. Hanns, Writer and Educator, Leland Stanford
Wallace Harrison, Architect, New York, N.Y.
Henry Russell Hitchcock, Writer and Educator, Wesleyan University
John Haynes Holmes, Preacher, New York, N.Y.
George Howe,* Federal Architect, Washington, D.C.
Dean Hudnut, School of Architecture, Harvard
Robert N. Hutchins, President, University of Chicago

F. Jayne, Assistant Director, Metropolitan Museum of Art
Dr. Alvin Johnson, Director, New School of Social Research

Albert Kahn, Architect, Detroit
Edgar J. Kaufmann, Sr., Capitalist and Merchant, Pittsburgh
Fiske Kimball, Director, Philadelphia Art Museum

Judge J. M. Landis,* Baseball Commissioner, Chicago
Lloyd Lewis, Writer, Chicago

Archibald MacLeish, Librarian, Congressional Library
Otto T. Mallary, Economist, Philadelphia
Tom Maloney, Editor, U.S. Camera, New York
Alexander Meikeljohn, Adult Education, Berkeley

Carl Milles, Sculptor, Bloomfield Hills, Michigan
Robert Moses, Civil Engineer, New York, N.Y.
Howard Myers, Editor, Architectural Forum, New York, N.Y.

Georgia O'Keefe, Painter, New York, N.Y.

Daniel Catton Rich, Director, The Chicago Art Institute
Nelson Rockefeller,* Capitalist, Washington and New York
Sterling Rockefeller, Capitalist, New York, N.Y.

Eliel Saarinen, Architect, Bloomfield Hills, Michigan
Ferdinand Schevill, Historian, Chicago
Robert Sherwood, Writer, New York, N.Y.
Ludd H. Spivey, President, Florida Southern College
C. L. Stevens, Capitalist and Efficiency Engineer, Baltimore
Alfred Stieglitz, Photographer and Critic, New York
Edward D. Stone, Architect, New York and Washington
Kenneth Stowell, Editor, Architectural Record, New York

Frances Henry Taylor, Director, The Metropolitan Museum of Art

Mies Van der Rohe, Architect and Educator, Illinois Institute
Donald Garrison Villard,* Writer, New York, N.Y.

Alexander Woollcott (see letter) [sic]
Walter Wanger, Producer and Director, Hollywood
Franklin Watkins, Painter, Philadelphia
Thornton Wilder, Writer, Washington, D.C.
William Allen White,* Editor and Public Servant, Emporia

*Signatures not yet received.

Bibliography

Manuscript Collections

Until the Frank Lloyd Wright Foundation undertakes to build the vault and museum to contain his papers and 9,000 drawings, which Wright requested in his will, it is unlikely that scholars will be allowed access to either. In theory they can obtain it; but in practice a heavy fee is demanded as well as the right of approval over anything written.

For collections of Wright's letters see Robert Twombly, *Frank Lloyd Wright: An Interpretive Biography,* Harper & Row, New York, 1973, pp. 358–359. To this list can now be added collections by Curtis Besinger, Helen and George Beal, and Elizabeth Gordon, all at the Kenneth Spencer Research Library, University of Kansas, Lawrence, Kansas.

Books by Wright

Architecture and Modern Life, with Baker Brownell, Harper and Bros., New York, 1938.
An Autobiography, Longmans, Green & Co., New York, 1932, 1943, books 1–5.
An Autobiography, book 6, Broadacre City, Taliesin Press, Spring Green, Wis., 1943.
The Disappearing City, William Farquar Payson, New York, 1932.
The Future of Architecture, Horizon Press, New York, 1953.
The Living City, Horizon Press, New York, 1958.
The Natural House, Horizon Press, New York, 1954.
An Organic Architecture: The Architecture of Democracy, Lund Humphries & Co., London, 1939.
A Testament, Horizon Press, New York, 1957.
When Democracy Builds, University of Chicago Press, Chicago, 1945.

Principal Articles by Wright

Architectural Forum, vol. 68, January 1938. Whole issue.
Architectural Forum, vol. 88, January 1948. Whole issue.
Architectural Forum, vol. 94, January 1951. Portfolio of Wright houses.
"At Taliesin," articles in *The Capital Times,* Madison, Wis.
"Broadacre City," *The American Architect,* vol. 146, pp. 55–63, May 1935.
"Broadacre City: An Architect's Vision," *The New York Times Magazine,* pp. 8–9, Mar. 20, 1932.
"Broadacre City: A New Community Plan," *Architectural Record,* vol. 77, pp. 243–254, April 1935.
"The House of the Future," *National Real Estate Journal,* vol. 33, pp. 25–26, July 1932.
"A Little Private Club," *Life,* vol. 5, pp. 331–340, Sept. 26, 1938. (Contains Wright's letter to the Blackbourn family in "Houses for $5000–6000 Income." Reprinted in *Architectural Forum,* vol. 69, pp. 331–340, November 1938.)
"Taliesin," Spring Green, Wis., 1934, 1935.
"Taliesin: The Taliesin Fellowship Publication," Spring Green, Wis., October 1940, February 1941.

"A Taliesin Square-Paper: A Non-Political Voice from our Democratic Minority," nos. 3–15, Taliesin Press, Spring Green, Wis., 1941–1951.
"Weekly Home News," Spring Green, Wis., May 9, 1935. (Radio address by Frank Lloyd Wright at the opening of the Industrial Arts Exposition in New York City.)

Selected Readings

Banham, Reyner: *Los Angeles. The Architecture of Four Ecologies,* The Penguin Press, London, 1971.
———: *The Architecture of the Well-Tempered Environment,* Architectural Press, London, 1969.
Edward Bellamy: *Equality,* Appleton & Co., New York, 1897.
———: *Looking Backward: 2000–1887,* Ticknor & Co., Boston, 1888.
———: *The Parable of the Water Tank,* Independent Labour Party Publishing Department, London, 1925.
Bester, Arthur E., Jr.: *Backwoods Utopias,* University of Pennsylvania Press, Philadelphia, 1950.
Borsodi, Ralph: *Flight from the City,* Harper & Row, New York, 1933.
Bromfield, Louis: *Malabar Farm,* Ballantine Books, London, 1971.
Büchi, John Henry: *Free Money: A Way out of the Money Maze,* Search Publishing Co., London, 1933.
Collins, George: "Broadacre City: Wright's Utopia Reconsidered" (Paper to Four Great Masters of Modern Architecture Symposium at Columbia University, 1961, in the Avery Library, Columbia University, New York).
De Nevi, Donald: "The Educational Thoughts of Frank Lloyd Wright and Their Implications for the Education of Teachers" (Thesis for Department of Education, University of California at Berkeley, 1969).
Dos Passos, John: *U.S.A. Big Money,* Houghton Mifflin Co., Boston, 1946.
Drexler, Arthur: *The Drawings of Frank Lloyd Wright,* Horizon Press, New York, 1962.
Eaton, Leonard: *Two Chicago Architects and Their Clients: Frank Lloyd Wright and Howard van Doren Shaw,* M.I.T. Press, Cambridge, Mass., 1969.
Elsner, Henry, Jr.: *The Technocrats: Prophets of Automation,* Syracuse University Press, Syracuse, N.Y., 1967.
Emerson, Ralph Waldo: *Self-Reliance,* Pauper Press, Mount Vernon, N.Y., 1967.
Frank, Edward: "Organic Philosophy, Organic Architecture and Frank Lloyd Wright" (Paper in the Avery Library, Columbia University, New York, 1963).
George, Henry: *Progress and Poverty,* Appleton & Co., New York, 1882.
Gesell, Silvio: *The Natural Economic Order,* Phillip Pye, ed., Berliner Frohnan: Neo Verlag, Berlin, 1929; republished by P. Owen, London, 1958.
Goldman, Emma: *Living My Life,* Alfred Knopf, New York, 1931; republished by Dover, New York, 1970.
Goodman, Paul and Percival: *Communitas,* Random House, New York, 1947.
Goodman, Robert: *After the Planners,* Pelican Books, London, 1972.
Gutheim, Frederick, ed.: *Frank Lloyd Wright on*

Architecture, Duell, Sloane & Pearce, New York, 1941.
Henken, Priscilla: "A Broadacre Project," *Town & Country Planning,* vol. 23, June 1954.
Hitchcock, Henry Russell: *In the Nature of Materials,* Duell, Sloane & Pearce, New York, 1947.
Howard, Ebenezer: *Garden Cities of Tomorrow,* Faber & Faber, London, 1946.
Kropotkin, Peter: *Fields, Factories and Workshops: Or Industry Combined with Agriculture and Brainwork,* Houghton Mifflin & Co., Boston, 1899.
March, Lionel: "Imperial City of the Boundless West: Chicago's Impact on Frank Lloyd Wright," *The Listener,* vol. 83, no. 2144, Apr. 30, 1970.
Maxwell, Robert S.: *La Follette,* Prentice-Hall, Englewood Cliffs, N.J., 1969.
Meiklejohn, Alexander: *Education between Two Worlds,* Harper & Row, New York, 1942.
Mohri, Takenobu: *Bruce Goff in Architecture,* Kenchiku Planning Center Co. Ltd., Tokyo, 1970.
Morris, William: *News from Nowhere,* 1890; republished by Asa Briggs, ed., *William Morris,* Penguin Press, London, 1962.
Morton, Terry B., ed.: *The Pope-Leighey House,* National Trust for Historic Preservation, Washington, D.C., 1969.
Nelson, George, and Henry Wright: *Tomorrow's House,* Architectural Press, London, 1945.
Noyes, John Humphrey: *History of American Socialism,* 1870; republished as *Strange Cults and Utopias of Nineteenth Century America,* Dover, New York, 1966.
Okakura, Kakuzo: *The Book of Tea,* Fox, Duffield & Co., New York, 1906; republished by Dover, New York, 1964.
Rosow, Irving: *Modern Architecture and Social Change,* unpublished M.A. thesis, Wayne State University, Detroit, Mich., 1948.
Ruskin, John: *Fors Clavigera,* vol. 8, *Letters to Working Men,* letter 89, September 1880, "Who's Fault Is It?: To the Trades Unions of England."
Smith, Norris Kelly: *Frank Lloyd Wright: A Study in Architectural Content,* Prentice-Hall, Englewood Cliffs, N.J., 1966.
Schumacher, E. F.: *Small Is Beautiful: Economics As If People Mattered,* Harper & Row, New York, 1975.
Streich, Eugene: "An Original Owner Interview Survey of Frank Lloyd Wright's Residential Architecture," William J. Mitchell, ed., *Environmental Design: Research and Practice,* U.C.L.A. EDRA 3/AR 8 Conference, January 1972.
Thoreau, Henry David: *Walden,* New American Library, New York, 1960.
Twombly, Robert: *Frank Lloyd Wright: An Interpretive Biography,* Harper & Row, New York, 1973.
Veblen, Thorstein: *The Theory of the Leisure Class,* Chatto & Windus, London, 1925.
White, Lucia and Morton: *The Intellectual Versus the City: From Jefferson to Frank Lloyd Wright,* Harper & Row, New York, 1942.
Williams, Raymond: *The Country and the City,* Chatto & Windus, London, 1973.
Wright, John Lloyd: *My Father Who Is on Earth,* G. P. Putnam Sons, New York, 1946.
Zevi, Bruno: *Frank Lloyd Wright,* Il Balcone, Milan, 1954.

Index

Acapulco, Mexico project, 86
Addams, Jane, 127, 128. *See also* Hull House
Adelman house (Fox Point, Wisconsin), 86, 145
Adelman house (near Phoenix, Arizona), 144
Adler, Dankmar, 118
Affleck house (Bloomfield Hills, Michigan), 68, 70, 112, 118, 119
Alsop house (Oskaloosa, Iowa), 148
American Institute of Architects (AIA), 99, 144
Architectural Forum, 16, 19, 21, 138, 148
Architectural Record, 123
Armstrong house (Ogden Dunes, Indiana), 51, 118
Arnold, Thurman, 136
Arts and Crafts Movement, 97–98
Autoworkers' cooperative homestead, 82. *See also* Cooperative homesteads

Baird house (Amherst, Massachusetts), 21, 56, 112
Bauhaus, 96
Bavinger house (Norman, Oklahoma), 162, 164, 166
Bazett house (Hillsborough, California), 11, 61
Beal, George, 100, 119
Beal, Helen, 99, 100
Beard, Charles A., 128
Bellamy, Edward, 123, 133
Berger house (San Anselmo, California), 86, 140, 143–144
Bergson, Henri, 14
Berm-type house, 76
Bernoudi, William, 28
Besinger, Curtis, 32, 74, 100, 102, 106
Blackbourn design, 139–140
Blockwork house, 22
Borsodi, Ralph, 122, 134, 167
Brauner project, 51, 78
Broadacre City, 11, 13, 22, 72, 76, 78, 79, 97, 98, 122–136, 138, 146, 156, 167, 168; decentralization, 123–126, 167; life as learning, 135; major failure of, 170; model for, 123–126; philosophy of, 122; rights of man, 133; significance to Wright's work, 126–127
Burlingham house (El Paso, Texas), 38, 40
Burnham, Daniel, 128

Carlson house (Phoenix, Arizona), 86, 145
Carson, Rachel, 167
Chadwick, Gordon, 112, 118
Chase, Mary Ellen, 98
Cheyney, Mrs. "Mamah," 96
Chicago City Club competition, 72
Christie house (Bernardsville, New Jersey), 40, 118
Commons, John R., 129
Community Church (Kansas City, Missouri), 118
Cooperative experiments: Shakers, Fourierists, True Inspirationists, New Harmony, Modern Times, 97
Cooperative homesteads (near Detroit, Michigan), 76, 78–80. *See also* Autoworkers' cooperative homestead
Corbusier, Le, 123

Darrow, Clarence, 12
Davison, Allen "Davey," 106

Delano, Frederick, 136
Department of Interior, National Parks Division, 119
Depression, the, 132–134
de Reuss, Jimmy, 112, 151, 154
Dewey, John, 98, 127, 128, 135, 136
Dos Passos, John, 12
Douglas, C. H., 133
Drought, Jimmy, 104

Eaton, Leonard, 97
Edison, Thomas, 166
Einstein, Albert, 136
Ely, Richard, 128
Emerson, Ralph Waldo, 122
Engels, Friedrich, 127, 128
Erdman Company, 145, 146
Euchtman house (Baltimore, Maryland), 56
Evans house, 20

Falling Water (Bear Run, Pennsylvania), 104. *See also* Kaufmann house
Federal Housing Authority (FHA), 23, 78, 139, 148
Field, Dorothy J., 30
Ford, Henry, 134
Ford house (Aurora, Illinois), 162
Foreman, Clark, 136
Fourier, Charles, 122
Frank, Edward, 14
Friedman house (Pleasantville, New York), 88, 161
Froebel, 20
Fuller, Buckminster, 11, 136, 146

Galesburg Country Homes (near Kalamazoo, Michigan), 79, 144
Garrison project, 51
George, Henry, 122, 123, 128, 129, 133
Gesell, Silvio, 130, 132, 133
Goetsch, Alma, 78
Goff, Bruce, 12, 161–166; architect-client relationship, 161; concept of organic homes, 161
Goldman, Emma, 127, 129
Goodman, Paul and Percival, 122
Goodrich, Burton, 112
Gordon, Elizabeth, 138
Grangers, the, 127
Grant house (Cedar Rapids, Iowa), 86, 140
Greene, Herb, 161
Gropius, Walter, 119
Gruntvig, N. S. F., 98
Guggenheim Museum, 32, 81, 85
Gurdjieff, Georgi, Institute for the Harmonious Development of Man, 99

Hanna house (Palo Alto, California), 11, 22, 36, 40, 60, 118; description of, 32–33
Haussman, Baron, 128
Haymarket martyrs, 127
Hein project (Chippewa Falls, Wisconsin), 56, 86
Henken, David, 79
Henshaw, Paul, 14
Hexagonal planning, 32. *See also* Frank Lloyd Wright, hexagonal designs
Hillside Home School, I, II (Spring Green, Wisconsin), 98
Hodnut, Dean, 119
Hoover, President Herbert, 119

Hoult house (Wichita, Kansas), 23, 110
House and Home, 138, 146, 148, 151, 154, 156
House Beautiful, 138, 148
Housing project (Pittsfield, Massachusetts), 74
Howard, Ebenezer, 122, 123
Howe, John, 23, 98, 99, 100, 102, 104, 106, 108, 118
Hull House, 98, 122, 138. *See also* Jane Addams
Hunt house (La Grange, Illinois), 30
Hyde house (Kansas City, Kansas), 162, 164, 166

Integrated Life-Support Systems Laboratories (New Mexico), 167
Internationalists, the, 54
International Workers of the World (IWW), 127

Jacobs house (Madison, Wisconsin), 16–23, 27–30, 110, 138, 140; budget, 27; planning innovations, 16–19; polliwog design, 40, 85, 86; second Jacobs house (Middleton, Wisconsin), 82, 85. *See also* Solar-hemicycle house
James, William, 128
Jefferson, Thomas, 122, 133, 136, 140, 166
Jester house (Palos Verdes, California), 36, 40, 85
Johnson house, "Wingspread" (Racine, Wisconsin), 118
Johnson Wax Company, Administration Building (Racine, Wisconsin), 16, 27, 118, 148
Jurgensen project, 51

Kaufmann house (Bear Run, Pennsylvania), 16, 32. *See also* Falling Water
Kaufmann, Edgar, 123
Kelly, Mrs., 127
Kenny, Sean, 99
Keynes, John Maynard, 130, 168
Kolb, J. H., 133
Kropotkin, Peter, 122, 123

Ladies Home Journal, 138
La Follette, Robert, 129
Lamberson house (Oskaloosa, Iowa), 148
La Miniature (Pasadena, California), 104
Lansing cooperative, 78
Lao-tse, philosophy, 14, 28, 140, 156
Laurent house (Rockford, Illinois), 85
Leighey house, 19
Letchworth, 122. *See also* Ebenezer Howard
Lewis house (Libertyville, Illinois), 19, 66
Life magazine, 46; feature on eight architects, 139
Little, Francis, 108
Lloyd-Jones family, 70, 98, 127
Loveness home, 140
Lusk house (Huron, South Dakota), 23
Lynch, Kevin, 99

MacArthur, Charles, 66
McCartney house (at Parkwyn Village, Michigan), 145
MacCormac, Richard, 20
McKenzie, R. C., 133
MacLeish, Archibald, 136
Manson house (Wausau, Wisconsin), 51
March, Lionel, 122, 127, 128, 129, 133, 138
Marcus project (Dallas, Texas), 51

Marting house (Akron, Ohio), 85
Martin house, 20
Marx, Karl, 128–129, 130
Masselink, Gene, 23, 102
Meiklejohn, Alexander, 98, 122
Meyer house (Galesburg, Michigan), 85
Minimum houses, 22
Mobile home, 11
Morgan, Mabel, 100, 104
Morris, William, 98, 123, 127
Moses, Robert, 136
Mumford, Lewis, 122
Myers, Howard, 138

Napoleon III, 128
National Association of Real Estate Boards, 146
National Resources Planning Board, 134
National Trust for Historic Preservation, 48
Nearing, Scott and Helen, 134
Nelson, George, 140
Neutra, Richard, 96
New Alchemy Institute (Massachusetts), 167
New Deal, the, 122, 132, 134, 138, 167
Newman project, 51
New Towns (Britain), 122, 168
Noel, Miriam, 129
Northwest Architect, 140

Oboler "Eaglefeather" (Los Angeles, California),
    56, 58
Ocatillo, 104
Ogburn, William, 133, 138, 139, 148
Okakura, Kakuzo, 28
Organic architect, 160–166
Organic architecture, 11, 12, 13–14, 16, 28, 30,
    80, 81, 86, 88, 96; direct instruction, 154–156;
    do-it-yourself architecture, 138, 140–143;
    homemade homes, 166–167; housing context
    at the time, 138–140; influence of, 156;
    methods of achieving organic architecture,
    138–140; popularizing by magazine,
    148–154; prefabricated houses, 145–146;
    problem of rising prices, 140–156; self-build
    methods, 146–148; spreading the organic
    idea, 138. See also Usonian houses
Organic community, the, 167–170
Organic design: alternative communities, 167;
    implications of, 160–170
Organic education, 98, 167

Palmer house (Ann Arbor, Michigan), 86
Panshin project, 51
Parker, Colonel Francis, 98
Parkwyn Village (near Kalamazoo, Michigan),
    79, 144
Parsons, Talcott, 138, 139
Pauson house (Scottsdale, Arizona), 40, 56, 58
Pearce house (Bradbury, California), 85
Pencil Points, 134
Peters, Svetlana, 102
Peters, Wesley, 99, 102
Peterson (formerly Edith Carlson) project, 56
Pew house, 68, 70, 138
Pfeiffer, Bruce, 23
Pope house (Falls Church, Virginia), 30, 40,
    48–51, 112, 138
Populism, 127, 170
Prairie houses, 19, 20
Prefabrication, 11. See also Organic
    architecture, prefabricated houses
Price house (Phoenix, Arizona), 86
Price, Joe, 161

Progressive party, 129
Proudhon, Pierre-Joseph, 122
Pullman, town of, 128
Quadruple homes, 22, 72, 74, 138

Read, Herbert, 122
Rebhuhn house (Great Neck, New York), 40,
    118
Richardson house (Glen Ridge, New Jersey), 64
Rockefeller, Nelson, 136
Rodia, Simon, 166
Roosevelt, Franklin D., 136
Rosenbaum house (Florence, Alabama), 21, 40,
    42, 86, 112, 118
Rosow, Irving, 139
Rousseau, Jean Jacques, 97
Ruskin, John, 98, 133

Sandberg, Carl, 66
Schapiro, Meyer, 122–123
Schevill, Ferdinand, 136
Schindler, Rudolph, 96
Schmidt, Arnie, 166
Schneider, Mrs., 102
School for Living (near Suffern, New York), 167
School for the Allied Arts, 96
Schwartz, Bernard, 108, 112, 139. See also
    Schwartz house
Schwartz house (Two Rivers, Wisconsin), 40,
    46–48, 112
Scott, Howard, 132
Smith house (Bloomfield Hills, Michigan), 86
Smith, Norris Kelly, 19, 96, 97–98, 127
Solar-hemicycle houses, 82, 85
Soleri, Paolo, 99, 166
Sondern house (Kansas City, Missouri), 22, 40,
    48–51
Special Committee to Investigate Industrial
    Centralization, 134
Spencer, Dudley, 140
Standard Detail Sheet, 110. See also Taliesin
    Fellowship, working drawings
Stevens plantation, "Auldbrass" (Yamassee,
    South Carolina), 60
Streich, Eugene, 108
Sturges house (Brentwood Heights, California),
    52, 54
Sullivan, Louis, 118, 128, 129
Sundt project (Madison, Wisconsin), 64
Suntop homes (Ardmore, Pennsylvania), 72,
    118

Tafel, Edgar, 104, 112
Taliesin archives, 40
Taliesin Associated Architects, 40, 99
Taliesin Fellowship, 19, 22, 79, 88, 96–119, 123,
    167; apprentices, 110, 112, 166;
    clerks-of-works, 112; clients, 106, 108; design
    development, 108; effect of, 119; finances and
    apprenticeship, 98–99; husbandry, 102;
    internal newsheet, 100; master-builders, 112,
    118–119; practice in, 100–102; production,
    106; students, 106; variations in construction,
    112; working conditions, 104; working
    drawings, 108, 110
Taliesin homes, 32; Spring Green, Wisconsin,
    40, 96, 104; Taliesin West (Phoenix, Arizona),
    40, 96, 104
Taliesin magazine, 13, 22, 30
Taliesin press, 102
Technocracy movement, 132

Tennessee Valley Authority, 134
Thoreau, David, 122
Time magazine, 46
Tonkens house (near Cincinnati, Ohio), 144
Turkel house (Detroit, Michigan), 144
Turner, Harold, 40, 62, 70, 78, 112, 118, 119
Turner house (Bloomfield Hills, Michigan), 119
Turner, John, 166
Twombly, Robert, 19
Two-zoned house, 22, 30

Usonia I, 78
Usonia II (Lansing, Michigan), 56, 78
Usonia III (Wheeling, West Virginia), 78
Usonia, definition of, 16. See also Organic
    architecture
Usonia Homes (Pleasantville, New York), 79, 80;
    postwar difficulties, 80
Usonian Automatic, the, 144
Usonian clients, 40
Usonian concept, evolution of, 22, 32, 140
Usonian construction: board and batten walls,
    19; planning grid, 19–20; privacy and the
    family, 30; underfloor heating, 20–21
Usonian cooperative, 40
Usonian democracy. See Frank Lloyd Wright, on
    democracy
Usonian houses: cost, 27; diagonal Usonian, 40,
    51; differences from standard American
    house, 12; furniture, 19; geometric variations
    on, 40; heating, 11–13, 28–29, 112, 118;
    hexagonal Usonian, 40, 60–64; influence on
    American architecture, 140; in-line Usonian,
    40, 52–58, 86; least successful aspects of,
    29–30, 112, 118, 119; performance of
    construction, 28; planning innovations, 16–19;
    plans for, 110; polliwog Usonian, 21, 40–51;
    public reaction to, 119; raised Usonian, 40,
    66–70; success of, 27–28; technological
    limitations of, 112; Usonian "kit," 21, 108
Usonian Manifesto, 16

van der Rohe, Mies, 13, 14, 54, 136
Veblen, Thorstein, 19, 128, 129, 132, 133

Walker house (Carmel, California), 86
Wall house, "Snowflake" (Plymouth, Michigan),
    62, 86, 118, 140
Wampler, Jan, 166
Wells, H. G., 123
Weltzheimer house (Oberlin, Ohio), 86
Welwyn, 122. See also Ebenezer Howard
Wend, Milton, 167
White, William Allen, 136
Whitehead, Alfred North, 14
Whitman, Walt, 122
Willey, Dean Malcolm A., 133
Willey house (Minneapolis, Minnesota), 22
Williams, Raymond, 170
Wilson house (Millstone, New Jersey), 145
Wiltscheck, Ben, 112, 118
Winkler, Catherine, 78
Winkler-Goetsch house (Okemos, Michigan),
    54, 78, 118
Woolcott, Alexander, 66
World's Fair (Columbian Exposition), 127–128
Wright, Henry, 140
Wright house (Phoenix, Arizona), built for David
    Wright, 85, 145
Wright, Frank Lloyd: anarchism, 122;
    architect-client relations, 138; as seen by his
    critics, 122, 123, 127, 136; clients, 97, 106,

108; construction methods, 112–119, 138; cooperative communities, 167; early career abandoned, 96; emphasis of last decade's work, 81; hexagonal design, 32, 33; idea of the organic architect, 160; influenced by Eastern philosophy, 28; influenced by Gesell, 130, 132; influenced by the Southwest, 129–130; influences in early life, 127–130; in Wisconsin, 129; Kahn lectures, 123; lifestyle, 97; method of working, 104, 106; on conscription, 127; on decentralization, 119, 122–126, 133–134 (*See also* Broadacre City); on democracy, 122, 127, 128, 133, 135; on heating, 29; on self-sufficiency, 40, 78; philosophy of architecture, 12–14, 81, 96; philosophy of education, 98, 119, 160; problem of low-cost housing, 16, 40, 81, 138, 140–156; problems with FHA, 78, 139; Prairie house career, 96; proselytizing his ideas, 138; quadruple homes, 72; relation to American radicalism, 122, 127; second Usonian career, 96; self-build methods, 146–148; significance of Broadacre City, 126–127; significance of Wright's contribution to architecture, 167–170; studio in Chicago, 96; textile block building system, 144–145; transcendentalism, 122; Wasmuth portfolio, 96. *See also* Organic architecture, Taliesin Fellowship

Wright, Frank Lloyd, writings: *The Art and Craft of the Machine,* 128; *An Autobiography,* 23, 96, 98, 126, 129, 133; *Architecture and Modern Life,* 123; *Broadacre City,* 30; *Disappearing City,* 123; *The Living City,* 74, 123, 129, 132, 133, 136, 146, 160; *The Natural House,* 11, 144; *When Democracy Builds,* 123

Wright, Henry, 140

Wright, John Lloyd, 36, 97, 129

Wright, Olgivanna, 96, 99, 100, 102

Wright, Robert Llewelyn (house at Bethesda, Maryland), 85

Young, Brigham, 97

Young, Owen D., 130

Zimmerman house (Manchester, New Hampshire), 86, 156

Zoned house, 22